Rice and Slaves

Rice
and Slaves

*Ethnicity and the Slave Trade
in Colonial South Carolina*

DANIEL C. LITTLEFIELD

Louisiana State University Press
Baton Rouge and London

Designer: Albert Crochet
Typeface: VIP Bembo
Typesetter: G&S Typesetters, Inc.
Printer and Binder: Thomson-Shore, Inc.

Published with the assistance of the Council on Research,
Louisiana State University

LIBRARY OF CONGRESS CATALOGING IN PUBLICATION DATA

Littlefield, Daniel C
   Rice and slaves.

   Bibliography: p.
   Includes index.
   1. Slavery in the United States—South Carolina.
2. Slave-trade—South Carolina.   3. South Carolina—
Race relations.   4. Rice trade—South Carolina—History.
I. Title.
E445.S7L57   975.7'00496   80-27332
ISBN 0-8071-0794-8

To the memory of my mother,
Ophelia Marie Broadway

Contents

Illustrations
and Tables

Preface and Acknowledgments

The concerns of this study developed in the Seminar on Atlantic History and Culture at the Johns Hopkins University in 1972. I had, at the time, already tentatively settled on a thesis topic, but ideas engendered during a series of discussions concerning African contributions to the development of plantation society and culture in the New World, and particularly in South Carolina, set me off on an entirely different course. The notion that blacks were active rather than passive (if often unwilling) participants in the founding of American civilization, that they were sometimes both physically and culturally better suited than their masters to the tasks of survival and construction in a new environment, and that Europeans were occasionally both perceptive and acquisitive of African capabilities, were concerns that, although not new, increasingly occupied the attention of American historians and other scholars. The North American black population, previously largely ignored except where posed as a problem of American life, became suddenly the focus of attention, and attempts were made to relate North American society more closely to other New World societies where blacks and whites were in intimate and often intense contact. South Carolina, settled relatively late, possessing a preponderantly black population, a large number of African imports, and an unusually remunerative crop by North American standards, provided a convenient locale for viewing the African component in the formation of a plantation society in North America. There, perhaps more clearly than elsewhere in British North America, one can contemplate interchange between Africans and Europeans.

I have been fortunate in being able to work with certain people. My mentor, Jack P. Greene, Andrew W. Mellon Professor at Johns Hopkins, was a continuing source of support, encouragement, and enthusiasm. I owe an especial debt of gratitude to Professor George C. Rogers, Jr., of the University of South Carolina, editor of the Laurens Papers. He extended extraordinary kindness to me, graciously permitting my use of typescript copies of unpublished papers, provided comfortable facilities in his office, and allowed me to benefit from his immense knowledge of South Carolina history, thereby speeding my research and rendering my stay in Columbia more enjoyable. He has been equally kind and helpful on my subsequent visits. He took time away from a busy schedule to read and comment on the entire manuscript, which is better for his efforts. Ronald Walters, John Russell-Wood, Ray Kea, and David Cohen, all of Johns Hopkins, read and made useful comments on all or part of the manuscript when it was a thesis. Edward Kopf, James T. Moore, Michael Messmer, and Philip J. Schwarz, of Virginia Commonwealth University, and Robert A. Becker, of Louisiana State University, read and commented on parts of the manuscript at a later date.

The staffs at all of the libraries, archives, and repositories I used, in England, Scotland, and America, were unfailingly courteous and helpful. Particular thanks are due to the registrar, D. M. Hunter, and to Mr. Ian Grant and other members of the staff at the National Register of Archives in Scotland, where I did research in 1973. Their aid both in finding documents and in securing permission for me to see them went far beyond what I had any reason to expect. Special thanks are due also to Sir Ewen Macpherson-Grant for his kindness in allowing me to visit Ballindalloch Castle and see some of his family papers, and again to Mr. Ian Grant for shepherding me in northern Scotland.

Rice and Slaves

Introduction

When Ulrich Bonnell Phillips considered American slavery at the beginning of the twentieth century, he made a laudable attempt to consider the African background of the servile population. "Only to the unpractised eye," he wrote, "could all Africans look alike."[1] Few, excluding even Phillips, gave the fact much emphasis in terms of its effects on slavery and race relations in the colonial South. This was partly because Phillips, like many others, tended to view slavery as a monolithic institution and approached it from the vantage point of the nineteenth century. It was, too, because he wrote in a period of intense racism that vitiated his perceptions and limited his conceptual approach, and, finally, because he imposed on an earlier epoch the attitudes and assumptions of his own. As a white Georgian born in a white supremist society, he had, from one point of view, an eminently comprehensible outlook; from another, however, his perceptions seem strangely blunted. A white contemporary in the sister state of South Carolina evinced greater perceptivity and attached meaning to the varied African background of the black population. "The so-called race problem," he said, "is not one of the relations of a single negro race, but rather one of a number of white races with a number of negro races. The negro population of the United States is probably as much mixed as the white population."[2]

Perhaps this awareness is a measure of the difference between South Carolina and Georgia and an aspect of the former's uniqueness. For South Carolina was distinctive, even though many of its singular characteristics are apparent only by contrast. An outlying section of the South Atlantic System, it was on the fringes of a complex of commercial relationships based on the production of staples for European consumption and achieved through the im-

1. Ulrich B. Phillips, *Life and Labor in the Old South* (Boston, 1929), 190.
2. Daniel A. Tompkins, *Cotton and Cotton Oil* (Charlotte, North Carolina, 1901), 48.

1

portation and utilization of African labor. It was part of, but often atypical of, British colonies in temperate North America. These colonies, so different from British settlements in the tropical zone, were yet so closely related to them. But South Carolina was a *méti*, an anomaly whose semitropical climate permitted it to produce one of the most profitable crops grown in British North America but whose geography limited the scope of production and modified the direction of social development. Its slave code, and even slavery itself, was taken from British possessions in the Caribbean, especially Barbados, whence many early Carolina settlers came. Some years ensued before statutory precepts, particularly governing definition of the institution, fell in line with those prevailing in more northerly English colonies.[3] In its subsequent evolution, too, slavery in colonial South Carolina was something of an aberration, containing elements and conditions usually associated with the West Indies but modified by Carolina's position on the North American coastline.[4] Hence, in more ways than one, South Carolina occupied an intermediate position between North America and the tropics, and if the continent as a whole was just on the fringes of the South Atlantic System, South Carolina was more completely a part of it than any other portion of eighteenth-century North America.

3. A slave was defined in Barbados and other parts of the West Indies as real or freehold property, except in cases of the master's indebtedness when he could be transferred as personal chattel. Freehold property entitled its holder only to service, not to absolute ownership: the master was entitled to the slave's service but not to his person, and the slave possessed some of the qualities of the serf. By contrast, chattel slavery, a uniquely North American creation, attached the slave to his master as personal property, transferable at will. Not until 1740 did South Carolina legally exchange the former for the latter, though its usage developed earlier. See, especially, M. Eugene Sirmans, "The Legal Status of the Slave in South Carolina, 1670–1740," *Journal of Southern History*, XXVIII (1962), 462–73. He refutes older views in Edward McCrady, "Slavery in the Province of South Carolina, 1670–1770," *American Historical Association Report* (1895), 629–73, and Oscar and Mary F. Handlin, "Origins of the Southern Labor System," *William and Mary Quarterly*, Third Series, VII (April, 1950), 199–222; see also Peter H. Wood, *Black Majority: Negroes in Colonial South Carolina from 1670 through the Stono Rebellion* (New York, 1974), 51–52.

4. Winthrop Jordan has done the best work in this regard. See his "American Chiaroscuro: The Status and Definition of Mulattoes in the British Colonies," *William and Mary Quarterly*, Third Series, XIX (April, 1962), 183–200; "The Influence of the West Indies on the Origin of New England Slavery," *William and Mary Quarterly*, Third Series, XVIII (April, 1961), 243–50; and, of course, *White Over Black: American Attitudes Toward the Negro, 1550–1812* (Chapel Hill, 1968), especially 136–50.

These reflections suggest that South Carolina may be best understood by reference to the larger system. Too minute a focus on one area can blind the scholar, not only to possible answers, but even to conceivable questions about his subject. This has been especially true regarding North American slavery and race relations, particularly before publication of Frank Tannenbaum's seminal essay *Slave and Citizen* in 1947 broadened the discussion.[5] The tendency (among historians anyway) before Tannenbaum had been to emphasize, implicitly at least, the uniqueness of American institutions and thereby to miss by default some of their real individuality. Phillips, the first serious student of North American slavery, considered other regimes but did not do much explicit comparison.[6] Others, notably anthropologist Melville J. Herskovits, have tried to look at the African population in America from a hemispheric perspective. But his work, though groundbreaking, was so wide ranging and his generalizations so broad as to be, in many cases, discredited or dismissed.[7] A proper balance, therefore, must be maintained between the particular and the general in order to spur rather than stifle further study.

When a hemispheric approach is adopted, thoughts suggest

5. Frank Tannenbaum, *Slave and Citizen: The Negro in the Americas* (New York, 1947).

6. Phillips did consider the West Indies and made some contrast between slavery there and on the mainland. Eugene Genovese writes, in fact, that "long before Frank Tannenbaum, not to mention Stanley M. Elkins, Phillips drew attention to the different kinds of New World slavery, to the importance of divergent cultural traditions, and to the separate developments of the ruling classes. . . . Even in his background explorations, if we leave aside those which succumbed completely to his racist bias he asked more and better questions than many of us still are willing to admit." However, this "racist bias," this inability to "take the Negro seriously" as Tannenbaum and Elkins both did, prevented him from asking questions that might earlier have changed the way we look at slavery. See Ulrich B. Phillips, *American Negro Slavery: A Survey of the Supply, Employment, and Control of Negro Labor as Determined by the Plantation Regime* (Baton Rouge, 1966)—quotes by Genovese taken from the Foreword of this edition—and *Life and Labor in the Old South*.

7. Herskovits is perhaps best noted for his *Myth of the Negro Past* (New York, 1941), but this was the culmination of years of research and prior publications. See, for an example of his earlier work, a collection of his essays edited by Frances S. Herskovits, *The New World Negro: Selected Essays in Afroamerican Studies* (Bloomington, 1966). For an example of criticism see E. Franklin Frazier's review of *The American Negro: A Study in Racial Crossing* in *American Journal of Sociology*, XXXIII (1928), 1010. Frazier's *The Negro Family in the United States* (Chicago, 1939), and Raymond T. Smith, *The Negro Family in British Guiana: Family Structure and Social Status in the Villages* (New York, 1956) both diverge from findings of Herskovits; note especially Smith's critique of Herskovits' methodological assumptions, pp. 228–33.

themselves that would not otherwise occur. Why, for example, has there been such a great recognition of African ethnic diversity in Brazil and so little in North America? More pertinently, why have North Americans only so recently come to realize that there was ever, on the northern mainland, a parallel concern? Part of the answer, of course, lies in the traditionally narrow focus of American history, which prevented the question from ever being asked and, when the fact was adduced, from being accorded much significance.

Peter Wood's recent study of colonial South Carolina slavery has given currency to a subject that has long been a matter of controversy in Brazil but has only lately been seriously considered in North America.[8] There are two aspects to the problem: the question of African diversity in America and the corollary problem of African contributions to the development of American society—not in music, where it is universally conceded that African influence has been strong throughout the Americas, but in technology. The questions are intertwined because the attribution of technical expertise requires a degree of specificity much greater than a general reference to Africa. In Brazil, as early as the end of the last century, there was an argument between Indianists and Africanists "as to whether the growing differences between Brazilians and Portuguese were due more to Negro or to native Indian and climatic influences."[9] Contemporaneously in the United States, differences between Englishmen and Americans were explained in terms of the frontier, or by reference to the plantation, but hardly ever in relation to Africans, either as immigrants or contributors.[10] Nor could it have been otherwise when the belief was prevalent that, labor aside, blacks had little to offer. The prevailing assumption was that their background and capacity unsuited them for

8. Wood, *Black Majority*.

9. José Honório Rodrigues, "The Influence of Africa on Brazil and of Brazil on Africa," *Journal of African History*, III, 1 (1962), 50. Also see Gilberto Freyre, *The Masters and the Slaves: A Study in the Development of Brazilian Civilization* (New York, 1966), *passim*.

10. See, for example, Ulrich B. Phillips (ed.), *A Documentary History of American Industrial Society* (4 vols.; Cleveland, 1910), I, 69–104. It is almost superfluous to mention Frederick Jackson Turner, of whom Phillips was both colleague and disciple and whose frontier thesis radically altered the concept of American history; but see also G. R. Taylor (ed.), *The Turner Thesis Concerning the Role of the Frontier in American History* (Boston, 1956).

anything else. Thus, as late as 1918, Phillips could write without fear of contradiction that "the climate [of Africa] . . . prohibits mental effort of a severe or sustained character, and the negroes have submitted to that prohibition as to many others, through countless generations, with excellent grace."[11]

Despite the ethnocentrism that infects all national groups and expands whenever divergent cultures come into close proximity, these attitudes of derogation may not have been so common, or at least not so blinding, as they were to become when racism was elevated to the status of a cornerstone of the American way of life. An English visitor to North Carolina during the two years before the Declaration of Independence commented, for example, that "the Negroes are the only people that seem to pay any attention to the various uses that the wild vegetables may be put to. For example, I have sent you a paper of their vegetable pins made from the prickly pear, also molds for buttons made from the calabash, which likewise serves to hold their victuals. The allowance for a Negro is a quart of Indian corn pr. day, and a little piece of land *which they cultivate much better than their Master*."[12] The statement bespeaks a certain separateness between master and slave, an initiative on the part of the slave, and a definite capacity on his part to offer skills and standards to the master, should he choose to accept them. Whether colonials were always attentive or receptive to such possibilities, the traveler's statement is the kind of evidence that historians have too often ignored in writing the history of slavery and of the meeting of African and European in North America. Ignorance begot by prejudice foreclosed whole areas of discussion. In view of prevailing racial attitudes in late-nineteenth- and early-twentieth-century United States, this situation is understandable. But it might have been neither so pervasive nor so persistent had a comparative approach to the study of American societies been adopted earlier. Whether Africans made great, little, or no contribution to the development of American civilization is less important than the fact that during long periods of American

11. Phillips, *American Negro Slavery*, 4.
12. Evangeline W. and Charles M. Andrews (eds.), *Journal of a Lady of Quality, Being the Narrative of a Journey from Scotland to the West Indies, North Carolina, and Portugal in the Years 1774 to 1776* (New Haven, 1921), 176–77. Italics added.

history the mere notion of such a contribution was, with rare exceptions, inconceivable. Hence, facts long existent were passed over in silence.

Within the past generation this situation fortunately has been reversed, to such an extent, indeed, that scarcely a year has passed during the last decade which has not seen the appearance of at least one major new historical work reassessing national and social institutions around the South Atlantic. As expressed by a French historian, it is now generally conceded in North America, as well as South America, that "the slave did not arrive in America [culturally] naked. He brought with him a sense of sedentary life and of agriculture, while his wife brought a concept of domesticity. . . . He brought as well culinary recipes, a sense of dietary balance . . . medical formulas and plants unknown in America."[13] He was, in short, equipped to be an active participant in the task of American colonization, fully capable of giving as well as receiving.

This inquiry is a result of this new consensus. It seeks to raise and answer questions relating to slavery and the slave trade with reference to South Carolina (and elsewhere) by focusing on the problem of why colonial South Carolinians preferred certain African ethnic groups over others as slaves. It deals with related questions such as whether they could distinguish one from another, whether it was important to do so, and why. The methodology is somewhat diffuse. The slave trade has traditionally been studied from the vantage point of either the African coast or of the region of debarkation. Seldom has an attempt been made to give equal emphasis to both in the same work. In this case, the need to discover whether the choice of South Carolinians was determined by conditions in Africa, in America, or in both seemed to require such a procedure. Nor is such an approach of value only to this study. A look at the African material immediately reveals a considerable lack of knowledge among historians about European contact with and reaction to Africans, in Africa as well as in

13. Frédéric Mauro, *L'Expansion Européenne (1600–1870)* (Paris, 1964), 217–18. Mauro referred to Brazil and was himself involved in the conflict between Indianists and Africanists, suggesting that Africans were more advanced.

America. Or perhaps it might be better to say that, with few exceptions, historians have usually failed to make a connection between the two settings. Such compartmentalization obviously did not obtain in the early colonial empires in which regions of Africa and America were invariably—and sometimes closely—related.

This study treats one area and aspect of an extended plantation system. The first chapter considers the attitudes of South Carolinians towards various African groups and compares and contrasts these attitudes with those of Europeans elsewhere around the South Atlantic. It assesses, in the process, some of the consequences of these variant perceptions. Chapter 2 concerns the trade on the African coast. It attempts to show that Europeans were in many ways much more knowledgeable about Africans, and at an earlier period, than is commonly assumed. Although some new facts are used, the presentation of new information in this chapter seems less important than showing that what was already known to African historians was relevant for American scholars as well. Chapter 2 is also intended to make clearer the discussions in Chapter 3, which also deals with linkages between Africa, Europe, and the New World in terms of ideas and information, and in Chapters 4 and 5, which treat relationships between Africans and Europeans in South Carolina. If, for example, Europeans possessed dependable knowledge about Africa and Africans, Peter Wood's suggestion that one reason Gambia slaves were preferred in South Carolina was because of their familiarity with rice production would be stronger. Chapter 4 treats rice and other aspects of this suggestion in detail. Chapter 5 deals more particularly with the interaction between Africans and Europeans by focusing on slave runaways. It uses the rich information about runaways to expand and support earlier suggestions about South Carolinians' perceptions of African ethnic groups and in the process indicates possible areas of further study.

This work obviously is not, nor is it meant to be, a final statement on the range of attitudes, relations, and perceptions of blacks and whites in colonial South Carolina. It is but one step in an ongoing endeavor, carrying forward ideas already suggested by other scholars and adducing new ideas for continuing discussion.

Chapter 1

Price and Perception

I

"Most white colonists," Peter Wood suggests in his recent study, "would have marveled at the ignorance of their descendants, who asserted blindly that all Africans looked the same."[1] In fact, European colonists concerned themselves quite closely with distinctions among African peoples, and paid great attention to such things as size, color, and cultural or other characteristics. This concern has long been recognized as having been present in Latin America and perhaps to a lesser extent in the West Indies. On the continent, quite as much as in the islands, British colonists were also concerned about where they got their slaves, what they looked like, and how they performed. Because potential customers had these concerns, moreover, merchants in Britain and America tried to cater to them, and one of the determinants of slave prices in South Carolina was the bondsman's provenance.

"The Slaves from the River Gambia are preferr'd to all others with us save the Gold Coast," merchant Henry Laurens wrote to one correspondent, adding that there "must not be a Callabar among them." To another he wrote, "Gold Coast or Gambias are best [;] next To Them The Windward Coast are prefer'd to Angolas."[2] Thus went the hierarchy of regional preferences. Slaves from the region of Senegambia and present-day Ghana were preferred, though more were imported from the former region than from the latter. Elizabeth Donnan, followed by Philip Curtin and others, states flatly that Gambias were the first choice, and that those from the Gold Coast were second.[3] Laurens himself often

1. Wood, *Black Majority*, 179.
2. Henry Laurens to Richard Oswald, May 17, 1756, Laurens to Smith and Clifton, July 17, 1755, in George Rogers, Jr., *et al.* (eds.), *The Papers of Henry Laurens* (7 vols.; Columbia, S.C., 1968–79), II, 186, and I, 295.
3. Elizabeth Donnan, "The Slave Trade into South Carolina Before the American Revo-

seemed to equate the two, though he was not always consistent. He wrote on one occasion that people from the Gold Coast had sold much higher than had been expected, "which shews that our People would give a preference to Slaves from that Quarter, for had they been Gambias we are almost sure they would not have brought so much by £20 [currency] per head." Later in the same year, though, he told an English merchant not to expect higher prices for his Gold Coast cargo than those at which Gambias had recently been sold, since the latter were as well liked as "those of any Country whatsoever." At the other end of the scale, the evidence is quite clear. "Few of our planters will touch Calabar Slaves when others can be had," Laurens cautioned a Liverpool merchant, and he advised another that such people sold from three to four pounds sterling per head less than those from more desirable regions.[4] The extremes, then, were Gambia and Gold Coast slaves on the one hand and Calabar (or Ibo or "Bite") slaves, from the Niger Delta, on the other, with Windward Coast and Angola slaves somewhere in the middle.

These regional types were presumed to embody valued characteristics. "Our Planters almost to a Man are desirous of large strong People like Gambias & will not touch small limb'd People when such can be had." Slaves sold better when they were tall, healthy, male (two times out of three), young (between eighteen and twenty-five was the optimum age for males; fourteen to eighteen for females), and free of blemishes.[5] Heavy emphasis was placed on the bondsman being as dark as possible.[6] These desirable

lution," *American Historical Review*, XXXIII (July, 1928), 816–17, and Philip D. Curtin, *The Atlantic Slave Trade: A Census* (Madison, 1969), 156–57.

4. In Rogers *et al.* (eds), *Papers of Henry Laurens*: Laurens to John Knight, February 12, 1756, II, 93; Laurens to Richard Nicholas and Co., September 11, 1756, II, 315; Laurens to Jonathan Blundell and Co., May 16, 1756, and, to the same effect, to John Knight, July 11, 1755, II, 182, and I, 29; Laurens to Devonsheir, Reeve, and Lloyd, May 22, 1755, I, 252; Laurens to Gidney Clarke, June 26, 1756, II, 230; Laurens to Samuel Linnecar, May 8, 1756, II, 179.

5. In *ibid.*: Laurens to Gidney Clarke, June 26, 1756, II, 230; Laurens to Smith and Clifton, July 17, 1755, I, 295; Laurens to Valentine Powell, November 9, 1756, II, 348.

6. Laurens to Lloyd and Barton, December 24, 1765, in *ibid.*, IV, 558. For similar ideas see James Laroche and Co. to Capt. Richard Prankard, May 29, 1733, in Jefferies Collection, XIII, f. 413, Bristol Central Library; and Elizabeth Donnan (ed.), *Documents Illustrative of the History of the Slave Trade to America* (4 vols.; Washington, D.C., 1930), II, 459. The concept that it was desirable for the slaves to be as black as possible was held by Africans as

attributes were all associated with people from the preferred regions. In addition, they were considered to be more dependable workers. Laurens, for example, complimented the governor of East Florida on servile laborers he had just obtained to work plantations in the newly acquired British possession but added that "the remainder should be fine Young Gambians or Gold Coast. They are fit to work immediately & the next Year will be as good hands as any & less inclined to wander."[7]

People who had the adverse of these traits, people who were small, slender, weak, and tended towards a yellowish color, were less desirable. Calabar or Ibo slaves, with whatever justice, seemed to epitomize these qualities.[8] Moreover, they were regarded as possessing a deplorable penchant for committing suicide. Slave dealers were advised that if Calabars and Ibos had to be sent, they should be "young People from 15 to 20" who were "not accustom'd to destroy themselves" like those who were older.[9] Laurens probably had the same thought in mind when, on another occasion, he advised that Calabar slaves should not be older than fourteen.[10]

---

well as Europeans. The Hausa at Kano (in northern Nigeria) thought that blacker slaves could better stand the sun and were less difficult to manage on the long march to the coast. They therefore raided among darker peoples to the south rather than among lighter peoples to the north, west, or east. See Melville J. Herskovits, "The Significance of West Africa for Negro Research," *Journal of Negro History*, XXI (January, 1936), 15–30.

In a table giving the average height of runaway slaves in Jamaica (in 1794, 1813, and 1814) by ethnic group, Mandingos, at 5'3", were shorter than any other group listed. This could have been an atypical sample, but it is not really contradictory, since Edwards remarked that the Mandingos consisted of "very distinct tribes" only *some* of which were "remarkably tall and black." (Coromantees, from the Gold Coast, at 5'5⅔", were the tallest group of the sample.) See Orlando Patterson, *The Sociology of Slavery: An Analysis of the Origins, Development and Structure of Negro Slave Society in Jamaica* (Rutherford, 1969), 138.

7. Laurens to James Grant, April 20, 1765, in Grant of Ballindalloch MSS, 0771/359, National Register of Archives, Edinburgh.

8. The association of these characteristics with slaves from the Niger Delta is found not only in the Laurens papers but in various other places. See, for example, Phillips, *American Negro Slavery*, 43; Bryan Edwards, *The History Civil and Commercial of the British Colonies in the West Indies* (Charleston, S.C., 1810), II, 280, hereinafter referred to as *History of the British Colonies*.

9. Laurens to John Knight, May 28, 1756, in Rogers et al. (eds.), *Papers of Henry Laurens*, II, 204. The observation about Ibos' predilection for self-destruction was also made by Edwards, *History of the British Colonies*, II, 281, and by the French, in Lucien Peytraud, *L'Esclavage aux Antilles Françaises Avant 1789* (Paris, 1897), 89.

10. Laurens to Smith and Baillies, March 1, 1764, in Rogers et al. (eds.), *Papers of Henry Laurens*, IV, 193.

How closely these stereotypes approached reality is problematical. Whether for the same or other reasons, however, a similar hierarchy of preferences extended beyond South Carolina to other English-speaking areas and to other European groups. A captain of the Royal African Company who had carried slaves from Barbados to Nevis in 1676 was asked by the governor to explain, in effect, why he slighted the latter by bringing down "byte" slaves instead of his original Gold Coast cargo. The company recognized such distinctions when in 1723 it offered to contract for slaves to Antigua at twenty-three pounds per head for Gold Coast and Whydah slaves and twenty pounds per head for those from Gambia and Cabenda.[11] And factors in Antigua, writing to Bristol merchants in November, 1740, also acknowledged this structure of preferences.[12] English merchants dealing with Spaniards were advised that they "buy Gold Coast & Whidaws before any other Country, after them Angolas & then Callabars."[13] Laurens noted in 1756, when the market for slaves in South Carolina was not so good, that he had a chance to sell some Windward Coast slaves to a Spaniard. He complained, though, that the Spanish were so used to accepting Calabars that "tis Very difficult to bring them up to Such prices for Others as they richly deserve."[14] This statement implies, not a divergence in assessments of worth, but in willingness or ability to pay, and it connotes some universal criteria of slave value.

II

Englishmen made various attempts in the eighteenth century to characterize in terms of temperament and disposition peoples

---

11. Donnan (ed.), *Documents*, I, 205; II, 303n.

12. Benjamin King and Robert Arbuthnot to Isaac Hobhouse and Stephen Baugh, November 1740, in City Museum, Bristol, England. These men expressed their preferences in almost precisely the same words as Laurens.

13. Tydall and Asheton to Isaac Hobhouse, February 17, 1729, in Jefferies Collection, XIII, f. 93. Several other letters to the same effect were exchanged between these correspondents and are located in the Jefferies Collection, XIII.

14. Laurens to Richard Oswald and Co., July 26, 1756, in Rogers *et al.* (eds.), *Papers of Henry Laurens*, II, 271.

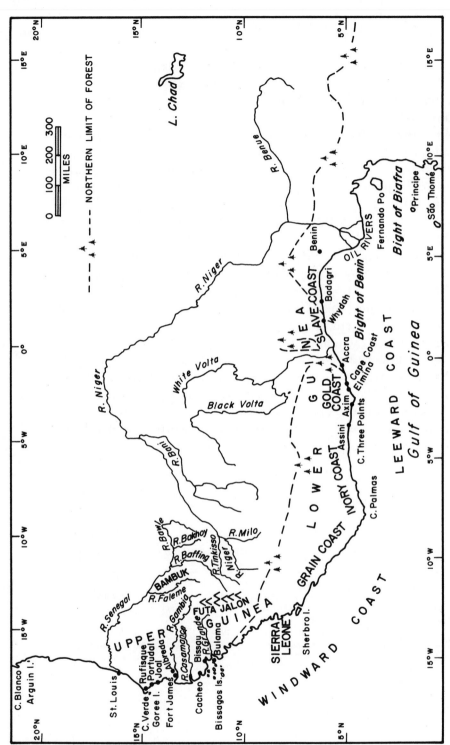

West Africa in the era of the slave trade
Map by Dean L. Pendleton

from the various regions that contributed slaves to New World plantations. Mandingos, from the Gambia region, were supposed to be physically more attractive to Europeans than were other Africans. Refined and possessed of a gentle nature, they were, some thought, not entirely trustworthy. Coromantees, from the Gold Coast, were said to be especially hardy, ferocious if angered, unmindful of danger, unwilling to forgive a wrong, but loyal if their devotion could be captured. "Papaws" and others from the region around Whydah on the Slave Coast were considered to be the most valuable of slaves imported. Accustomed to work, more even-tempered than Coromantees, they were skilled, complacent, and obedient. Ibos, from the Niger Delta, were commonly less desirable than other people imported, considered to be melancholy and suicidal, sickly, unattractive, and superstitious. Peoples from the regions of the Congo and Angola were supposed to be docile, comely, not especially strong, possessed of a peculiar predisposition towards the mechanic arts, but inclined to run away.[15]

These characteristics were assumed to make certain groups particularly suited to certain types of work. For example, Coromantees and Whydahs, because of their greater hardiness, were supposed to be especially desirable as field hands, whereas Ibos, Congos, and Angolas, allegedly weaker, were said to be more effective as house servants. Such, anyway, was the feeling in British colonies. These judgments appear at first to be entirely subjective, because it would seem that Latin Americans thought precisely the opposite. Roger Bastide writes that in the Iberian colonies "the Bantu [including some peoples from the Niger Delta, Congos, and Angolas] were chiefly valued for their physical strength and endurance, their capacity for work, their known skill

15. These characterizations, some in more elaborate form, are found in, among other places, Edwards, *History of the British Colonies*, II, 265–83; Anon., "A History of the Sugar Cane," *Gentleman's Magazine*, XXXIV (October, 1764), 487; Edward Long, *The History of Jamaica, or General Survey of the Ancient and Modern State of That Island with Reflections on its Situations, Settlements, Inhabitants, Climate, Products, Commerce, Laws and Government* (New edition; London, 1970), II, 403–404; Gonzalo Aguirre Beltrán, *La población negra de México: Estudio ethnohistórico* (Mexico, 1972), 141, 186–87; "Governor Codrington to the Council of Trade & Plantations," *Calendar of State Papers, Colonial Series: America and the West Indies* (London, 1910), XIX, 720–22; Peytraud, *L'Esclavage*, 85–90.

as agricultural labourers. While ethnic groups such as the Fon, Yoruba, and Mina were chosen as 'house servants.'"[16] So important were slaves from Angola to the sugar-producing regions of Brazil that the remark was current in the seventeenth century that "without sugar there is no Brazil and without Angola there is no sugar."[17]

It is easy to dismiss assessments of temperament and character as based on stereotypical perceptions; and it is striking that slaves from the same region, who were esteemed by Spaniards yet denigrated by English planters in Barbados during the seventeenth century, were the first choice of British colonials in South Carolina during the eighteenth century.[18] One might think, however, that a material quality such as physical strength would be susceptible to measurement and thus to objective evaluation. That even this quality was subject to variable interpretation is vividly illustrated not only by the dissimilar assessments of North and South Americans but more trenchantly by a change of opinion within a single region.

During the seventeenth century, when most slaves came from Angola anyway, Brazilians considered Angolas to be the best workers and did not regard Sudanese slaves (Fon, Yoruba, and Mina) highly. During the eighteenth century, an altered situation dictated the development of trade in the regions of current Togo and modern Benin, called the Mina Coast, and a pragmatic change occurred in slave preferences.[19] Portuguese officials writing in the first decades of the century indicated that Brazilian evaluation of

16. Roger Bastide, *African Civilizations in the New World* (New York, 1971), 106.
17. James Duffy, *Portuguese Africa* (Cambridge, 1961), 138–39.
18. Walter Rodney, "Upper Guinea and the Significance of the Origins of Africans Enslaved in the New World," *Journal of Negro History*, LIV (October, 1969), 341.
19. Trade with the Mina Coast was authorized by the Portuguese crown in the 1640s but was light before 1680. It greatly increased from the latter decade because of a smallpox epidemic in Angola and Bahia that restricted commerce at Luanda, and because the simultaneous discovery of gold in Minas Gerais redoubled the need for servile labor. The changes in slave preferences accompanied these altered conditions. See Charles Boxer, *The Golden Age of Brazil, 1695–1750: Growing Pains of a Colonial Society* (Berkeley, 1969), 45–46; A. J. R. Russell-Wood, *Fidalgos and Philanthropists: The Santa Casa da Misericordia of Bahia, 1550–1755* (Berkeley, 1968), 67–68, 290; Pierre Verger, *Flux et Reflux de la Traite des Nègres entre le Golfe de Benin et Bahia de Todos os Santos du XVIIe au XIXe Siècle* (Paris, 1968), 67–68.

the relative merits of Angolan and Sudanese slaves had reversed. Sudanese slaves were now considered to be stronger and better workers than Angolas, who, it was said, died more easily and were inclined to commit suicide.[20] Sudanese slaves were apparently more troublesome and predisposed to insurrection. But when the Portuguese king, to obviate this possibility, suggested in 1725 that only Angolas be sent to the mining regions, the viceroy replied that they were fit only for domestic labor and that adequate vigilance was sufficient to frustrate any Sudanese plot.[21]

These differences in perception can be laid to divergent local conditions or variant circumstances, most of which had little to do with the slave. For what he was expected to do doubtless affected how he was perceived. It would seem, though, that the observations are not so far apart as they initially appear. Gilberto Freyre, commenting that Bantu slaves (Congos and Angolas among others) were good for field labor, remarks that "those from Guinea, Cape Verde, and Sierra Leone were bad slaves but comely of body. Especially the women, for which reason they were preferred for domestic service." What Freyre apparently means by their being "bad" slaves was that they were "slack and lazy."[22] This could be read as *recalcitrant*, an aspect of rebelliousness that may have had something to do with their original rejection as less desirable.[23] But Angola's proximity and the absence of serious competition there quite possibly were more important.[24] However, the reason

20. Boxer, *Golden Age of Brazil*, 47; Russell-Wood, *Fidalgos and Philanthropists*, 68; Verger, *Flux et Reflux*, 71, 150, 61–157 *passim*.

21. Russell-Wood, *Fidalgos and Philanthropists*, 141. Patterson, *Sociology of Slavery*, 137–38, also remarks on the "'perverse' preference of Jamaican planters for slaves from the Gold Coast, despite their major role in the slave revolts of the island."

22. Freyre, *Masters and Slaves*, 302, 302n.

23. It could also be read as *intransigence*, but a less anomalous term would seem applicable, not merely because of the reputation of Sudanese slaves for rebelliousness but because "everywhere in the Americas a correlation existed between concentrations of African-born slaves and the outbreak of revolts." The term *intransigence* is anomalous because it often represented accommodation rather than resistance. Eugene D. Genovese, "Rebelliousness and Docility in the Negro Slave: A Critique of the Elkins Thesis," 307, and George M. Frederickson and Christopher Lasch, "Resistance to Slavery," 22–26, both in *Civil War History*, XII (December, 1967). Rodney, "Upper Guinea," 339, indicates that the opinions of Europeans about various African groups were often determined by the extent to which Africans cooperated with the slavers.

24. Under favorable conditions, a voyage from Angola to Bahia took forty days; to Pernambuco, thirty-five days; and to Rio de Janeiro, fifty days. Inclement weather increased

Sudanese were favored as house servants, according to Freyre, derived not from considerations of strength or capability but physical appearance. "It is easy to imagine," Freyre continues, that the women "were also employed as pleasing concubines . . . in those relations between master and slave girl which were so common with our colonial patriarchs." [25] By using the phrase *house servants* in quotes, Bastide seems to second this opinion.

Whatever personal prejudices, historical precedents, or psychological or sociological predeterminants modified Portuguese perceptions in seventeenth-century Brazil, by the eighteenth century their observations of the physical capabilities of various slave types agreed largely with those made by the English. French and Dutch appraisals seemed likewise coincident. [26] Comments to the contrary were evidently made exclusively in the earlier period. Bastide's assertion that Iberians preferred the Bantu because of their physical strength, therefore, is probably too sweeping.

That judgments made by the British were not entirely capricious is indicated by their analysis of the effects of diet and environment. A British slave trader distinguished among the several groups this way:

> Those from the Gold Coast, who are accustomed to Freedom and inhabit a dry Champain Country and feed on nutricious and solid Aliments, such as Flesh, Fish, Bread of Indian Corn &c are healthy and robust; little subject to Mortality; very hardy and turbulent, as well as much disposed to rise on the White People. . . . Those from the Grain Coast, which is also elevated, live chiefly upon Rice, Plantains, Potatoes &c are less hardy than the Gold Coast Slaves, but somewhat more so, than those from Angola, whose Situation and Mode of Living is in many Respects similar. But the Slaves from Bennin, Bony, & the Calabars, where the Soil is low, moist, and marshy, and the Com-

---

sailing time. Frédéric Mauro, *Le Portugal et l'Atlantique au XVIIe Siècle (1570–1670): Etude économique* (Paris, 1960), 171.

25. Freyre, *Masters and Slaves*, 303.

26. For the Dutch, see Johannes Postma, "The Origin of African Slaves: The Dutch Activities on the African Coast, 1675–1795," in Stanley L. Engerman and Eugene D. Genovese (eds.), *Race and Slavery in the Western Hemisphere: Quantitative Studies* (Princeton, 1975), 36; for the French, see M. L. E. Moreau de Saint-Méry, *Description Topographic, Physique, Civile, Politique et Historique de la Partie Française de l'Isle Saint Dominique* (Philadelphia, 1797), 45–59; and Peytraud, *L'Esclavage*, 85–90.

mon Food nothing else than Yams, Plantains, Cassava, Potatoes, and other soft and succulent Vegetables, are of all others on the African Coast, the most weakly and delicate.[27]

Interestingly enough, a similar ranking according to food value is reflected in modern nutritional studies. Among staples commonly cultivated in Africa, maize (of New World provenience but widely grown in western and south-central regions by the eighteenth century) is exceeded only by wheat and sorghum in the quantity of protein provided and by sorghum alone in the amount of most other nutritive components. It outranks rice, plantains, and manioc (or cassava) on practically every scale, while the former exceeds the latter two in every significant nutritive component except calcium, more of which is contained in manioc.[28] The foods are about equal in energy value, with the exception of plantains which, pound for pound, contain "little more than one-fifth the calorie value of a food grain such as rice or maize, and is somewhat less than the calorie value of roots and tubers."[29] To the extent, then, that the description is an accurate gauge of the diets of these peoples, the assessments appear to have considerable validity. He went on to assert that insurance premiums against mortality in slave ships were based on these beliefs, indicating that they were widely and firmly held.

These observations of strength and presumed suitability for hard labor led to certain African groups becoming more closely associated with one plantation region than another. A British official comparing the productivity of French and English sugar colonies at the end of the Seven Years' War argued that the French colonies were more productive because they used a better class of laborers. Gold Coast, Whydah, and Popo slaves were best qualified for labor in the sugar colonies; and because the French

27. In Liverpool Papers, Add. MSS 38416, British Museum: Henry Ellis to Lord Hawkesbury, April 12, 1788, CCXXVII, f. 160; also see James Jones to Lord Hawkesbury, July 26, 1788, CCXXVII, ff. 154–55.

28. Marvin P. Miracle, *Maize in Tropical Africa* (Madison, 1966), 9–11, and 87–100. Also see Woot-Tsuen Wu Leung *et al.*, *Composition of Foods Used in Far Eastern Countries*, USDA Agricultural Handbook No. 34 (March, 1952), 10–16. William O. Jones, *Manioc in Africa* (Palo Alto, 1959), 6–19, 118–21.

29. Bruce F. Johnston, *The Staple Food Economies of Western Tropical Africa* (Palo Alto, 1966), 106.

had more of these types, their colonies were more productive. British West Indian planters, he said, were forced to buy other, weaker Negroes because the desirable types were not sufficiently supplied. In discussing the suitability of types, however, he went beyond the dietary explanation by relating the environment to character development.

> The Gold Coast, Popo, and Whidah Negroes are born in a part of Africa which is very barren. . . . On that account, when able to take the hoe in hand, they are obliged to go and cultivate the land for their subsistence. They also live hardily; so that when they are carried to our plantation (as they have been used to hard labour from their infancy) they become a strong, robust people, and can live upon the sort of food the planters allow them. . . . On the other hand, the Gambia, Calabar, Boney, and Angola Negroes are brought from those parts of Africa, that are extremely fertile, where everything grows almost spontaneously. . . . They have every . . . necessary of life in great plenty. On that account, the men never work, but lead an indolent life, and are in general of a lazy disposition and tender constitution . . . so that when these people are carried to our sugar islands they are obliged to be nursed, to be taken care of, and brought to work by degrees.

The latter were better suited to North America than to the Caribbean because provisions were more plentiful and less expensive; thus they could be gradually strengthened and brought up to difficult field work.[30]

This official distinguished two rather than three general groups and reveals a lower level of specificity than does the previous writer. The vagaries of African ethnological, cultural, and ecological distributions are such that various degrees or criteria of discrimination are indeed possible. The area of western Africa south of the Sahara Desert and north of the tropical forests clothing the seaboard is composed of open grasslands and bush country or savanna. This region, stretching from Dakar on the Atlantic coast to Lake Chad in about the center of the continent, almost three thousand miles to the east, is called the Western Sudan. Peoples inhabiting it generally possess a food economy based on the production and consumption of diverse grains, while societies confined to the

30. Donnan (ed.), *Documents*, II, 515.

forest littoral subsist basically on tubers, fruits, and vegetables. There is perhaps no more sharp division between these food zones than between the geographical regions with which they coincide, desert, savanna, and forest shading gradually into each other as one moves south from arid Sahara to humid tropics along the coast. The coastline is punctuated by occasional breaks, where the plains meet the sea; peoples such as the Akan, Fon, and others in the region from modern Ghana to modern Benin, though technically in the forest zone, are, in their food crops and other aspects of culture, related to the Sudan, while the penetration of rice into the forest lands of Senegambia creates an exception to the general pattern.[31] This variegated pattern of interrelationships between land, crops, and peoples occasions slightly variant perceptions but accommodates both descriptions. The expansion of grain into the tropics of Upper Guinea would place peoples there in an intermediate position between those of the Sudan and others of the forest zone in terms of both diet and related cultural attributes. The same is true for peoples in the Congo-Angola region to the extent that their situation parallels that of Upper Guinea.

Whatever the validity of the early ethnic characterizations, it is clear that they were taken seriously and acted upon, for slaves from particular geographical regions and of certain specifications sold better in one colony than another. Of this fact, slave traders were highly conscious. "At Granada we hope Windward & Gold Coast Slaves may be wanted, and generally Sell [well] there," a Liverpool ship captain was advised.[32] Another company ordered its captain to trade at Whydah "where you must Barter your Cargos for Negroes Mostly Grown people if to be had, as your destiny will probably be Either to Jamaica or So Carolina."[33] Sometimes the orders were quite detailed. One captain was instructed to slave first on the Gold Coast and at Whydah. He could then

---

31. See Daryll Forde, "The Cultural Map of West Africa: Successive Adaptations to Tropical Forests and Grasslands," in Simon and Phoebe Ottenberg (eds.), *Cultures and Societies of Africa* (New York, 1969), 116–37; also see Roland Oliver, "The Problem of Bantu Expansion," *Journal of African History*, VII, 3 (1966), 363–66.

32. James Clemens and Co. to Capt. David Tuohy, July 9, 1768, in Tuohy Papers, 380 TUO 4/3, Liverpool Record Office.

33. William Earle and Co. to Joseph Caton, August 25, 1764, in Raymond Richards Collection, Account book *Sisters*, 1, University Library, Keele, England.

proceed almost anywhere in the West Indies where slaves were desired. But, if he could not get a full cargo at the first two places and had then to go to Angola, he was to take it to Jamaica; for Gold Coast slaves would sell well on the island, and Angolas could be reexported at good advantage to Cartagena.[34] William Davenport and Company, of Liverpool, required a ship to maintain its course for South Carolina even if it were to arrive later than the usual season for slave trading, for it was "certainly the only Markett for Gambia Slaves."[35] Of course, slave dealers periodically tried to meet a specific rather than a general demand. "There has not [been] a Cargo of Ebbo slaves sold here [for] a long time," a Barbados mechant told his supplier in 1730, "and many People are Enquiering for them."[36]

The region with which South Carolina was most closely associated was Gambia. It is evident, however, that this was a result as much of external as internal circumstances. We have seen that Henry Laurens appeared to equate Gambia and Gold Coast slaves and that Britons felt that the former were better suited to North American conditions. If South Carolinians would pay as much for one as the other, so much the better. There was a fortuitous conjunction of colonial desire with what British officials or merchants, or both, already thought was the best course. In fact, 80 percent of British imports of Gold Coast slaves went to Jamaica, the largest British sugar-producing region in the eighteenth century.[37] Whether the relationship between Gambia and South Carolina would have been as strong if the relationship between the Gold Coast and Jamaica had been weaker is an open question. But a judgment of preference based solely on the number of slaves im-

34. Richard Norris to Thomas Brownell and James Murray, October 10, 1700, in Norris Papers, 920 NOR 2/179, Liverpool Record Office.

35. William Davenport and Co. to Capt. Samuel Sachevall, January 29, 1755, in Richards Collection, *Davenport* Letter and Bill Book, 1748.

36. Thomas Morris to Isaac Hobhouse, January 12, 1730, in Jefferies Collection, XIII, f. 133.

37. Curtin, *Atlantic Slave Trade*, 161. See Frank W. Pitman, "Slavery on British West India Plantations in the Eighteenth Century," *Journal of Negro History*, XI (October, 1926), 584–650, and *The Development of the British West Indies, 1700–1763* (London, 1967), and Richard B. Sheridan, "Commercial and Financial Organization of the British Slave Trade, 1750–1807," *Economic History Review*, Second Series, XI (December, 1958), 249–63, hereinafter referred to as "British Slave Trade."

ported is not definitive anyway. For example, although South Carolinians expressed a proclivity for Gambia over Angola slaves, more Angolans were actually imported. That British merchants coupled Gambia with South Carolina more than with any other region, though, is suggested not solely by the statement of William Davenport and Company that South Carolina was the only market for Gambia slaves, but by statistics from the African coast in 1764, the only year for which such complete information has been uncovered. In that year, forty-three ships stopped at James Fort on the River Gambia. Five had just arrived and had not begun to slave when the year ended. Some picked up a few captives and continued down the coast to slave elsewhere. Others left for specific destinations on or near the African coast. One had left the previous August with a full cargo of bondsmen who had revolted, taken over the ship, run it ashore, and made their escape, leaving those of the crew who survived in the hands of the Portuguese at Cacheo, whence they and the ship had been recently salvaged and brought back. Of fifteen ships that left directly for the New World, seven, or almost half, were destined for the Carolina region—six of them to South Carolina.[38] Of the five ships that came into the Gambia at the end of the year, three arrived in South Carolina in 1765.[39]

III

The question naturally arises as to what extent colonials could actually distinguish one ethnic group from another. On this point, the evidence is mixed. For one thing, slaves were usually called after the region or port of embarkation, which might not have been where they originated. Consequently, the terms *Angola*,

38. "List of the Vessels arrived at and sailed from James Fort in the River Gambia in the Year 1764," in Dartmouth MSS., D 1778.251, County Record Office, Stafford, England. Other such lists probably exist, for agents of the Company of Merchants in Gambia were ordered to stop and inspect the registers and clearances of all ships that proceeded up the river. In Treasury Papers, Public Record Office, London: London Committee of the Company of Merchants, August 30, 1754, 70/29, f. 22; agents at James Fort, March, 1755, 70/30, ff. 112–13.

39. Donnan (ed.), *Documents*, IV, 412–13; William Davenport and Co. to William Patten, November 23, 1764, in Richards Collection, Account book *William*, 19–21.

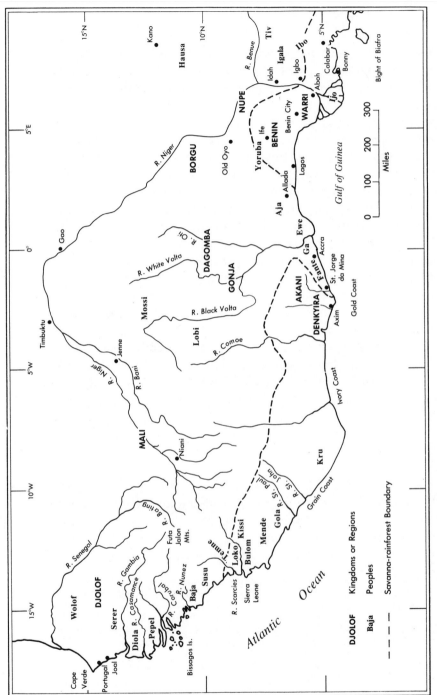

Peoples and states of the Guinea Coast

Map by Cartographic Section, School of Geoscience, Louisiana State University

DJOLOF Kingdoms or Regions

Baja Peoples

– – – Savanna-rainforest Boundary

Congo, Gambia, Whydah, Papaw are relatively imprecise when try-ing to identify particular groups. The terms *Ibo* and *Mandingo* are more precise but not necessarily correct. For example, terms such as *Ibo, Calabar, Bonny,* and *Bite* were sometimes used inter-changeably and are therefore vague if not inaccurate: the first des-ignates an ethnic group, the next two refer to political entities, and the fourth refers to a geographical area. Ibos inhabited the region containing all these features, but not all the people in the region were Ibos.[40] The term *Mandingo* was as loosely applied. Henry Laurens, after six years as a slave dealer (and more as a planter), complained to a correspondent in the West Indies that he had not included in the bill of lading the "Species" of slaves sent on con-signment.[41] Laurens thereby not only admitted his inability to de-termine slave origins on the basis of appearance himself but opened the possibility of perpetuating an error should his correspondent choose to mislead him.

Still, it is clear that South Carolinians had some attributes firmly in mind when they used these terms, and, whereas Bite, Bonny, Calabar, and Ibo are not coterminous, they do all pertain to the Niger Delta. Thus, although South Carolinians might not have been able to distinguish particular African ethnic groups with precision, they had some general sense of the difference between people from that region and from, say, the Congo. Moreover, be-cause peoples in various regions of Africa share elements of cul-ture and thereby constitute broad cultural areas, there is some le-gitimacy in such a conceptualization.

A culture area is "a classification of social groups according to their culture traits," or, better expressed, "a geographically delim-ited region, all the social groups in which share certain elements of culture not found in surrounding regions."[42] This concept, de-vised largely by American anthropologists, was applied by Mel-ville Herskovits to Africa in 1930. He suggested, at that time, the

40. Kenneth Onwuka Dike, *Trade and Politics in the Niger Delta, 1830–1855: An Introduc-tion to the Economic and Political History of Nigeria* (Oxford, 1966), 19–46.
41. Laurens to Law, Satterthwaite and Jones, December 14, 1755, in Rogers *et al.* (eds.), *Papers of Henry Laurens*, II, 38.
42. Irving Rouse, "Culture Area and Co-Tradition," *Southwestern Journal of Anthropol-ogy*, XIII (Summer, 1957), 124.

existence of nine major culture regions with two minor areas of transition.[43] The increase in ethnological knowledge in recent years has caused some of Herskovits' original suggestions to be modified and the total number of cultural zones to be greatly increased. Hermann Baumann, writing in 1947, designated twenty-six cultural groupings; George Peter Murdock, in 1959, found over forty.[44] Obviously, the more information one possesses about an area and the various peoples within it, the more refined the concept becomes.[45] It is not suggested here that eighteenth-century American colonials possessed the same kind of awareness as twentieth-century social scientists. But they did have a keen practical sense that dictated a judicious concern about things affecting their economic well-being, and the regional derivation of slaves was one of them.

Historians of Latin America commonly talk about two major slave types. In general, they label those people in West Africa from the Gulf of Guinea northward to the Sahara as Sudanese and those to the southward, in Central and Southwest Africa, as Bantu.[46] In this categorization they follow a disjunction made by anthropologists, philologists, and other African scholars—a division that is primarily linguistic but implies certain substrata of cultural commonality.[47] The Sudanese include such peoples as the Wolof, Mandingo, Bambara, Soninke, Mossi, Yoruba, Hausa, and Fulani, among others. The Bantu are equally diverse. A line formed by the Niger and Benue rivers at their juncture in Nigeria would seem to be a convenient geographical feature separating the Sudanese from an area comprising a series of Bantu-related lan-

43. Melville J. Herskovits, "The Culture Areas of Africa," *Africa*, III (January, 1930), 59–76; also in Herskovits, "Social History of the Negro," in Carl A. Murchison (ed.), *A Handbook of Social Psychology* (New York, 1967), 214–27.

44. H. Baumann and D. Westermann, *Les Peuples et les Civilisations de l'Afrique; Les Langues et l'Education* (Paris, 1970), 13–437; George Peter Murdock, *Africa: Its Peoples and Their Culture History* (New York, 1959).

45. See, for example, Alan P. Merriam, "The Concept of Culture Clusters Applied to the Belgian Congo," *Southwestern Journal of Anthropology*, XV (Winter, 1959), 375–95.

46. Mauro, *Le Portugal et l'Atlantique*, 152.

47. See Oliver, "Problems of Bantu Expansion," 361–76, and Forde, "Cultural Map of West Africa," 119–24. This distinction has been called into question; see Joseph Greenberg, "Linguistic Evidence Regarding Bantu Origins," *Journal of African History*, XII, 2 (1972), 189–216.

guages that shade gradually into the region of Bantu-speakers proper. There is thus no sharp break between Sudanese and Bantu-speaking peoples. This fact is particularly true at the lower reaches of the Niger (roughly below eight degrees north latitude) where the Ibo, linguistically related to Sudanese groups, extend east of the river and share cultural elements with delta peoples who are linguistically distinct. Frédéric Mauro distinguishes the Bantu from the Sudanese by their "smaller size, clearer complexion, smaller nose, less-acute prognathism. They have a slender neck, well-proportioned body, an underdeveloped calf, and large feet with prominent heels." [48] This description accords well with descriptions of slaves from Angola and the Niger Delta given by Henry Laurens. The distinction here, though, is in terms of physical type instead of culture. Physical type, however, was only one of the things that eighteenth-century planters were concerned about. As pointed out, they also assigned certain attributes to various ethnic groups, some of which had more to do with culture, perhaps, than with anything else. An Ibo and an Angola might not be physically dissimilar, but certain presumably local cultural traditions predisposed Ibos but not Angolas towards self-destruction (assuming the stereotype had any validity). Hence, knowledge of the provenance of the slave was as important as his appearance if he could not clearly be distinguished as different from a less-desirable group. In this light, Laurens' complaint that "you dont mention in your Bill of Loading of what Species they were" was evidence of a certain sophistication as well as an admission of his inability to make careful distinctions.

IV

Regional characterization might have less value, on the one hand, or divergent descriptions of people from the same region might be better explained, on the other, if it could be shown that people taken from the same port actually came from more than one cultural region, determined by distance inland rather than by distance

48. Mauro, *Le Portugal et l'Atlantique*, 153.

along the coast. Early descriptions of the slave trade often related
that the slaves had come from many miles away in the interior.
Recent historians have indicated, however, that with a few exceptions, most slaves were taken within a radius of several hundred
miles of the coast.[49] The most significant exceptions to this rule
are, perhaps, in Upper Guinea, where trade along the Gambia and
Senegal rivers permitted penetration for an extraordinary distance
into the hinterland, and in the Congo-Angola region, where long-
distance trade from Central Africa, and even beyond, was an important aspect of coastal exchange.[50] When slaves did originate
many hundreds of miles inland they were, especially in the latter
region, commonly less desirable than those captured closer to the
coast, because they arrived for sale in much poorer condition.[51]

Not only did most of the internecine conflict and slave raiding
that characterized "recruitment" for the trade involve coastal peoples, but even in cases that involved interior kingdoms—as at
Kano, which was about seven hundred miles from the sea—the
people actually captured and sold were from the south rather than
north of the kingdom.[52] Besides, there were many ways short of
hostilities in which slaves were recruited. Offenses against society
(commonly such crimes as witchcraft, murder, adultery, and theft)
or offenses against the king were often punished by selling the
transgressor to the Europeans. Some slaves, furnished as tribute
from one African group to another, were transferred to Euro-

49. See, for example, Melville J. Herskovits, "A Footnote to the History of Negro Slav-
ing," and "On the Provenience of New World Negroes," in Frances S. Herskovits (ed.),
The New World Negro: Selected Essays in Afroamerican Studies (Bloomington, 1966), 83–101.
Philip Curtin and Jan Vansina, "Sources of the Nineteenth Century Atlantic Slave Trade,"
Journal of African History, V, 2 (1964), 185–208.

50. Curtin and Vansina, "Sources of the Nineteenth Century Atlantic Slave Trade,"
189, and Rodney, "Upper Guinea," 327–45. Jan Vansina, "Long-Distance Trade Routes in
Central Africa," *Journal of African History*, III, 3 (1962), 375–90; David Birmingham, *Trade
and Conflict in Angola: The Mbundu and Their Neighbours Under the Influence of the Portuguese,
1483–1790* (London, 1966), 133–61; Phyllis M. Martin, *The External Trade of the Loango
Coast, 1576–1870: The Effects of Changing Commercial Relations on the Vili Kingdom of Loango*
(Oxford, 1972), 136–57.

51. Elena F. Scheuss de Studer, *La Trata de Negros en el Rio de la Plata durante el Siglo
XVIII* (Buenos Aires, 1958), 324. On this point, see also Donnan (ed.), *Documents*, I,
284–85, 458–59.

52. Melville J. Herskovits, "Significance of West Africa," 15–30.

peans.[53] Personal misfortune such as indebtedness, or natural disasters such as famines, caused many people to be sold, or to sell themselves or members of their families, into servitude, another practice from which Europeans benefited.[54] Thus, although in extraordinary cases particular slaves might have traveled as much as a thousand miles or more before being sold to Europeans on the coast, most came from among peoples with whom resident agents ought to have been familiar.[55] Therefore, tribal or regional characterizations might possess, if not total validity, at least greater dependability.

Because Europeans on the African coast possessed a certain knowledge of Africans, however, does not mean that all, or indeed that any, of this knowledge was necessarily transmitted to other Europeans or that others perceived the same types of differences. It is likely that few knew more about their human commodity than what vitally affected their own welfare. Nor was such knowledge as existed self-perpetuating. Donnan remarks in amazement on the speed with which the origins of Carolina blacks ceased to be important.[56] It might be ventured as a general, though not infallible, rule that Europeans were more conscious of distinctions among Africans in direct proportion to their involvement with the African coast. This consciousness was determined, though, not so much by geographical propinquity as by the way in which circumstances of the slave trade affected relationships between Africans and Europeans.

In dealing with this question, one has to distinguish four or, perhaps, five different sets of Europeans. There were those merchants who operated solely from Great Britain, who had no direct contact with the slaves at all, and whose awareness of slave differences was based entirely on hearsay. Distinctions were nonethe-

53. Extracts of Evidence of James Penny, Esqr., in Long's Collections for the History of Jamaica, ff. 24–26, Add. MSS 18272, British Museum; Donnan (ed.), *Documents*, I, 403, 294.

54. Donnan (ed.), *Documents*, I, 284; "Robert Norris, Esqr., Carolina Merchant of Liverpool, Evidence," in Long's Collections, ff. 11–17, Add. MSS 18272.

55. Curtin and Vansina, "Sources of the Nineteenth Century Atlantic Slave Trade," 190.

56. Donnan, "Slave Trade into South Carolina," 817*n*.

less important to them because they had much to do with profit and loss. Second, there were the captains and sailors who had direct contact with the slaves and gained some knowledge of them and of the African coast—an obligation dictated by a desire to make the best possible deal in the shortest conceivable time. Third, there were the agents of the various British companies who were stationed on the coast and whose cognizance of African tribal and ethnic distinctions and whose understanding of the complexities of African political and social life were expected, at least within a given region, to be most complete. Finally, there were the planters and slave dealers in America whose general awareness of African distinctions was a matter of self-interest but who could probably afford to be less aware than agents in Africa, whose position was so much more tenuous. Slavers thus occupied an intermediary position between colonials and resident agents in terms of knowledge as well as function. The fact that colonists usually expressed preferences in regional rather than more precise tribal or ethnic terms suited both agents and slavers, because their cargoes were, as often as not, composed of peoples from various tribal groups, and, unless there were obvious, significant differences among them, there was no reason to be more particular.

When ships traded in different regions, however, they usually kept an account of slaves taken from the various areas. Differential mortality was one reason for this practice; the ship *James*, for example, logged its incidents of sickness and death thus:

> Rec'd from Wyembah Sickned and would not eat anything.
> Rec'd from Anambooe departed this life of a flux.
> Rec'd from Agga and departed this life of a flux.[57]

Related to this concern with mortality was an interest in the sort of food that the captives preferred or that seemed best for them, which also varied according to the regional derivation of the unfortunates. Local food crops determined and differentiated tastes, and Africans preferred foods that most closely approximated those with which they were familiar. Thus, Calabar slaves were said to prefer manioc and yams to other staples that ships dis-

57. Donnan (ed.), *Documents*, I, 207.

pensed, because they had been raised on those foods.[58] Since traders were interested in bringing as many as possible of their cargo to port alive, they concerned themselves with making the food as attractive as circumstances would admit, which included obtaining those viands that particular groups most relished.[59]

A most serious consideration of distinction among Africans was propensity for insurrection. Certain groups, aboard ship and in the colonies, had a reputation for being more likely to revolt than others. One trader warned seamen to be aware that "Fida and Ardra slaves are . . . the most apt to revolt aboard ships, by a conspiracy carried on amongst themselves; especially such as are brought down to Fida, from very remote inland countries, who easily draw others into their plot."[60] The discernment here went beyond a mere regional characterization. It divided inland from coastal peoples and indicated a recognition that all the people of the area were not the same, though vagueness is evident in that they were all called Ardras or Fidas.[61] In other cases, the distinction was more precise. After a slave insurrection was repressed aboard a ship in 1700, the captain learned that the ringleaders were all Menbombe slaves (from Cabinda, on the Loango Coast).[62]

But although the distinction is more precise, it is not necessarily more accurate in terms of identifying a particular ethnic group. Phyllis Martin says of the trade in this region:

> There were different categories of slaves on sale at the three ports. At Loango Bay were to be found *Monteques*, *Mayombes*, and *Quibangues*; at Malemba were *Mayombes* and *Congues*; at Cabinda were *Congues*, *Sognes*, and *Mondongues*. These names did not, however, indicate the exact source of the slaves; rather they derived from the peoples who supplied the slaves or across whose territory the slaves had passed on route to the Loango Coast. This would explain, for example, why Mayombe slaves figured prominently at Loango Bay and Malemba.

---

58. *Ibid.*, 463.
59. Testimony of Robert Norris to the House of Lords, 1788, *Report of the House of Lords, 1789*, pp. 111–12, in Bristol Archives Office.
60. Donnan (ed.), *Documents*, I, 295.
61. A similar kind of distinction, though just as vague, was made by a French planter, who asserted that "true" Ardras could be distinguished from "the others" who were called by that name. Saint-Méry, *Description Topographique*, 50.
62. Donnan (ed.), *Documents*, I, 457.

These were not necessarily the Yombe inhabitants of the Mayombe region. They were rather given this name since the caravans going to Loango Bay or Malemba would pass through this region.[63]

This kind of inexactitude is a problem for the modern scholar in a way that it may not have been for the eighteenth-century trader. What the captain meant by a Menbombe slave might not be clear to us, but it was quite clear to him and, in fact, might have led to the development of a new stereotype and to other captains being warned to take particular care of captives of that type.

The way in which this kind of information was passed on and the sort of interaction that took place between various groups of Europeans is indicated in ship orders written in 1782. Captain Henry Moore of the ship *Nancy* was ordered to Cape Coast Castle to receive instructions as to where trade on the coast would be best—at Porto Novo (in present-day Benin), at Lagos (in Nigeria), or at "Portagery" (*i.e.*, Badagry, also in Nigeria). The shipowners admonished that at Lagos he would find "two kinds of Slaves, the one equal to the Whydahs; the other little if any better than Benins, which therefore desire you will be very cautious & not purchase any of the latter but get ev'ry Informations and Instructions before you leave Cape Coast regarding them, that on your arrival there you may not be at a loss to know the Difference." He was to get the same information about slaves at the other two places and to be just as careful. Because the document is mutilated, his instructions relative to Whydah are unclear. Apparently, the shipowners thought that even when there was no difference in the quality of slaves bought at Whydah and elsewhere, slaves at Whydah would still be more expensive. Wherever the slaves came from, the captain, when he got to the West Indies, was to put them all off as Whydah slaves "if possible."[64]

This document indicates clearly an awareness that all Africans were not alike, that some were valued more highly than others,

---

63. Phyllis Martin, "The Trade of Loango in the Seventeenth and Eighteenth Centuries," in Richard Gray and David Birmingham (eds.), *Pre-Colonial African Trade: Essays on Trade in Central and Eastern Africa Before 1900* (London, 1970), 150.

64. Francis Ingram and Co., ships orders to Captain Henry Moore, July 25, 1782, in Tuohy Papers, 380 TUO 4/9.

that ignorance of such distinctions could result in a pecuniary loss, and that the innocence of others in this regard was something of which one might be able to take advantage. Certainly, there were periodical complaints from inexperienced traders about being imposed upon by ship captains who passed off one type of slave as another, emphasizing the need for a knowledge of ethnic variations.[65] Such complaints would less likely have been made had the traders been able to do the same with the planters. As a practical matter, then, slave dealers were expected to be familiar with the African's provenience and with the characteristics thereto pertaining. This attitude is evinced by a London merchant who advised his contact in the West Indies that he could expect a slave ship from Sierra Leone, adding, "so you know what sort of Slaves those are."[66]

V

In their preoccupation with the ethnic background of their servile labor force, South Carolinians were atypical of English settlers in colonies to the north. "Virginians," according to Michael Mullin, "were unconcerned about the 'national character' of particular tribes, since Africans were expected to become Negroes as soon as possible."[67] In this statement he is surely mistaken if he means to suggest that they expressed no slave preferences. Their attitudes regarding the desirability of various African groups were consonant with those of colonists in South Carolina and elsewhere.[68] Mullin is doubtless correct, however, in the latter part of his state-

65. Report to the House of Commons on African Trade, London, 1775–76, in Papers relating to the West Indies, America, Africa, and the Canaries, 1696–1786, f. 189, Add. MSS 14034, British Museum.

66. Letter to Charles Caines, March 19, 1759, in "Instructions and Letters to Capt. Saml Bainbridge of the *Nancy*," p. 3, Wilberforce House, Hull Museum, Hull, England.

67. Michael Mullin (ed.), *American Negro Slavery: A Documentary History* (New York, 1976), 15. See statements to the same effect in Curtin, *Atlantic Slave Trade*, 156, and Donnan (ed.), *Documents*, IV, 234n.

68. See Darold D. Wax, "Preferences for Slaves in Colonial America," *Journal of Negro History*, LVIII (October, 1973), 371–401, whose conclusions support much of my work. Virginians differed from South Carolinians in that they had more regard for peoples from the Niger Delta and less for peoples from the Congo-Angola region. The latter aversion,

ment, and remarks on another occasion that when the important issue of job assignments arose, there were only two kinds of blacks in the Chesapeake, those born in Africa and those native to America.[69] Darold Wax's dictum, therefore, that "ideas concerning preferences were sometimes based less on direct evidence than on tradition" would seem to have particular application to the Chesapeake.[70] A dissimilar ecological setting, different agricultural interests, and a distinctive social development explain the relative lack of emphasis on ethnicity in the Chesapeake. The social and economic environment in South Carolina, by contrast, accentuated and prolonged a recognition of African ethnicity. Direct involvement of the region in the slave trade, determined by these circumstances, was one factor responsible for a continued and increasingly sophisticated awareness.

according to Wax, resulted from the long voyage from Africa, which left slaves in a weakened condition, from which they might not recover. Still, less brute strength was required in Virginia, which explains the regard for Niger Delta peoples. Also see Wax, "Black Immigrants: The Slave Trade in Colonial Maryland," *Maryland Historical Magazine*, LXXIII (March, 1978), 30–45.

69. Gerald Mullin, *Flight and Rebellion: Slave Resistance in Eighteenth Century Virginia* (Oxford, 1972), 17.

70. Wax, "Preferences for Slaves in Colonial America," 389.

Chapter **2**

Agents and Africans
The Trade Overseas

I

The need or desire to know about Africans that was expressed at the end points of trade was even more pronounced at the source. For the reality of commerce on the coast obliged a close attention to the actions and attitudes of Africans who controlled it. Frequently hazardous, slave trading was not often haphazard, and though the best-laid plans sometimes came to naught, there was an overall and intricate design. Myriad factors had to be considered closely for a slave voyage to yield adequate returns, and no element was more important than the Africans themselves. Varying groups, regions, and political circumstances had to be dissected and cataloged, and the resulting information used coherently and consistently, despite unavoidable limitations deriving from insufficient knowledge. Henry Laurens in South Carolina might have occasionally revealed confusion about the origin and type of slave, but coastal traders would have been more exact. Indeed, it is striking how much Europeans, confined to the seaboard, knew about African ethnology, politics, and customs.

Although people commonly talked about the "African trade," of which slaving was the most noted part, the expression, as K. G. Davies points out, was a generic term, and people actually involved in it were likely to be more specific. It made a great difference whether one traded at Whydah (in Benin) or at Cape Coast Castle (in Ghana), for the circumstances of trade were not the same at the two places, even though they were not very far apart. Even when regions were incorrectly identified or tribal names were used inaccurately, the frame of reference was likely quite particular. Whether as resident agents or in coasting vessels, Europeans working on the African coast had to be precise in their designations. Profits depended upon it. Differences between a Fanti or an Ashanti, who might both be called Coromantees (as opposed to an "Ibo," who may not have been Ibo at all), might have been of little moment to the South Carolinian or Barbadian purchaser interested only in more general characteristics; but they were of crucial importance to traders and officials responsible for maintaining British influence on the coast. Whether a slaving captain went ashore at one point or another or treated with one ethnic group or another had a direct bearing upon matters of profit or loss. The reason was that, to a degree often unappreciated, Africans played a major role in determining the character of the slave trade. As entrepreneurs and victims, Africans had to be judged carefully by Europeans. Some of the more important European perceptions of Africans are suggested by a survey of trading practices in two major regions, Upper Guinea and Congo-Angola.

During its high point in the eighteenth century, the slave trade was controlled on the African side by coastal middlemen who were highly conscious, and jealous, of their position. They had a monopoly on trade with the interior and insisted that business be conducted through them. They refused to be bound by any one European power and largely determined the conditions and mechanisms of trade, even in areas where nominal European control existed. They decided what goods would be traded, how long the trading sessions would go on, and where the trade would take place. In disparate parts of the coast, however, the trade proceeded in various fashions.

In Upper Guinea, from about Cape Verde in Senegal to Cape Mount in Liberia, the method of trade was what K. G. Davies has called "sloop and factory" trade.[1] During the seventeenth century the British had established major settlements or "factories" along the coast, of which the most important was James Fort in the River Gambia, with lesser settlements at Bence Island in Sierra Leone and York Island in the Sherbro River; the former was four hundred miles to the south and the latter, five hundred. The region, dominated by no single polity, African or European, consisted of a number of local kingdoms and principalities whose

1. K. G. Davies, *The Royal African Company* (New York, 1970), 216–20.

conflicting interests were complicated—though trade was facilitated—by the presence of a mulatto class of Afro-Europeans.[2]
These competing local interests, in association with European
competition, made it impossible for the three large English establishments to engross the trade. Therefore, out-factories sprang up
at strategic points along the coast—Rufisque, Portudal, and Joal,
north of the Gambia; up the Gambia at Barra Kunda, Buruko,
Sangrique, and elsewhere; and south of the Gambia on the Rivers
Casamance, Nunez, and Pongo. At these places, two or three
company employees were posted to secure trade to the English.[3]
These outposts were supplemented by small sloops of about thirty
tons and longboats that traveled between major settlements and
the outposts to collect trade goods. They sometimes engaged in
trade themselves, as in the Rivers Grande and Cacheo;[4] and it was
in such places as these, where no posts were set up, that Afro-
Europeans were particularly important, for they had the contacts
that made the trade work.

Although both methods were necessary and complementary,
the use of sloops was preferred to the system of outposts because,
as one agent expressed it:

> A factor once settled ashoar is absolutely under the command of the
> king of the country where he lives, and liable for the least displeasure
> to loose all the goods he hath in his possession with danger also of his
> life. Besides in case of mortallity it is very difficult to recover of the
> negroes any thing that was in the hands of the deceased. Whereas in a
> sloop if the factor die the vessell is soone brought down to the Island,
> and if he find no trade in one port may goe to another and not [be]
> lyable to sell their goods at the pleasure of the kings.[5]

For the right to establish factories along the coast, Europeans
had to pay various charges to local potentates, including ground
rents, tributes, and customs duties, before trade could proceed.
These charges, in Upper Guinea, were known collectively as *cole*.
The Royal African Company paid cole to the king of Sherbro for

2. Christopher Fyfe, *A History of Sierra Leone* (London, 1963), 3; Walter Rodney, *A History of the Upper Guinea Coast, 1545–1800* (Oxford, 1970), 200–22.
3. Davies, *Royal African Company*, 216; Donnan (ed.), *Documents*, I, 192.
4. Donnan (ed.), *Documents*, I, 192 and II, 394; Davies, *Royal African Company*, 216.
5. Quoted in Davies, *Royal African Company*, 217–18.

use of York Island; to the king of Bagos for rights at Bence Island; to the king of Barra to locate at James Island.[6] Ships operating independently of the company also had to pay customs, especially for the right to obtain water and to gather firewood, wherever and whenever they stopped, whether or not they traded in the vicinity.[7] Failure to pay was to risk attack, capture, and detainment until satisfaction was forthcoming. If such a vessel eluded capture, another of the same nationality might be held responsible for the dereliction of its compatriot ship. Indeed, a major complaint of the Royal African Company against the separate traders was that they too often disregarded the common practices of the coast, causing others to be held liable, to the detriment of English trade. The company was concerned about such breaches not only because they disrupted commerce but because its agents were particularly vulnerable to retaliation. For example, in 1701, when a separate trader carried a slave away from Joal without paying for him, the local potentate took over the Royal African Company factory and confiscated its goods. He refused to return them even after the company had replaced the stolen slave.[8]

Europeans also needed establishments to maintain their influence against that of competitors as well as to facilitate trade by the collection of goods. The larger settlements furnished the out-factories with goods that were then either exchanged at the post or entrusted to Africans or Afro-Europeans who took them into the hinterland and returned with desirable trade articles.[9] These in turn were stored in the factories until they could be shipped to Europe or America. The obvious desirability of such posts and the

6. Fyfe, *History of Sierra Leone*, 4, 5; Harry A. Gailey, *A History of the Gambia* (New York, 1965), 22–23; Gailey uses the term *purchased* in this regard, which may be an incorrect expression, since it is unlikely that Africans renounced ultimate title to the land. See J. M. Gray, *History of the Gambia* (London, 1966), 40.

7. Donnan (ed.), *Documents*, II, 394–95; Fyfe, *History of Sierra Leone*, 3. The position of the Barra king apparently hardened in this regard as the century advanced, for in the 1730s ships proceeding upriver had the option of paying customs or continuing without taking on wood and water if they could get by without it, while in 1754 company merchants reported that the ruler insisted that all English ships pay customs no matter what their needs or trade destination. London Committee to Governor and Council at James Fort, August 30, 1754, in Treasury Papers, 70/29, f. 20.

8. Gray, *History of the Gambia*, 130.

9. Fyfe, *History of Sierra Leone*, 5.

insistence of Africans upon determining the conditions of trade meant that Europeans had to conform to, if not respect, African ways of doing things.

European competition helped ensure that Africans could get their own way. By the eighteenth century, the contest in Gambia was mainly between the French and the English. Although the English claimed the right of exclusive trade in the Gambia, the French maintained a factory at Albreda near James Island and were anxious to take advantage of misunderstandings between the English and their clients, allies, and partners to advance their own cause. Thus, the English in their sphere (and the French in theirs) had to be careful not to offend native sensibilities or chance the diversion of trade towards their adversaries. If company agents on the coast forgot, in exasperation, this fact of life, the erosion of their position in the locality and pressure from the company at home were quick to bring them to their senses.

Such an incident occurred in December, 1750, when Captain Gother of the *Penelope* from Liverpool was fired on by the French at Albreda during his passage up the Gambia. His assessment of blame for the incident is instructive. In his report to the committee of the Company of Merchants in London, Gother charged that this "Insolence in the French" derived from "the Countenance shewn them by the Natives." This was a consequence, he thought, of the "mistaken Behavior of the English Factory who have neglected to ingratiate themselves by making little Presents to the principal Men" of the country. English trade, as a result, was "quite at a Stand." As a remedy, the company could only "insist strenuously" that those at the fort exert every effort to reestablish harmony between themselves and the local peoples and to try by their good behavior to convince the latter to break off trade with the French and return to the English. To improve "the good Harmony between you . . . to the highest Pitch," the committee continued, "you are from Time to Time to advise us what further Presents (& of what Sorts) are necessary to be sent out for this purpose."[10] This attitude is quite different from that adopted during

10. London Committee of the Company of Merchants to James Skinner, James Fort, August 21, 1751, in Treasury Papers, 70/143, ff. 99–100.

the late nineteenth century and indicates how dependent Europeans were upon Africans, how closely they had to work with them, and, as a consequence, how much more perceptive they had to be about them. Maintenance of a special position within a region was strictly a function of how well they got along with the people who inhabited it.

South of the Gambia, along the Windward Coast, a different method of trade prevailed. The limits of this region are variously defined. Geographically, the area extends from Cape Palmas northward to the vicinity of Cape Verde, but for purposes of trade the Royal African Company specified the end points as Cape Mount in the north and Cape Three Points to Leeward.[11] In my description Sierra Leone from the Isles de Los will be included as well. In this region, no traders constructed permanent establishments, and "ship trade" prevailed. In the early years, according to Davies, natives would light fires or send up smoke signals to notify ship captains of their readiness to barter. They would then either come in canoes and board the ship or wait on shore for the arrival of the ship's party. If this method was characteristic of the seventeenth century, the trade would appear to have undergone some evolution by the eighteenth, for it was much more systematic.[12] Ships stopped at regular points along the coast to treat with the local authority. Here, too, if the polity was large enough, customs had to be paid, and in some places, as at Cape Mount, business could not proceed in the absence, or without the permission, of the king.[13]

Ships also stationed themselves at various points off the coast and sent yawls, pinnaces, and longboats to trade. If a captain were a frequent visitor to the region, he made acquaintances ashore and might receive the king of the local polity aboard ship and present him with gifts to assure himself a favorable reception and an expe-

11. See, for example, cartography in John D. Fage, *A History of West Africa: An Introductory Survey* (Cambridge, 1969), 71; Davies, *Royal African Company*, 222.

12. Davies, *Royal African Company*, 222, laments the lack of evidence that hampers his description; so it is possible that even in the seventeenth century the pattern was more complex than he indicated.

13. *African* Journal, 1752–53, f. 155, and 1753–54, ff. 270–71, in National Maritime Museum, Greenwich, England.

ditious voyage his next time around.[14] Ships often contracted with local chiefs to give them a preference of trade or to furnish so many slaves.[15] The Royal African Company, which had such an engagement with "Kentaun, King of Bassam," even promised to set up a factory in his territory if he could make it worth their while (an honor he might very well have preferred to forego).[16] In Sierra Leone, the Afro-English were especially instrumental in making and performing engagements with ship captains. During the eighteenth century, in various regions, their influence rivaled and in some cases superseded that of native peoples, to whom they were related by economic and consanguineous ties.[17]

Because of the relative fluidity of trade in the region some unscrupulous slavers engaged in a practice called "panyaring," in which unsuspecting Africans were kidnapped and sold into slavery. In response to this practice, coastal peoples took retribution on the next ship from the same port or nation.[18] Sometimes they required hostages, or "pawns," to guarantee the safety of local traders. Europeans who were regular traders on the coast recognized the repercussions likely to result when the rights and prerogatives of Africans were disregarded, and they deplored the activities of those who were unmindful of these facts. On the other hand, they also had to be careful of those parts of the coastline where local traders were unfair. Two captains agreed, in the middle of the eighteenth century, to go together to the region of Grand Lesters and Cape Palmas in order to "assist and protect each other," for the peoples thereabouts had "got to such a head in their villainy . . . that it is judged precarious for a single ship to venture near them."[19] In an incident in 1751, a captain belatedly learned that a European he had placed in charge of a longboat had shot an African on the ship's previous voyage. This had occurred "some-

14. See, for example, the *Black Prince* Journal, *passim*, in Bristol Central Library, and *Duke of Argyle* Journal, ff. 42–43 and *passim*, in National Maritime Museum.
15. *Duke of Argyle* Journal, 1750, f. 31 and *passim*; *African* Journal, 1753–54, f. 313.
16. Ship's orders to Captain Pariss, March 7, 1722, in Treasury Papers, 70/64, ff. 142–43.
17. *Duke of Argyle* Journal, ff. 38, 66.
18. Fyfe, *History of Sierra Leone*, 8.
19. *African* Journal, 1753–54, f. 276.

where below Cape Mount," to which region the longboat had been sent again. "I never heard a word of it till today," the captain lamented. "If I had known it at first, should not have sent her down there again, nor any where else in his Charge; but I begin to fear they have either surpriz'd or overpower'd him, out of revenge, for unless first provoked I am well assured, the natives are not inclin'd to quarrel on this side Rio Junque, & I ordered him not to pass Cape Manserado."[20]

The practice of consigning goods to coastal traders to take into the hinterland to secure slaves was one among a number of considerations influencing Europeans to make distinctions: in some cases on a personal basis (as when the captain of the *Duke of Argyle* refused credit to a Mr. Osborne, apparently an Afro-European, in Sierra Leone because he did not think him trustworthy in his current circumstances), and in other cases on a regional basis (as when the sloop *Kite* was ordered to trade in Sierra Leone).[21] If the voyage could not be completed there, the captain was authorized to go as far south as Cape Mount and the surrounding area. In that eventuality, however, he was "not to trust any Goods to the Natives on any Account whatsoever on forfiture of your commissions & privileges . . . for the trusting of Goods to them has been the totall defeat of many a Voyage on Account of there Defaults of payment." Or, as he put it on another occasion, "When you trust them you never see them again."[22]

Slaving on the Windward Coast was a tedious process, and vessels usually traded there en route to an ultimate destination somewhere else. In this region and in Senegambia, slaves were only one of many articles of trade and perhaps not the most important one. It is possible, in fact, that this section of the coast was at least as important, if not more so, as a granary than as a source of slaves, for rice in particular was of far greater consequence than whatever slaves were obtained if the ship was not to do its major slaving

20. *Duke of Argyle* Journal, f. 66.
21. *Ibid.*, f. 44; also see *African* Journal, 1753–54, f. 272.
22. In Robert Bostock Papers, Liverpool Record Office: Robert Bostock to Stephen Bowers, June 19, 1788, 387 MD 54, ff. 28–29, and Bostock to Capt. Peter Reme, July 2, 1787, 387 MD 54, ff. 18–19.

there. It was especially common for ships destined for Angola to stop first at points along the Windward Coast to gather rice, because provisions to succor the presumptive cargo through the middle passage were not plentiful where the slaves were actually acquired.[23] Elsewhere, such as the Gold Coast, similar conditions obtained, and vessels engaged in the Windward Coast trade were equally, if not more, interested in taking on rice, wood, water, malaguetta pepper, and other provender as in acquiring the vendible commodities of slaves, ivory, wax, gold, and camwood.[24]

In southwestern Africa, from about Cape Lopez in the north to perhaps Cape Negro in the south, was the region that English traders commonly called Angola. In fact, the kingdom of Angola, or more properly the Mbundu Kingdom of Ndongo, was only a very small part of this region and during the eighteenth century was a Portuguese sphere of influence. Foreign trade took place (illegally) all along the coast but was concentrated in an area north of the Congo River and south of the Kwila River and extended south of the Congo to the River Dande.[25] Between the Congo and the Dande was the kingdom of the Kongo. Between the Kwilu and the Congo was Loango.[26] The major ports of trade were Malemba (Melimba) and Cabinda in Loango and Mpinda and Ambriz in Kongo; therefore, the most intense northern European slaving activity was not in "Angola" at all, though the source of slaves may well have been largely the same. Luanda was the center of Portuguese slave exports, and for this reason other Europeans did not

23. See, for example, ship's orders to Capt. John Owen, October 17, 1721, in Treasury Papers, 70/64, f. 72; Thomas Leyland to William Young, in Account book *Spitfire* (June, 1795), MS/10/49, University Library, Liverpool; William Davenport and Company to Capt. Pat Dwyer, April 1, 1748, in Richards Collection, *Davenport Letter and Bill Book*, 1748; Extracts of Evidence of James Penny Esqr to Privy Council, March 6, 1788, in Long's Collections, ff. 24–26, Add. MSS 18272.

24. See letter to James Phipps, September 7, 1721, in Chancery Papers, 113/35, Part I, No. 142, Public Record Office; Francis Ingram to Capt. George McMinn, December 31, 1783, in Tuohy Papers, 380 TUO 4/10; Parke, Heywood and Co. to Joseph Fayrer, September 10, 1782, MS/10/46, University Library, Liverpool; Donnan (ed.), *Documents*, I, 393–94; Royal African Company ship's orders to Capt. John Owen, October 17, 1721, in Treasury Papers, 70/64, f. 72.

25. This region is described in Birmingham, *Trade and Conflict*, 1–20, 133–61.

26. This region actually comprised three kingdoms—Loango, Kakongo, and Ngoyo—but was dominated by the Vili kingdom of Loango until the eighteenth century.

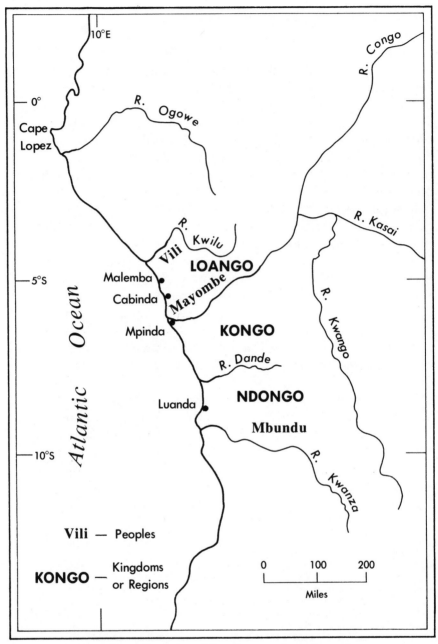

Peoples and states of the Congo–Angola region

Map by Cartographic Section, School of Geoscience, Louisiana State University

often go there. South of Ndongo, in Benguela on the Ovimbundu
Plateau, the Portuguese developed another sphere of influence
during the eighteenth century, but their position was not as secure
there as it was farther north because tribes in the hinterland and
other Europeans on the coast continued to frustrate their claim to
hegemony. English and French ships continued to pick up slaves
along this coast on their way to Loango.[27]

Outside Portuguese possessions, trade in the Congo-Angola region (using the modern terminology) perhaps most closely approximated Davies' "sloop and factory" trade in Upper Guinea.
Here, too, the coast was characterized by the existence of numerous polities with which Europeans had to deal. Relationships on
the Loango Coast in particular, though, appear to have modified
the "sloop and factory" method. Kingdoms were strong and du-
rable. One observer commented, in fact, on the greater facility
with which trade was conducted in the area. The ease of trade, he
thought, was a "consequence of the greater refinement of the natives, which have some resemblance to those of the Asiatics. The
country is more beautiful and presents better accommodations
and the Climate is healthier."[28] The whole region had once been
the scene of large stable political entities, notably Ndongo and
Kongo, before European discovery and the development of external commerce. But by the eighteenth century, the former had
been reduced to the status of a Portuguese colony and the latter
had been transformed into "a series of chiefdoms" that as Jan Vansina asserts, "somewhat in the manner of the Holy Roman Empire," professed to recognize a single king but were practically
independent.[29]

27. Birmingham, *Trade and Conflict*, 140–41, 154–55, 157–58; in Treasury Papers,
70/64: Royal African Company to Capt. Henry Cornwall, April 5, 1722, f. 113, and May
16, 1721, f. 53. Winds and currents determined that a ship sail farther south than the port he
wanted to reach before approaching the coast because coastal streams flowed strongly
northward. See Henry Trafford and Co. to Alexander Speers, September 28, 1772, and
Speers, Tuohy and Co. to Capt. Luke Mann, April 5, 1774, both in Tuohy Papers, 380
TUO 4/6 and 4/7 respectively.
28. Privy Council, March 6, 1788, Extracts of Evidence given by James Penny, Esqr., in
Long's Collections, ff. 24–26, Add. MSS 18272.
29. Jan Vansina, *Kingdoms of the Savanna: A History of Central African States until European Occupation* (Madison, 1968), 189.

On the Loango Coast, the traditional kingdoms of Loango, Ngoyo, and Kakongo survived into the nineteenth century.[30] They were comparatively small; and here, too, permission to trade and set up factories was obtained from local potentates, and coastal kingdoms mediated commerce between foreigners and the hinterland, setting the conditions and articles of trade. Here, as elsewhere, mutual cooperation was necessary to ensure orderly exchange.

These facts made intimate knowledge of the coast desirable and inhibited crass generalizations about Africans. This obviously was not the result of any particular humanitarian concern or philosophical bent. It was dictated by hard commercial realities. The apparently vague usage of *Angola* conceals a firm grasp of the political and social conditions on the coast. Consider the following instructions to a slaving vessel ordered to the Loango Coast to inquire about the trading situation farther south, in the area of Ambriz: "If you are Inform'd that you can Slave with Safety woud recommend it to you to proceed there directly. . . . Shou'd it so happen that you cannot Slave [there] . . . then you are to fix at Cape Benda [Cabinda] Provided the Prince of Sawney is not King there; if he is you are to fix either at Melimba or Loango, the latter we [would] have you fix at, if Prince Vaba, who is a friend to the English [is] there, and there to barter your Cargoe." Another merchant revealed the same kind of concern. He wrote his employee, "If you should fav^r me with a Letter soon pray let me know how Cabenda is governed whether the Same Villains are there or who is the King."[31] And one company indicated an entirely different but equally noteworthy concern when it counseled special care in the choice of slaves at Angola. "You must be far more particular than is usual on the Windward Coast of Africa where you have been generally employed."[32]

30. *Ibid.*, 195.

31. Henry Trafford and Co. to Alexander Speers, September 28, 1772, and David Tuohy to Mr. Chilcott, December 15, 1772, both in Tuohy Papers, 380 TUO 4/6 and 2/1 respectively.

32. Leyland, Penny and Co. to Charles Wilson, January 4, 1783, MS/10/47, University Library, Liverpool.

II

Regional variations in slave prices likewise forced Europeans to be particular. During the seventeenth century, slaves were cheaper to leeward—that is, on the Gold Coast, at Whydah, and in the Niger Delta, where they averaged about three pounds sterling at the end of the century—and more expensive to windward and in the Congo-Angola region (about four guineas each in the latter).[33] During the eighteenth century, these conditions changed, perhaps because of more stringent competition to leeward, the greater desirability of Gold Coast and Whydah slaves, the effects of inland wars that disrupted trade routes, or some combination of these reasons. A correspondent wrote in the middle of the eighteenth century that the price of slaves on the Gold Coast had increased from £12 to £16 sterling per head and on the Windward Coast from £9 and £10 to between £12 and £14 per head.[34] However, Royal African Company agents had complained as early as 1724 that the price of slaves at Whydah had reached £14 sterling, and the company agent at Cape Coast Castle lamented in 1721 that the best men cost £15 sterling in nearly all the region between Cape Three Points and Accra.[35]

Slaves from the Congo-Angola region also cost less than Gold Coast blacks in the eighteenth century.[36] But there, as elsewhere,

33. Davies, *Royal African Company*, 236–37; Martin, *External Trade of the Loango Coast*, 77.

34. Mr. Pownal's Account of the Slave Trade, circa 1753, in Liverpool Papers, CCXXVII, ff. 221–24, Add. MSS 38416. Pownal indicated that prices in the colonies had undergone a proportional rise, from between £28 and £30 sterling prewar to between £35 and £40 postwar for Gold Coast slaves and from between £20 and £25 to between £28 and £30 for Windward Coast slaves. The agent in charge of James Fort reported in 1755 that prices paid for the slaves up the Gambia River were 100 bars each, or about £12 sterling, in Treasury Papers, 70/30, ff. 112–13.

35. See Donnan (ed.), *Documents*, II, 309n. The former sterling figure is derived from cowries; the cost was "45 Sletias or 300 lbs cowries." Conversions are given in Karl Polanyi, "Sortings and 'Ounce Trade' in the West African Slave Trade," *Journal of African History*, V, 3 (1964), 389; the latter sterling price was converted from the given price of "Seven ounces Eight Ackeys." James Phipps to William Baillie, November 30, 1721, in Chancery Papers, 113/34, Part I, No. 10.

36. John Merewether and Edward Manning to Peter Burrell, January 6, 1736, in Donnan (ed.), *Documents*, II, 455.

prices rose over the century. Phyllis Martin reports that at Cabinda in 1700 seven or eight pieces of cloth, the currency in the region, was a reasonable price for slaves; this had almost doubled by about 1713 to between ten and fifteen pieces per slave, had risen to between twenty and thirty pieces by the middle of the century, and was commonly thirty pieces by 1770.[37]

A trader wrote in 1772 that when last at that port, he had paid for slaves an amount equal to more than thirty pieces. Since the value of goods relative to pieces became fixed during the eighteenth century, slaves would have cost less on the Loango Coast than on the Gold Coast or at Whydah, if the same trade commodities could be obtained more cheaply in Europe or elsewhere or if less expensive goods could be put off in Africa at the same value they had formerly possessed.[38] To some extent, this was possible. A Liverpool trader advised a prospective employer in London regarding a slave voyage that "a Cargo to Ambross [Ambriz] is much the same as to Cabenda with this difference that the goods need not be so good in quality . . . for Instance Coarse baffts or Byron pants will do in the room of Superfine."[39] If things went well, such advice could represent a savings. Another merchant reported two years later, in fact, that slaves at Cabinda cost almost twice as much as those at Ambriz, though the ship's turnover would be faster at the former.[40] The cost of slaves on the Leeward Coast could not be so easily lessened, among other rea-

37. Martin, *External Trade of the Loango Coast*, 113. In Donnan (ed.), *Documents*, I, 456, James Barbot gives a breakdown of the measurements in use: "The stick is eighteen inches; three sticks are accounted a fathom, and four fathoms make what is here call'd a piece."
38. D. Tuohy to M. Barber, January 13, 1772. Barber was in London. Tuohy wrote: "Perhaps you will be surprised when I tell you that I was giving when last at Cabenda 5 bafts on Slaves with 10 other p[iec]es of India goods 5 pons [?] & 2 gunne." He wrote later that bafts went at three pieces. D. Tuohy to M. Barber, January 22, 1772, both in Tuohy Papers, 380 TUO 2/1. Martin, *External Trade of the Loango Coast*, 109, relates that a gun equaled one piece. Assuming that the unidentified articles (5 pons) were equal to one piece each, the price would be thirty-two pieces per slave. By contrast, perhaps because of the disruption of trade during the American War of Independence, a slave ship sent to Cabinda in 1783 was expected to pay no more than between fourteen and sixteen pieces for slaves and even less—between ten and twelve pieces—if he loaded in the River Ammoris. Leyland, Penny and Co., ships orders to Charles Wilson, MS/10/47, University Library, Liverpool.
39. D. Tuohy to M. Barber, January 13, 1772, in Tuohy Papers, 380 TUO 2/1.
40. Speers, Tuohy and Co. ship's orders to Capt. Luke Mann, in *ibid.*, 380 TUO 4/7.

sons, because African merchants at Whydah and on the Gold Coast demanded a certain proportion of the price of slaves in cowries and gold respectively, the value of which in terms of goods increased over the eighteenth century.[41]

The rise in slave prices during the eighteenth century, as Karl Polanyi has shown, was due in part to the establishment of a fictitious unit of account that was one-half the real value of commodities in Europe or gold on the coast, causing Africans to demand more in compensation.[42] Nevertheless, the factor of competition cannot be underrated. Ships of the Royal African Company were specifically instructed to pay more for slaves if a separate trader was in the vicinity, and it goes without saying that costs rose to meet increased demand.[43] Moreover, the various European nations were constantly trying to outbid each other in one fashion or another. In the Gambia, for example, the French were able to outbid the English by using better goods. The result was that the French could get slaves for the value of 70 bars (the local unit of account) while the English had to pay 120. The English were further disadvantaged by being required to use foreign goods.[44] At Loango, the local king's agent tried to encourage the French to establish a permanent representative in the region to oversee French interests and mitigate complaints that might cause French traders to withdraw, because such an act would have decreased competition and caused prices to fall. At Cabinda the price of slaves increased on one occasion despite a previous agreement to the contrary, because more ships arrived. (Africans simply ceased to bring slaves to market, obliging the Europeans to offer more money.)[45]

The fact that slave prices and other aspects of commerce varied

41. See Donnan (ed.), *Documents*, II, 547. The difference in price between regions may be one reason that Anstey discovered an increasing number of Angola slaves being imported in the second part of the eighteenth century. See Richard Anstey, "The Volume and Profitability of the British Slave Trade, 1761–1807," in Engerman and Genovese (eds.), *Race and Slavery*, 13.

42. Polanyi, "Sortings and 'Ounce Trade,'" especially 392–93.

43. See, for example, Royal African Company, ship's orders to Capt. Wm. Minzeis, African House, November 20, 1721, in Treasury Papers, 70/64, ff. 86–89; Donnan (ed.), *Documents*, I, 445.

44. Governor O'Hara to [?], January 12, 1767, in Papers relating to the state of British settlements in Africa, ff. 30–31, King's MSS 200, British Museum.

45. Donnan (ed.), *Documents*, II, 551; I, 454–55.

not only between regions but within them was a further consideration requiring punctilious distinctions. This was true all along the coast but was quite noticeable at its extremities. A French trader supplied the British with lists of commodities and rates of exchange current in the Senegal when that river was captured during the Seven Years' War. He informed them that values were different and goods more expensive in the region of Galam than they were downstream because of the proximity of the Senegal in this area to the Gambia.[46] Galam, however, is several hundred miles from the river's mouth. The distance did not have to be so great.

Charles Quinsac, a Gambia trader employed by the Company of Merchants, was involved in an unfortunate enterprise in 1755 and 1756. Captain James Gaul, of the sloop *Cannon Hall*, belonging to Benjamin Spencer of London, died even before he left the river. His death, along with that of his second in command, prompted Quinsac to accompany the cargo to Antigua. During the voyage, many of the crew and slaves became sick and died—the former from overwork, the latter from bad treatment, and both from lack of sufficient provisions. These and other mishaps contributed to an unsuccessful venture. In the recriminations that followed the debacle, Quinsac made a number of criticisms, one of which related to the purchase of slaves. "I was very anxious to go with the late Mr. Gaul to assist him in making Trade & advised him to buy his Slaves at Barsally & not Fettick or Fowey [Fowel] the Jolliffs being full as cheap as the Barbazeens & always Prime, Healthy Slaves."[47] The two areas mentioned are within a radius of less than forty miles of each other, but Captain Gaul's ignorance of specifics and rejection of advice contributed to failure.

Unfortunately, there was more. Not only had the vessel come to the coast with inadequate provisions, Quinsac wrote, but it had come at the wrong time of year if it expected to supply itself on the coast. Captain Gaul, he thought, had "met with some friend in London (probably Doctor Carlisle) who informed him Corn [*i.e.*, rice, in this case] might be had in Gambia in the rainy Season but it

46. Charles Rossin, Etablissement du Senegal, in Dartmouth MSS, D1778 V 255, County Record Office, Stafford, England.
47. Charles Quinsac to Benjamin Spencer, March 14, 1756, in Spencer-Stanhope Muniments, 60549/179, Sheffield Central Library, Sheffield, England.

never was my Opinion & the late Mr. Gaul never consulted nor dealt with me in that friendly Manner which I often & in vain sought for." Trade in the Gambia was seasonal, he expounded; a vessel ought to be in the area "some time from May to October any of those Months being a proper time for a cheap Purchase & no other Season."[48] In this observation he is supported by other traders. One noted that although coastal middlemen went upriver to gather slaves at all periods of the year, "ye chief time for selling them upon ye Coast is about August & Sept[r] which is ye rainy season." By contrast, on the Leeward Coast and in the Congo-Angola region, trade was dependent solely on the supply of slaves and the absence of conflict, and these conditions were no more likely to obtain in one season than another.[49]

Quinsac, in referring to the cost of slaves, demonstrated how drastically the price could vary. He remarked that Captain Gaul had obtained servitors at an average of less than forty shillings per head, which was one-third less than Quinsac had estimated they would cost. Even at the higher rate they would have been considerably below the usual price. This variation can be explained by the shortage of provisions on the coast that year.[50] More than one observer noted that slaves were especially cheap when provender was scarce. The significance of this variable is accentuated by the degree to which it affected the ability of the company to preserve captives as well. Agents at James Fort notified their superiors in London in June, 1736, that slaves had been collected in such abundance, the local crop was so deficient, and the season was so advanced that "we have thought it for your interest to take up 113 Slaves on our Accounts of Wages, and send them on freight to South Carolina per Capt. Coe." In September they reported: "In proportion to our Slaves we have had a great Mortality among

48. Charles Quinsac to Benjamin Spencer, March 7, 1756, in *ibid.*, 60549/185.
49. In Long's Collections: Extracts From the Evidence of Jno. Matthews Esqr. given to ye Committee of Privy Council, March 4, 1788, ff. 1–6, Robert Morris Esqr., Carolina Mercht. of Liverpool, Evidence, July 27, 1775, f. 11, and Extracts from the Evidence of James Penny Esqr. given ye Committee of Privy Council, March 6, 1756, ff. 24–26.
50. In Spencer-Stanhope Muniments: Charles Quinsac to Benjamin Spencer, March 7, 1756, 60549/185, and Capt. James Gaul to Benjamin Spencer, July 20, 1755, 70550/296; also see Charles Quinsac to Benjamin Spencer and Co., August 7, 1755, and September 21, 1755, 10549/183 and 60549/177 respectively.

them likewise and if we had missed of freighting the 113 Slaves per Capt. Coe the[y] must have perished, for it was with the greatest difficulty that we with short allowance could feed them and the Castle Slaves."[51]

The matter of securing the right trade goods was also crucial to economic management of the trade. One observer alleged at the end of the eighteenth century that slaves could be had as much as eight pounds cheaper if African traders could be supplied with precisely what they desired rather than larger amounts of commodities that were in less demand.[52] Clearly that trader who had the most-sought-after articles did better than he who had something else. Brazilian tobacco from Bahia, for example, became a favored trade commodity on the Leeward Coast during the eighteenth century, and attempts by the Royal African Company to substitute Virginia tobacco as the preferred article of exchange failed. The Company of Merchants, therefore, was forced to direct its agents to make an exception to company rules against trading with other Europeans in order to obtain tobacco from the Portuguese.[53] The success of New England rum on the Gold Coast influenced even chief agents of the Company of Merchants at Cape Coast Castle to disregard company policy and British mercantile restrictions by accepting an article they knew would sell.[54]

But the vagaries of trade were such that even a preferred article might be out of favor at any particular moment. One observer wrote that no cargo was ever so well assorted but that one-fourth of it was out of demand or entirely unsalable at its arrival on the coast.[55] This had an adverse effect on the price of slaves, because

51. Letters dated James Fort, June 15, 1736, rec'd. December 10, 1736 and James Fort, September 18, 1736 rec'd. March 5, 1736/7, in Treasury Papers, 70/4, ff. 87, 88.

52. John Roberts, "Tracts and Papers on African Trade," December 14, 1779, in Papers relating to the Commerce of Africa, f. 17, Egerton MSS 1162B, British Museum.

53. Verger, *Flux et Reflux*, 25–35; Council at Cape Coast Castle to Wm. Baillie and Tho. Bound at Whydah, in Chancery Papers, 113/34, I, No. 10; James Phipps at Cape Coast Castle to Wm Baillie at Whydah, February 27, 1719, in Chancery Papers, 113/34, Pt. I, No. 10; Committee of the Company of Merchants to Tho. Melvil at Cape Coast Castle, April 17, 1751, in Treasury Papers, 70/143, ff. 84–85.

54. "Report of the House Commons on African Trade," circa 1775–76, in Papers relating to the West Indies, America, Africa, and the Canaries, 1696–1786, f. 187, Add. MSS 14034.

55. John Roberts, "Tracts and Papers on African Trade," December 14, 1779, in Papers relating to Africa, f. 16, Egerton MSS 1162B.

captains attempted to put off unwanted goods anyway by offering larger amounts than normal and thereby increasing the price of slaves to the company. Moreover, the cost of unsold goods had to be averaged as part of the profit or loss of a voyage. Hence, constant vigilance was necessary to determine which goods were best able to facilitate a profit—a consideration that required a detailed knowledge of the commodities, people, and circumstances involved.

III

Finally, the relationship between the situation in Africa, the market in America, and conditions in Europe had to be taken into account.[56] We have seen that the Gambia trade was seasonal, not only because of the dearth of slaves in some periods, but also for health reasons.[57] Trade in the Niger Delta, or portions of it, was also geared to the calendar; a ship left Liverpool for Bonny only in April or May.[58] Naturally, there was a need to collate the period of trade on the African coast with that at the port of debarkation. Thus, a Liverpool company advised its ship captain in 1797:

> We do not wish you to arrive in Jamaica before the end of October that you may escape the Hurricane Season and avoid all the disadvantages attending the Sale of Slaves in those months, do not therefore be in too great a hurry in Bonny; propose to the leading Traders very low Barrs to begin with, and if they do not comply therewith, seem indifferent as to the length of your stay, nay you may even shew them a disposition to go to New Callabar, and thus you will most likely bring them to moderate terms and avoid the hurry and confusion which always attends the receiving great numbers of Negroes on board at the same moment.[59]

56. An official complained about British restrictions on trade in 1788 because, although legally binding only one year, the date from which they would take effect meant that they would effectually last two since there were particular seasons when most of the slave trade was carried on and ships had to be fitted out accordingly. James Jones to Lord Hawkesbury, July 26, 1788, in Liverpool Papers, CCXXVII, ff. 154–55, Add. MSS 38416.

57. John Roberts, "An Account of the Gum Coast and the River Senegal," in Papers relating to Africa, ff. 15–16, Egerton MSS 1162A.

58. David Tuohy to Messrs. Ryan and B—— [?], October 5, 1775, in Tuohy Papers, 380 TUO 2/4.

59. Richard Bollin and Co. to Geo. Bernard, Account book *Earl of Liverpool*, April 5, 1797, MS/10/50(1), University Library, Liverpool.

In November, 1764, however, when William Davenport and Company ordered William Patten, captain of its brigantine *William*, to trade in Gambia for 120 Negroes "Suitable for ye Carolina Markett," it cautioned him not to "stand with the Traders for four or five Barrs a Head in ye Latter end of your Purchase in order to gett Dispatched out of ye River that you may be one of the Earliest Ships at S° Carolina." The reason was that "by being an early Ship there in all Probability you'll Obtain upwards of £40 Stg. for your Cargo round whereas by being a late Ship the prices will be reduced." Nevertheless, he was not to arrive in South Carolina before the first of March.[60]

IV

The slave trade was thus not conducted on the haphazard basis that many have assumed. To prepare a successful voyage, European traders needed precise information from resident agents or ship captains who had previous experience. The mechanics of trade varied from one region to another as did the commodities in demand. Goods suitable for one area were unsuitable for another, and ships trading to more than one region had to prepare separate cargoes for each.[61] Timing was also essential. Although these and other considerations compelled Europeans to treat Africans with great regard, not all European attitudes diverged from those of a later period.

Ethnocentrism shaped the opinions of Europeans, but it did not blind their business sense. Much of what was perturbing about their African venture accentuated an awareness of racial as well as cultural distinction and expressed itself, at times, in racialistic terminology. An English pamphleteer wrote in 1709 that the "Natives are generally so very Poor and Avaricious, and naturally so very Mercenary and Trecherous, even to one another, as well as to *Europeans*; that the most solemn Engagements can never secure their Fidelity longer than it makes for what they think to be their

60. William Davenport and Co. to William Patten, Capt., November 23, 1764, in Richards Collection, Account Book *William*, ff. 19–21.
61. See, for example, Dalby Thomas to [?], April 9, 1710, in Treasury Papers, 70/2, f. 16, and Donnan (ed.), *Documents*, I, 353.

Interest at the time." They were, he thought, "cunning" and "deceitful."[62] A French trader in Senegambia expressed surprise to find that the settlement of a European post on the Isle of Saint Louis near the mouth of the Senegal had encouraged local peoples to cultivate circumjacent land "with an ardor unexpected from the natural laziness of this Species of Mankind."[63] An Englishman wrote in the same vein, referring to an attempt to introduce cotton gins into the Gold Coast, that "we hope there will be no Danger of ye Natives falling into the method of cleaning Cotton by Gins [of their own initiative] as their natural Inclinations of Sloth seem no ways tending to make improvements."[64]

Lest these statements be taken to allude to condition rather than skin color, others were more explicit. A Frenchman spoke of a caboceer in Senegal as being illiterate but possessed "of such pride and vanity which is so natural in those of his color."[65] And an Englishman lauded a local chief, noting that he had "indeed shewed more spirit than is usual among negroes; but the spirit of a negro is little better than indolence compared to the trading genius of white men."[66] This posture was to some extent a function of the type of relationship—one in which each group was constantly trying the will and resolution of the other. In a different situation, a preexisting bias might be altered. A British doctor in Sierra Leone wrote in 1792 that the people in the region of Freetown were of the Timmany nation and opined that "upon the whole I think the females may be considered as really handsome; indeed I have now been so much accustomed to people of this complexion that I can see as much beauty in a Timmany negro, as I have formerly done in my own country women."[67] Whether Africans were admired,

62. R. E., *Reflections upon the Constitution and Management of the Trade to Africa* (London, 1709), 20, 10, in Lennox of Woodhead MSS, 0616/1, National Register of Archives, Edinburgh.

63. Charles Rossin, "Memoire pour My Lord Comte Dartmouth, Chef du Conseil de Commerce," in Dartmouth MSS., D 1778 V 255, f. 4.

64. Committee at Cabo Corso Castle to London Committee of the Royal African Company, July 2, 1722, in Chancery Papers, 113/36, Pt. I, No. 1541, ff. 18–19.

65. Rossin, "Memoire," in Dartmouth MSS., D 1778 V 255, f. 12.

66. John Hippisley, "On the Necessity of Erecting a Fort at Cape Appolonia," in *Essays* (London, 1764), 46–56.

67. Private Journal, March 7–April 25, 1792, in Clarkson Papers, IV, Add. MSS 41264, British Museum.

they had to be respected, and despite misconceptions, variant groups had to be distinguished. Europeans simply could not afford, in the first centuries of contact, the kind of arrogant disregard for African sentiments, perceptions, and usage they later adopted during the Age of Imperialism in the later nineteenth and early twentieth centuries.

The interest of colonial South Carolinians in the geographical origins of their slaves created a parallel situation in America. While such knowledge as resident agents possessed was not transferred *in toto*, merchants and planters acquired enough to help them make intelligent choices, though local circumstances determined their reaction to various groups. Seamen active in the trade carried much of their information and many of their attitudes to the province, and the quality of information appeared to increase during the eighteenth century. Consequently, general regions were commonly mentioned in sale notices of new Africans in, for example, the 1730s: "Negroes imported . . . directly from the River *Gambia*"; "a fine Cargoe of young healthy Slaves, just imported . . . from the Gold Coast and Angola"; "just imported . . . directly from the Windward and Gold Coast of *Guinea*."[68] But in the second half of the century, advertisements were frequently much more specific. Thus, in the 1770s South Carolinians learned of the arrival of slaves from Cape Coast "mostly of the Fantee Country"; "from WHYDAH on the Gold Coast"; from "CAPE-MOUNT, a Rice Country, on the *Windward Coast*"; or "from ANGOLA," slaves "Mostly of the MASSE CONGO Country." If designations were too specific, explanations were appended, thus: "WHYDAH is esteemed to be the finest Country in AFRICA, and Slaves from thence usually sell in all WEST INDIA Islands, for *Five Pounds Sterling* per Head more than Negroes of any other Country," and slaves from the "MASSE CONGO" were "esteemed equal to the Gold Coast Negroes."[69] Whether the more precise information had a more particular effect in determining who came over, it was

68. South Carolina *Gazette*, August 14, 1736, and July 19, 1735.
69. South Carolina *Gazette and Country Journal*, July 28, 1772, July 2, 1772, and June 11, 1771.

quite important in identifying those who already had, a consideration to be further explored in another connection.

But not only did the collection of information in Africa have
some influence on what went on in South Carolina, other events
there did so as well. Accordingly, South Carolinians learned in
1759 that a sloop commanded by Captain Ingledieu, while "slaving up the River *Gambia*, was attacked by a number of Natives,
about the 27th of *February* last, and made a good Defence; but
the Captain finding himself desperately wounded, and likely to
be overcome, rather than fall into the Hands of such merciless
Wretches, when about 80 Negroes had boarded his Vessel, dis-
charged a Pistol into his Magazine, and blew her up," everyone
perishing. Another vessel, they read, had similarly been lost.[70] Incidents such as these could not help but make them reflect upon
the nature of their servants. Consequently, the close connection
between Africa, Europe, and the New World, the ethnic awareness and concern for African events and circumstances, influenced
the nature of slavery at every step of the way, from capture and
sale in Africa to arrival in South Carolina. This linking of three
continents helped to make slavery in the colonial period distinctive from the institution that developed in a later era, when both
master and slave were products of a common environment.

70. *Ibid.*, June 30, 1759.

Chapter **3**
Plantations, Paternalism, and Profitability

I

If the circumstances of trade overseas affected the social environment in the colony, the colonial social matrix also influenced the trade overseas. The effect is suggested by a document in Wilberforce House, Hull, England, which gives an account of the sale of 143 slaves in South Carolina in June, 1773, and completely illustrates the method and rationale of sale.[1] One of the most arresting facts about the cargo was that a majority of the unfortunates was female. This incident excites various considerations, such as to what extent this was a chance occurrence and how often, whether by fortune or design, it happened. Speculations of this nature are encouraged by an enterprise of Benjamin Spencer and Company of London in 1755 and 1756. Its agents on the African coast shipped on its account in September, 1755, twenty-five slaves to Antigua, composed of fifteen men, five women, three girls, and two boys; in the same month ten slaves, comprising three men, two boys, two women, and three girls were dispatched for either Barbados or South Carolina, landing in the latter. The cargo with the disproportionate number of males to females went to the West Indies, while that with the more equal sex ratio ended in South Carolina.[2]

Subsequent events are more intriguing. The cargoes arrived in America just after four merchantmen, among them two French

1. "Sales of One Hundred & forty three Negroes received [from] the Snow *Robert*, Luke Mann Master from Africa on Account of Messrs. Robert Grimshaw & Co.," in Wilberforce House.

2. In Spencer-Stanhope Muniments: Charles Quinsac to Benjamin Spencer, November 19, 1755, November 20, 1755, and November 30, 1755; John Guerard to Spencer, December 23, 1755, copy included with letter of February 2, 1756. Document numbers, respectively, are 60549/180; 60549/181, 60549/182 and 60549/150. Bills of lading for slaves shipped to Antigua, dated James Fort, September 20, 1755, to Barbados, dated James Fort, September 30, 1755, and to Charlestown, dated Saint Johns, [Antigua], November 19,

slavers, had been taken as prizes of war, with the result that over eight hundred slaves had been deposited in Antigua and prices had been generally depressed. Therefore, after selling ten of the original cargo (nine had died in passage), the supercargo decided to send the rest, along with a few others from another vessel, to South Carolina, where prices were higher. This shipment of twenty-four Africans consisted of two men, eleven women, three boys, and four girls for the company's account and three women and one boy for the supercargo's account. The sale did not go as well as expected because the threat of war lowered the value of Carolina produce, and the sex ratio was not helpful. As the merchant who took up the consignment mildly protested, "Had they been Chiefly men instead of Women would have Answer'd better." Nevertheless, these documents suggest a tendency to ship more women to the continent than to the islands or reflect an expectation that women would sell better in one place than in another. The questions become, then, how widespread was this practice or this expectation and was it significant.

Some aspects of the slave trade contribute support to ideas already extant about the relationship between the type of plantation system and the ability of the slave population to reproduce itself, which in turn is connected in some measure with the sex ratio of the servile class. Historians have often observed that the black populations in the West Indies and in Latin America failed to reproduce themselves, in contrast to those in North America.[3] So striking was this difference, in fact, that the idea developed in some quarters during the eighteenth century, based on the West Indian experience, that blacks were less fertile than whites.[4] The

---

1755, numbered respectively 60550/299, 60550/359, and 60550/358. The ten slaves shipped on September 30 were actually directed to "Barbados or some of His Majesty's Colonies in America" and were shipped on freight with a larger cargo in the ship *Gambia*. Quinsac in his letter of November 30 indicated that South Carolina was foremost in his mind, though Barbados might do.

3. See, for example, Franklin W. Knight, *Slave Society in Cuba During the Nineteenth Century* (Madison, 1970), xvii; Philip D. Curtin, "The Slave Trade and the Atlantic Basin: Intercontinental Perspectives," in Nathan I. Huggins *et al.* (eds.), *Key Issues in the Afro-American Experience* (New York, 1971), 92.

4. Henry Ellis to Lord Hawkesbury, March 31, 1788, in Liverpool Papers, CCXXVII, ff. 69–70, Add. MSS 38416. Ellis opposed the manumission of slaves in the West Indies, even of children, because such a move would cause planters to discourage reproduction.

presence or absence of a reproductive propensity has recently been related to a more-intense versus a less-intense plantation system. As Peter Wood has argued, the rapid expansion of staple crop production in South Carolina seems to have adversely affected the situation of the slave population, which experienced a sharp decrease in its natural growth rate.[5] He has also demonstrated that in the first decades of the eighteenth century the black sex ratio generally mirrored the specifications of slave traders for cargoes composed of two males for every female. There is, of course, no absolute correlation between these proportions and the ability of the slave population to reproduce itself, as Wood has admitted.

Obviously, the more equal the ratio of male to female, the greater the reproductive capacity, other circumstances permitting. But whereas a black population composed of 62 percent males and 38 percent females had a reproductive rate of 5.6 percent in the years prior to 1721, a growth rate which exceeded that of the white population (and which some scholars think is too high),[6] its natural growth decreased thereafter, despite the fact that the sex ratio remained largely the same or, in some cases, improved. In

---

"Favored as the Negroes now are in this respect, their Numbers do not encrease." They were not even prolific in Africa, he thought, and concluded that blacks normally reproduced less than whites. By contrast, John Hippisley, "Essay on the Populousness of Africa," in *Essays*, 1–18, defended continuing the slave trade by reference to the fertility of the country and the people, which would prevent the continent from being depopulated. Thus, two reactionary views are defended, in Ellis' case, partly by the inability of Africans to reproduce and, in Hippisley's, by their greater reproductive tendencies.

5. Wood, *Black Majority*, 142–66. Richard Dunn has found a situation in the West Indies roughly parallel to what Wood found in South Carolina. In the seventeenth century, although more men than women were imported, differential mortality created an equal sex ratio. There was even a desire on the part of some large plantation owners to see that the sex ratio was balanced on their lands; but varying treatment affected the birthrate despite the sex ratio, and in the eighteenth century the condition of sexual equality in numbers was altered with an imbalance of males. See Dunn, *Sugar and Slaves: The Rise of the Planter Class in the English West Indies, 1624–1713* (Chapel Hill, 1972), 314–25. Richard Sheridan writes that the slave population increased naturally only on Barbados, but not until the British Parliament prohibited the African slave trade in 1807. Among the causes of slave mortality in the West Indies were the high proportion of male to female imports, the difficulty of acclimating newly imported slaves, unstable sexual unions, high infant and child mortality, malnutrition, hard labor, cruel punishment, diseases, and accidents. See Sheridan, "Mortality and the Medical Treatment of Slaves in the British West Indies," in Engerman and Genovese (eds.), *Race and Slavery*, 286–87, and "Africa and the Caribbean in the Atlantic Slave Trade," *American Historical Review*, LXXXVII (February, 1972), 19–26.

6. Stanley Engerman to the author, April 6, 1979.

Saint George's Parish, in 1726, for example, although the sex ratio among slaves was 129 males to 100 females, virtually the same as that of the white population, its natural increase had declined from that of the earlier period and was half that of the whites. Wood goes on to point out that the general sex ratio is not always an accurate measure of specific possibility because the sexes may be (and in this case were) disproportionate on individual plantations. But if sex ratio alone is not a sufficient determinant of reproductive capacity, it is undeniably an important component, and the absence of a desire to secure a more nearly equal sexual distribution among slaves may be an important index in determining the character of a plantation system.

Despite the fact that the usual demand for slave cargoes seems to have been universally in the proportion of two males to one female, slave dealers were aware that disparate colonies had a differential predisposition to accept a greater or lesser percentage of one or the other gender.[7] A London merchant instructed his correspondent in 1732 not "to meddle with any Negroes but men for Sale to the Portuguese, they seldom give Gold for any other."[8] Similarly, a Liverpool company advised a ship captain whose cargo was destined for Havana in 1803 that his vessel was legally permitted to carry four hundred slaves and added, "We request that they may all be males if possible to get them, at any rate buy as few Females as in your power, because we look to a Spanish market for the disposal of your Cargo where Females are a very tedious Sale."[9] A merchant house desiring its ship to deliver slaves

7. See Herbert S. Klein, "The Portugese Slave Trade from Angola in the Eighteenth Century," *Journal of Economic History*, XXXIII (December, 1972), 914n. Also see Davies, *Royal African Company*, 299–300, who reports that despite the preference, an analysis of 60,000 slaves delivered to the West Indies between 1673 and 1711 indicated a ratio of 60 percent male to 40 percent female. This ratio, along with differential mortality, would be a partial explanation for the more equal sex ratio in the seventeenth-century West Indies, but it was a response to a different kind of society than was later to develop. Sheridan states that when the situation altered as the eighteenth century advanced, and the emphasis shifted from settlement and conservation of human capital, the condition of a nearly equal sex ratio ceased to obtain. See Sheridan, "Mortality and Medical Treatment of Slaves in the British West Indies," 287, and "Africa and the Caribbean," 20–26.

8. Letter dated London, June 23, 1732, in H. M. Drakeford MSS, 36, County Record Office, Stafford, England.

9. Thomas Leyland to Caesar Leyland, Liverpool, July 18, 1803, in Thomas Leyland Papers, 387 MD 43, Liverpool Record Office.

to the West Indies in 1761 specified that "as its most likely you'll sit at some of the windward Islands, middle size strong young Slaves will sell better than the heavy, or overgrown, avoiding too great a number of females."[10]

These cargoes were also planned with contingent destinations in mind, as when an 1803 voyager was admonished not to get any slave over twenty-four years old in case he had to go to Jamaica, where the legislature had imposed an extra duty on slaves older than that.[11] A greater than usual disproportion of men to women seems to have confined the alternatives to either the West Indies or Latin America. Thus an Angola vessel was ordered to collect an assortment of three males to one female, which would "answer for a Spanish Contract shou'd there be one at any of the [West India] Islands."[12] A vessel trading on the River Congo was advised to buy only males if females were difficult to obtain, for the males were certain to "make the highest Average in the West Indies," and "particularly at Havannah." Indeed, he was ordered to "avoid females as much as possible."[13] Hence, one is brought to wonder if (and doubt that) the shipment to South Carolina in 1773 of a cargo containing more females than males was a matter of chance.[14] Even if the composition of the cargo was not predetermined, the destination likely would be.

In none of the regions noted by the merchants above did the slave population grow naturally, whereas by the second half of the

10. John Maine and Co. to William Hindle, February 17, 1761, in Richards Collection, Account book *Tyrell*, 15–17.

11. In Leyland Papers: Thomas Leyland to Caesar Leyland, July 18, 1803, 387 MD 32, and to John Whittle, Liverpool, July 2, 1798, 387 MD 41.

12. James Clemens and Co. to Capt. William Speers, June 3, 1767, in Tuohy Papers, 380 TUO 4/2, ff. 1–3. African imports into Cuba between 1790 and 1794 reflected this ratio. See Herbert S. Klein, "North American Competition and the Characteristics of the African Slave Trade to Cuba, 1790 to 1794," *William and Mary Quarterly*, XXVIII (January, 1971), 98.

13. Thomas Leyland to Capt. William Young, June, 1795, in Account book *Spitfire* MS/10/49, University Library, Liverpool.

14. The argument here is not that ships with such a sex ratio never went to the West Indies or elsewhere, as this clearly was not the case. See, for example, the account of 503 slaves imported in the ship *Golden Age* from Whydah into Jamaica in December, 1784, in the Liverpool Museum. Printed as Item 12 in Liverpool History Teaching Unit, No. 2. There were various attempts in the West Indies, especially in the latter part of the eighteenth century, to encourage reproduction among the slaves, but there was more consistency in this regard in North America.

eighteenth century in South Carolina a more settled society probably encouraged a more stable slave population. In any case, South Carolina planters periodically expressed a concern to create or maintain slave families. Henry Laurens, for example, indicated in 1765 that he disliked to divide families even of new Negroes, and some months earlier he had written to the overseer on his Mepkin plantation: "I send up a stout young Woman to be a Wife to whome she shall like best amongst the single men. The rest of the Gentlemen shall be served as I have opertunity. Tell them that I do not forget their request."[15]

A similar situation existed in the Chesapeake. Russell B. Menard and Wesley Frank Craven have shown that in the seventeenth century the black population in Virginia and Maryland had an imbalance of males and females and was unable to reproduce itself. Craven warns against too ready an assumption that seventeenth-century planters promptly recognized the advantage of a self-perpetuating labor force.[16] Whether the advantage was immediately recognized or not, by the eighteenth century, blacks in the region were beginning to show a natural increase.[17] Menard places the watershed for natural increase in Western Shore Maryland in the 1720s. This increase was not a result of a more nearly equal sex ratio and thus, Menard asserts, did not reflect, on the part of those masters who were wealthy enough to alter the sexual balance on their possessions, a proper regard for black reproduction. The increase was caused, rather, by the growth of a creole population better adjusted to the environment. Allan Kulikoff suggests the beginnings of natural increase in Virginia a few years earlier, for similar reasons.[18]

15. Laurens to Elias Ball, April 1, 1765, IV, 595, and Laurens to Timothy Creamer, January 26, 1764, IV, 148, in Rogers *et al.* (eds.), *Papers of Henry Laurens.*
16. See Russell R. Menard, "The Maryland Slave Population, 1658 to 1730: A Demographic Profile of Blacks in Four Counties," *William and Mary Quarterly*, Third Series, XXXII (January, 1975), 29–54; and Wesley Frank Craven, *White, Red, and Black: The Seventeenth Century Virginian* (Charlottesville, 1971), 98–103.
17. Menard, "Maryland Slave Population," 42–45; and Edmund Morgan, *American Slavery, American Freedom: The Ordeal of Colonial Virginia* (New York, 1975), 301.
18. Allan Kulikoff, "A 'Prolifick' People: Black Population Growth in the Chesapeake Colonies, 1700–1790," *Southern Studies*, XVI (Winter, 1977), 391–428; also see "The Origins of Afro-American Society in Tidewater Maryland and Virginia, 1700 to 1790," *William and Mary Quarterly*, Third Series, XXXV (April, 1978), 226–59, and "The Beginnings of

But if western Maryland planters failed promptly to recognize the advantage of redressing the imbalance among their slaves, it ought not to be too much to assume that the realization came earlier in the older settlement of the Chesapeake. Certainly Robert "King" Carter of Corotoman, for one, perhaps the leading planter of his day, encouraged the creation of stable family units.[19] But whether for this or a different reason, by the third decade of the eighteenth century the latter area had established a reputation that encouraged the shipment of a larger percentage of women. Accordingly, in September, 1721, the Royal African Company complimented the handling of a cargo by James Phipps, their agent at Cape Coast Castle, commenting, "We take Notice what you write as to the Assortmt. of Capt. Bulcock's Cargo of Slaves and approve very well your Care and prudence in enlarging the Numbr of Women, boys & Girls, since there is so little difference in prices at Virginia and so great on the Coast."[20]

Gerald Mullin has contrasted the paternal-autarkic nature of Virginia plantation society with what could be styled as the modern-industrial nature of South Carolina slave society.[21] This typology ought, perhaps, to be extended to include the West Indies (and other, similar societies) at one end of the scale and the Chesapeake at the other, with South Carolina somewhere in the middle, containing elements of both. This dichotomy is comparable to Eric Wolf's distinction between "old-style" plantations,

---

the Afro-American Family in Maryland" in Aubrey C. Land *et al.* (eds.), *Law, Society and Politics in Early Maryland* (Baltimore, 1977), 171–96.

19. Kulikoff, "A 'Prolifick' People," 399–400.

20. Captain John Bulcock, of the galley *Sarah* of London, left the Gold Coast for Virginia in April, 1721, with 250 slaves and arrived at her destination June 26, 1721, with 233 slaves. Donnan (ed.), *Documents*, IV, 184. In Chancery Papers: London Committee to James Phipps, September 7, 1721, 113/35, Part I, No. 142. A slaver on the Gold Coast in 1717 paid four ounces, twelve ackies of gold dust for men, and for women two ounces, thirteen ackies, six tackoes. Cabo Corso Castle, March 30, 1717, 113/35, Part II, No. 25. In 1720 a ship paid six ounces, eight ackies for men and four ounces, eight ackies for women. Cape Coast Castle, August 2, 1720, in Treasury Papers, 70/4. In 1771 a report had men at ten and women at eight ounces; Donnan (ed.), *Documents*, II, 542. (*Ackies* and *tackoes* were measurements used on the African coast and represented divisions of the ounce.)

21. Gerald W. Mullin, "Religion and Slave Resistance," paper prepared for the American Historical Association Meeting, New Orleans, 1972, pp. 2–7. Also see his *Flight and Rebellion, passim,* and Michael Mullin (ed.), *American Negro Slavery: A Documentary History, passim.* Gerald Mullin used the term *autarkic* but not the words *modern* or *industrial* in his paper and is thus not responsible for this typology.

which have a traditional, paternalistic ethos, and "new-style" plantations, which have a free-labor, capitalistic ethos.[22] The former is characterized by a great interest—extending even to interference—in the personal life of the servant. This tightly circumscribed his autonomy and hampered his initiative but demonstrated a greater concern for his material well-being and a respect for familial cohesiveness—which in itself dictated a sex ratio that was closer to equal. The latter style is typified by a comparative lack of concern about the private affairs of the bondsman, his household social structure, or his material welfare; its preeminent consideration is business efficiency; and it would result in a relatively greater amount of individual freedom but also an unequal sex ratio. The more nearly equal sexual distribution, in association with other aspects of the paternal system, would encourage reproduction; the less nearly equal sex ratio, in association with other aspects of the industrial system, would discourage reproduction.[23]

The argument here is not that masters were more or less humane in one type of society as opposed to the other but that they perceived their interests differently and thereby acted in such a way that, in one case, the slave received greater physical benefits. This conjunction can clearly be seen in East Florida, where the British attempted between 1763 and 1783 to establish a plantation colony modeled somewhat after that of South Carolina. Governor James Grant requested permission from London to purchase state slaves to be used for provincial construction.[24] One of his corre-

22. Eric Wolf is quoted in Eugene D. Genovese, *The World the Slaveholders Made: Two Essays in Interpretation* (New York, 1969), 11. Genovese goes on to say, "The plantations of the British Caribbean, even with slave labor, exhibited most of the characteristics of Wolf's 'new-style' while they did retain certain important features of the old." Also see Eric R. Wolf, "Specific Aspects of Plantation Systems in the New World: Community Sub-Cultures and Social Classes," in Pan American Union, *Plantation Systems of the New World* (Washington, D.C., 1959), 136–46.

23. Peter Wood has outlined the retrogression in South Carolina from one type of system to the other, where largely West Indian settlers were encouraged by the Society for the Propagation of the Gospel in Foreign Parts to exercise more supervision over their slaves than had previously been their practice, eventuating in greater strictures on the servitor's liberty and cultural vitality. *Black Majority*, 131–42. The material benefits, therefore, might have been offset by greater psychological stress. A capsule series of comparisons can be found in Laura Foner and Eugene Genovese (eds.), *Slavery in the New World: A Reader in Comparative History* (Englewood Cliffs, 1969).

24. James Grant to the Board of Trade, July 16, 1765, in Grant of Ballindalloch MSS, 1771/Letterbook.

spondents, in supporting his plan, wrote in 1765: "It must manifestly appear to every person to be a saving to the Publick, as the Slaves will rather increase than diminish in Value or number and will always at least be worth the original purchase, in so healthy a Country as East Florida. The young ones will even do more than keep up the number. A few likely young Wenches must be in the parcell, & [he added in a phrase which calls attention to the sexual predisposition of some white colonials] should their Husbands fail in their duty, I dare say my friend Sweetinham & other publick Spirited Young Men, will be ready to render such an essential service to the Province as to give them some help." [25] The use of the word *husband* in this case could have been rather casual, and the desire to have the slaves reproduce did not necessarily oblige the creation of an equal sex ratio, force a regard for monogamous family units, or mandate stability. But the attitude of the above writer indicates a concern for progeny without any sensitivity to human considerations requisite for procreation. (This might not, in fact, mean that he had no such awareness, as the offending phrase could simply be an example of the kind of gross jocularity with which men probably have contemplated sex since time immemorial.) But however else the response is interpreted, it explicitly recognizes a regard for natural increase and therefrom a need for women.

The men actually engaged in building plantations had myriad reasons for wishing a more nearly equal balance between male and female. Richard Oswald notified the governor in 1767 that he was taking advantage of a ship going to Saint Augustine via the African coast to send some females to the colony, as "it might be of bad Consequence if the Men Slaves now on the Plantation, remained longer unprovided with Wives." [26] The earl of Egmont wrote in 1769 that he hoped soon to reap a profit from the slaves who already occupied his property, out of which he proposed that more slaves be bought.

25. John Graham to James Grant, July 19, 1765, in *ibid.*, 0771/401. Punctuation has been modernized slightly.
26. Richard Oswald to Grant, May 20, 1767, in *ibid.*, 0771/295.

And I Shd. be obliged to Yr. Excellency, for advising those who may be concerned for me, in such Encrease of Negroes, not so much to Consult my most Immediate Profit, as to render the Negroes I now have happy and contented, wch I know they cannot be without having each a Wife. This will greatly tend to keep them at home and to make them Regular and tho the Women will not work all together so well as ye Men, Yet Amends will be sufficiently made in a very few years by the Great Encrease of Children who may easily [be] traind up and become faithfully attached to the Glebe and to their Master.[27]

As if to confirm that the solicitude of these gentlemen was not idle worry, Grant's overseer wrote the departed governor in 1781 advising that five hundred pounds which were to be used in another way be spent instead "in purchasing young wenches for the plantation, which suffers much by having so few, for you not only lose by your negroes not increasing, but frequently the labour of the young fellows, who are either absenting themselves after the Wenches in town or inducing them to run away and concealing them in the woods in the neighborhood of your plantation. I have had frequent complaints on this head, and their excuse is what must they do for Wife."[28]

The concerns for permanence and stability as well as the foresight implicit in these statements, entirely aside from the benefits accruing to the slave, were uncharacteristic of the exploitation mentality associated with the industrial plantation model. Rather than trying to make as much profit as possible in the least imaginable time, regardless of consequences, as was typical of planters in the West Indies and in areas of Latin America, the posture expressed here is a willingness to defer immediate, temporary earnings for measured, long-term gains. This outlook, of course, was entirely pragmatic and reflected a realistic appraisal of continental possibilities. Richard Oswald, for instance, admitted to Governor Grant in 1768 that many of the worthies involved in the East Florida venture had become discouraged because they "lookt upon having a Tract of Land in Florida, as having a Plantation; & with-

27. Earl of Egmont to Grant, May 14, 1769, in *ibid.*, 0771/264.
28. David Yeats to Grant, February 3, 1781, in *ibid.*, 0771/250.

out giving themselves the trouble of further enquiry, were too easily amused with the idea of a Similarity to that respectable denomination when applied to a West India possession." But when they received a host of bills for implements, slaves, and supplies, he went on, with little prospect of a ready return on their outlay, their enthusiasm waned. He concluded by expressing the hope that a common acquaintance might "be cautious, & not overburden his scheme with too great preliminary expense, Since Circumstances in North America are so different from the West Indies, that it will in any event be a long time before they can be fetched up, by the fruits of the Settlement, & if half these late [discouraging] reports are true," he noted with pessimism, they "never will." [29] It is possible, therefore, that the more paternal attitude was determined by the economics of the situation, that the return on some crops was such that their production would not be profitable if the labor force had to be continually replaced.

A judgment of the extent to which this was true will ultimately depend upon a comparative analysis of the economics of production in the three major agricultural regions of the old empire, an endeavor beyond the scope of the current study. It is certain that rice, Carolina's primary crop, in association with its subsidiary, indigo, yielded much higher returns than did Chesapeake tobacco. It created, in fact, the greatest plantation wealth on the continent, though the riches of Carolina planters paled compared with that of their compatriots in the West Indies. But, as Edmund Morgan asserts, to make a profit, island planters worked their slaves to death, while mainland planters did not have to.[30] He argues, indeed, that the development of slavery in Virginia was inhibited initially in part because of the high death rates among whites and blacks alike.[31] Slaves were more expensive than servants (they cost about twice as much), and there was no reason to pay more for one than the other if a black man might live no longer than a white man could be indentured. When, among other things, survival rates improved, slavery took hold, marking a clear recogni-

29. Richard Oswald to Grant, February 19, 1768, in *ibid.*, 0771/259.
30. Morgan, *American Slavery, American Freedom*, 301.
31. *Ibid.*, 297–98.

tion of longevity as a consideration in economical plantation management.

Rice cultivation was more strenuous than raising tobacco but does not seem to have been so hazardous to life as sugar production. The life expectancy of a slave imported into the sugar islands was from five to seven years, it being considered more economical to use the slave in such a way that he died within that period than to improve or create conditions wherein his life could be longer preserved. Even if, as one scholar asserts, slaves managed to survive longer than that, the attitude is instructive.[32] In South Carolina, by contrast, planters estimated that a slave paid for himself within four or five years, so that the real profit from his labor came after that span. They looked upon slaves as an investment from which the owner could "reasonably expect above 16, 20, and 25 per Ct." when rice gave a "tolerable Price."[33] But for the master to realize this remuneration the slave had to survive. Moreover, the worth of slaves conditioned, or native, to the country was more than strictly economic. Governor James Glen, writing to the Board of Trade in 1751, after having valued the forty thousand blacks in the province at twenty pounds sterling per head, continued:

> But this Valuation does not satisfie me, for when it is Considered that many of these are Natives of Carolina, who have no Notion of Liberty, nor no longing after any other Country, that they have been brought up among White People, And by white people have been made, at least many of them, useful Mechanicks, as Coopers, Carpenters, Masons, Smiths, Wheelwrights and other Trades and that the rest can all speak our Language, for we imported none during the War, I say when it is Considered that these are pleased with their Masters, contented with their Condition, reconciled to Servitude, seasoned to the Country, and expert at the different kinds of Labour in which they are em-

32. Herbert S. Klein, in *The Middle Passage: Comparative Studies in the Atlantic Slave Trade* (Princeton, 1978), 246, rejects this statement on the five-to-seven-year survival rate of slaves, but somewhat ambiguously, since his comment refers to all the Americas, whereas the traditional statement refers specifically to the West Indies and modern studies seem to support it. See note 36 below.

33. James Glen to the Board of Trade, July 15, 1751, in Colonial Office Papers, ff. 155–57, 5/373, Public Record Office.

ployed, it must appear difficult if not impracticable to ascertain their instrinsick Value, I know a Gentleman who refuses five Hundred Guineas for three of his Slaves and therefore there is no guessing at the Value of strong seasoned handy Slaves by the prices of weak Raw New Negroes.[34]

Although their intrinsic value might not be ascertainable, their market price, fortunately, can be. For the attitude towards slaves as an investment, along with their pecuniary worth, was also expressed in East Florida. James Grant notified the earl of Egmont, who balked at paying £140 sterling for a servile tradesman, that skilled slaves sold in Charleston often as high as £200 sterling and noted that he would "rather give that price for a good [black] Tradesman, than employ white Indented Servants." He currently possessed, he wrote, about forty slaves, the first eight of whom had been purchased "before I came from England and cost at the rate of seventy pounds sterling a piece. They were all Country born but only common field Slaves. They have turned out remarkably well; for tho' I have lost three Negroes by Death I should sell those remaining for more Money than the whole cost me." He could get £100 for some of them, he went on.[35] While the assessment of worth for skilled or seasoned slaves would be equally applicable to a select number of bondsmen in the West Indies, the general philosophy of investment surely was not. The facts of slave treatment there are prima facie evidence to the contrary.[36]

An indication of some of the details of economical plantation management in South Carolina is suggested by a report on a successful venture in 1757. The owner had died, and an executor de-

34. James Glen to the Board of Trade, March 1751, "An Attempt towards an Estimate of the Value of So. Carolina," received with letters dated June 24, 1751, in *ibid.*, f. 137, 5/373.

35. Grant to Earl of Egmont, February 9, 1769, in Grant of Ballindalloch MSS, 0771/Letterbook.

36. See J. Harry Bennett, Jr., "The Problem of Slave Labor Supply at the Codrington Plantations," *Journal of Negro History*, XXXVI (October, 1951), 406–41, and XXXVII (April, 1952), 115–41; Else M. Goveia, *Slave Society in the British Leeward Islands at the End of the Eighteenth Century* (New Haven, 1965), 103–51, gives numerous examples of the thoughtless and wasteful exploitation of the slave population. Also see Pitman, "Slavery," 584–650, and *Development of the British West Indies*, 61–90, and Sheridan, "Africa and the Caribbean," 26.

scribed the condition of his plantation to a relative in the West Indies.

> There are near 100 slaves great and small upon the plantation but of these scarce 40 can be deemed working hands capable to go into the field, with these hands there was made last year 1780 weight of good Indico and 240 Barrels of Rice, both of which were shipt home. If the Indico arrived and was sold at 5 sh. ster. per. lb. which by the bye is a very moderate price for good Indico, the amount will be 445 Sterling. Deduce from this 30 per Cent for freight and Insurance and there will remain about £312 neat proceeds. The Rice would not produce less than 3£ Sterling per Barrel at home which is you know 720£ amount. But then the freight which was at £4:10 & £5 per Ton, with the Insurance at 15 per Cent being deduced, the neat proceeds will not be more than about £350, so that this year the Estate has produced upwards of 600£ sterling neat from which there may be probably a Deduction for Cloaths to Negroes and overseers wages, if a fund is not raised to pay these from the Corn &c planted besides the Indico and Rice.[37]

More than half the slave population of this plantation were not full working hands, and consequently the estate was supported by 40 percent of the labor force. Significantly, this percentage was sufficient. Most of the rest could be looked upon as a trust that would yield at some future date. This state of affairs may not have been possible in the West Indies, where many of the foodstuffs to support the slaves had to be (or in any case were) imported. This circumstance made the keeping of slaves more expensive. On the mainland, supplementary food crops frequently were a source of income as well as subsistence. In addition, they could be raised by

---

Richard Dunn, *Sugar and Slaves*, 251, 251*n*. writes that in seventeenth-century Jamaica, as in eighteenth-century North America, planters tried to keep a fairly even sex ratio among the slaves so as to avoid unrest. He gives examples of large Jamaica slaveholders who had a more or less proportionate number of men and women, remarking that lesser planters had more difficulty. In the eighteenth century, however, when sugar production in Jamaica rapidly expanded, Dunn writes that men heavily outnumbered women in the big slave gangs and provides facts that suggest support for the dichotomy between more- and less-intense plantation systems. Sheridan says explicitly that "slavery in the infancy of the sugar industry was considerably milder than it became in a later period of intensive culture." See "Africa and the Caribbean," 20. Also see Sheridan, "British Slave Trade," 240–63, and Michael Craton, "Jamaican Slavery," in Engerman and Genovese (eds.), *Race and Slavery*, 241.

37. John Murray to Sir Robert Laurie, July 12, 1757, in Murray of Murraythwaite MSS, ff. 48–49, GD 219/290, Scottish Record Office, Edinburgh.

less than full hands, that is, by older or younger men and women; these excess slaves, far from being a drag on the plantation, were an asset—both in the years before they reached their full potential, and after their prime. They paid their keep and still made a contribution. Further, their contribution was very important in gauging the worth of a plantation. Accordingly, James Grant wrote a plantation adventurer, telling him that "the Gentlemen were too sanguine who informed your Lordship that 33 Negroes ought to clear £500 a year." (The optimum number for beginning a rice plantation was about thirty slaves.)[38] He went on:

> I think a Planter does a great deal if he makes at the rate of eight pounds a Year of his Negroes, clear of all expences. To do that a plantation must be well established, and the Slaves must all be seasoned able working hands. There are Instances of Indigo planters doubling their Capital in a Year, but at an average Carolina planters do not make so much as I have mentioned, I mean of produce to go to Market, so as to remit the Money to Europe, for many things are consumed in a plantation which are of great utility in point of Living, tho' they cannot be converted into Cash, and I have always reckoned that an Intelligent Carolina Planter with a Capital from two to three thousand sterling (if his Negroes & Lands were to be disposed of) lives as well as any Man can do in Great Britain with an Income of £500 a year.[39]

The picture here is of a stable planter living off the land, committed to the country, and content to live more or less within his means. This situation did not usually obtain in the Caribbean.

The patriarchal spirit inherent in the profile above, though a concomitant, and not a determinant, of economic management, nevertheless had some humanizing aspects. Thus Laurens wrote of one slave that "he is a quiet orderly old Man, not able to do much Work and therefore is never drove to Labour, but suffer'd to go his own way. I observe he makes larger Crops of Rice and Corn for himself than most able Young Negroes, which I believe is greatly owing to their Aid for they all Respect and Love him."

38. See Thomas Nairne, *A Letter from South Carolina Giving an Account . . . of That Province* (London, 1710), 52–53, and John Murray to his mother, March 6, 1757, in Murray of Murraythwaite MSS, GD 219/287/11.

39. Grant to Earl of Egmont, February 9, 1769, in Grant of Ballindalloch MSS, 0771/Letterbook.

Laurens continued, "I shall order proper Care to be taken of him, if his Life shall happen to surpass his Strength for Labour . . . and continue to make the same Annual Allowance during all the Time that he is able to perform any Work."[40] The same motivation prompted a Georgia planter to offer to sell to the same man the family of a slave he had sold previously. The fellow, he said, "writes to his Wife frequently, and appears by his letters to be in great distress for want of her." He added that the slave would not have been sold except that "he disobliged me," but he thought the slave's punishment had now been sufficient. He concluded that "a separation of those Unhappy people, is adding distress to their unfortunate condition; for that reason I have taken the liberty to mention this matter to you; And if it is agreeable I will send them, and leave the value to your own or the Judgement of any other person after you have seen them."[41] On the other hand, it was probably just a matter of business that caused a slave dealer to report that he had obtained for a planter "a remarkable choice family. They cost no less than £290 [sterling], consists of a fellow, his Wife, two fine Grown Boys & a Girl. . . . I had no directions to buy his family, but I could not get him without them."[42]

Various suggestions have been advanced to explain the divergence between North America and other South Atlantic plantation systems in their ability to achieve slave propagation. Philip Curtin has adduced the novel proposal that this phenomenon might be a concomitant of a higher proportion of preseasoned slaves arriving on the mainland, a consideration vitiated by the fact that the majority of imports into North America came directly from Africa.[43] But the different rationales of the varying plantation systems might be partly responsible. The reasoning in

40. Rogers *et al.* (eds.), *Papers of Henry Laurens*, IV, 148n.
41. William Simpson to Grant, June 15, 1767, in Grant of Ballindalloch MSS, 0771/243.
42. John Graham to Grant, March 1, 1768, in *ibid.*, 0771/401.
43. Philip Curtin made this suggestion in a personal communication to Herbert Klein. See Klein, "Slaves and Shipping in Eighteenth-Century Virginia," *Journal of Interdisciplinary History*, V (Winter, 1975), 287n. Closer attention ought to be paid to this proposition, though, in view of Menard's work in Western Shore Maryland, where a native-born population was one aspect of an increase in the ratio of children to women, while the sex ratio had not improved. "Maryland Slave Population," 44–48.

one case not only provided better treatment but required a more equal balance between men and women. This logic might not have been as strong in every period and in every region. But over the long haul it would have encouraged the importation of relatively more African women into North America than any place else around the South Atlantic, and the greater population growth would be partly a function of this greater human capability. Certainly documents of the slave trade support this view.

II

In another direction, the social environment that encouraged more women imports may also have influenced the ethnic mix of the incoming slave population. For the source of slaves had something to do with the percentage of women likely to be obtained. We have already mentioned a ship trading on the River Congo in 1795 that was ordered to push its purchase in men if it found "the usual scarcity of Females" in the region. Herbert Klein argues, indeed, that all plantation societies had a more nearly equal valuation of women than commonly assumed and that supply conditions may have been more important than anything else in determining the normal disproportion of men to women.[44] Still, it seems that North America established a distinctive reputation as a market for females, and in this case, regions where women were more available might have been prominently represented on the continent partly for that reason. In this regard, a British official wrote in the 1780s that "few Women are allowed to be had on the Gold Coast & those never Approved in the West Indies, being Old. Eboe Women (from Bonny & New Calabar) are very fine and may be had." A month later he wrote that more women "and better" could be had at those two ports than anywhere else on the coast.[45] This fact might help to explain why such a large percentage of North American slave imports, especially in the Chesapeake, were from the Bight of Biafra. It was not simply that slaves from this region

44. Klein, *Middle Passage*, 240–41.
45. James Jones to Lord Hawkesbury, June 27, 1788, and July 26, 1788, in Liverpool Papers, CCXXVII, ff. 131 and 154, Add. MSS 38416.

were slighted elsewhere (including South Carolina), but, too, there was the greater probability of a larger quantity of women in cargoes collected there. Indeed, this reasoning might be a partial explanation for the Niger Delta figuring so prominently in the British slave trade as a whole, despite misgivings about these slaves in some quarters. But the official's statement increases the significance of Phipps's actions regarding Captain Bulcock's cargo, since it indicates that even where women were not easily obtained, more were likely to be shipped to North America.

Finally, the patriarchal ethos that mandated a more nearly equal sexual balance, a greater valuation of women, and better slave treatment, and that conceivably modified the ethnic composition of the slave population obliged closer attention to the slave. James Glen's inability to judge the "intrinsick Value" of country-born slaves, as opposed to the economic worth of new Negroes, indicates this kind of concern. In such a situation, the value, capacity, or utility of all slaves might be more easily recognized, including any connection between African ethnic groups and particular skills or crafts. Such recognition would spur slave preferences and be a further example of the way in which the plantation ethos affected the slave trade and the ethnic composition of the slave population. When South Carolinians were struggling to establish a new colony and grow a new crop, planters may have observed with even greater acuity the behavior patterns of their slaves. African knowledge, therefore, might have been more than welcome.

Chapter **4**

Rice Cultivation and the Slave Trade

I

"Fifty years ago," Stanley Elkins wrote in 1959, "if the American Negro was congratulated for anything, it was his remarkable advancement from a state of primitive ignorance. Now, however, looking back upon the energy, vitality, and complex organization of West African tribal life, we are tempted to reverse the question altogether and to wonder how it was ever possible that all this native resourcefulness and vitality could have been brought to such a point of utter stultification in America."[1] This stifling process began, he asserts, the moment a peaceful villager was torn from his tranquil existence in Africa and continued by progressive stages to his abject dehumanization in America. But if stultification ever existed, it was never so complete as Elkins imagined, and the indescribable horrors of their ocean passage did not numb Africans beyond recovery nor render them entirely forgetful of their background.

This is not to deny that the experience of enslavement involved trauma, whether in Africa or America, or that the degree of "shock and detachment" was more acute the more alien the circumstances surrounding the enslaved. The fear excited when a captive was first taken probably did not begin to equal his apprehension as he was taken away from the African coast. Traders reported that this was the time slaves were most likely to revolt.[2] Their continuing anxiety about their fate is illustrated by the ease with which panic was created aboard a slave ship newly arrived at Saint Christophers in 1737, during which a large number of slaves

1. Stanley Elkins, *Slavery: A Problem in American Institutional and Intellectual Life* (Chicago, 1968), 93.
2. See, for example, the Memorandum of Capt. Debat Relating to Gambia, to the Earl of Dartmouth, 1765, in Dartmouth MSS, D 1778/V/254.

succeeded in jumping overboard and committing suicide. The incident occurred when an experienced slave with a "perverted sense of humour," in the words of John Pope-Hennessy, "trotted on board to tell the new arrivals that they were first to have their eyes put out and then be eaten." But the degree of resilience these people possessed is seen by the fact that even under such horrifying conditions as the middle passage they were able to regain their spirits—the women and children much sooner than the men, it is said—and to form such a community of mutual support and suffering that there remained forever afterwards a special feeling of comradeship among those who had come over in the same vessel.[3]

The emotional suppleness displayed on slave ships and the often fairly rapid adjustment of Africans to a new overseas environment derived from, and were facilitated by, African religious and cultural beliefs. The African historian Kenneth Onwuka Dike indicates that in many cases tribal "oracles," particularly in the Niger Delta, conditioned Africans to accept slavery fatalistically as divine retribution and thus mitigated a destiny that might otherwise have been considered unjust and incomprehensible.[4] This assertion is confirmed in South Carolina by a minister of the Society for the Propagation of the Gospel, who wrote in 1724 that "our Negro Pagans have a Notion of God & of a Devil, & dismal apprehensions of Apparitions, Of a God that disposes absolutely of all things, for asking one day a Negro Pagan woman how she happen'd to be made a Slave [she] reply'd that God would have it so & she cou'd not help it."[5]

Africans, therefore, were much better prepared psychologically and, as we shall see, technologically, to be active participants in the creation of New World society than has often been realized. Perhaps nowhere was this background more suitable than in the case of Africans from Upper Guinea who were brought into

3. John Pope-Hennessy, *Sins of the Fathers: A Study of the Atlantic Slave Traders, 1441–1807* (London, 1967), 105–106, 103; testimony of John Newton, *Report of the House of Lords, 1789*, p. 110; testimony of Archibald Dalzell, *Report of the House of Lords, 1789*, pp. 113–14, Bristol Archives Office.

4. "The Question of 'Sambo,'" *Newberry Library Bulletin,* V (December 1958), 27; Dike, *Trade and Politics,* 13, 37–41.

5. Francis Vernod to secretary, January 13, 1724, in A-18, pp. 69–75, Society for the Propagation of the Gospel in Foreign Parts Archives, London.

South Carolina. Nor is it by any means inconceivable that their contribution to the development of rice cultivation in South Carolina was greater than has been recognized.

When the British attempted to establish a plantation colony in East Florida, one of the participants in the endeavor described his quest for slaves thus: "As to the Negroes, I must get them either in Carolina or Georgia, and must choose such as are used to the different Cultivations I begin with as Rice, Cotton, Indigo etc."[6] This quote highlights the role that slaves often played in the foundation of new settlements, as a source not only of brawn but of technical skills. It is evidence, too, that planters frequently recognized and were eager to make use of those skills. Although this particular statement relates to East Florida, a similar attitude can be seen in South Carolina with reference to slaves brought from Africa: bondsmen already familiar with crops the colonials desired to produce were extremely high priced.

Peter Wood has recently suggested that certain Africans might have known more about the cultivation of rice than their masters during the early period of Carolina's settlement; undeniably, South Carolinians placed a positive value on slaves brought from rice-growing regions throughout the eighteenth century.[7] In fact, slaves brought from some regions of Africa were probably familiar with all three of the crops mentioned by the East Florida speculator. An eighteenth-century Frenchman traveling in the Senegambia region after the rainy season in November, 1749, reported that the countryside around Galam, up the Senegal River, "had now a very different face from what it wore at the time of my first voyage. Instead of a dry barren plain, I beheld an agreeable champaign, intersected with morasses, where rice grew naturally without being sown. The higher grounds were covered with millet; and there also the indigo and cotton plants displayed a most lovely verdure."[8] A British official wrote of the same region in 1766 that it "abounds in prodigious Quantities of Wax, Rice, Cotton, In-

6. William Stock to Earl of Cassillas, June 14, 1763, in Ailsa MSS, GD 25/9/27, Scottish Record Office, Edinburgh.
7. Wood, *Black Majority*, 34–62.
8. M. Adanson, *A Voyage to Senegal, the Isle of Goree and the River Gambia* (London, 1759), 151.

digo and Tobacco. The latter is of the same sort as the Growth of Brazil. The Cotton that has been carried from Senegal to Europe has been repeatedly proven to be the finest in the World."[9]

In the Gold Coast region a similar condition obtained, at least in relation to cotton and indigo. An official at Cape Coast Castle reported that these crops grew very well on the coast, and he endeavored to get the Royal African Company to send out authorities from the West Indies to improve production. He reported that he had written to the chief agents at the various company factories located along the coast, asking them to "promote the planting and improveing of Cotton & for the Natives encouragement to employ themselves therein we have offered them a Damboy or two Pence half penny per pound for whatever Quantitys of un Clean Cotton their peoples labour shall produce and hope in a few years Your Hon[rs] will reap the benefit of it by receiveing Quantitys home." (It is interesting to ruminate about how history might have been changed had his suggestion been followed and the endeavor become successful.) He continued his report with the statement that "there is a Sort of Indigo grows wild here that the Natives make use of and is of a very lasting Dye; therefore if we had People Skilled in that Art and proper Cisterns set up we are of Opinion that great Improvements might be made thereof as well at this place, Commenda and Accra as at Quittah where ye West India sort, as we are informed, is a Weed of ye Country."[10] Obviously, Africans from these regions of the coast were familiar with all of the major crops cultivated by slave labor on the North American continent.

Being familiar with a crop, however, is a different matter from being familiar with the cultivation of a crop. Even in the latter case, it is possible that if the circumstances and methods of production in the New World radically diverged from those in the Old, prior experience could have inhibited rather than facilitated the apprehension of new methods (though this is hard to imagine). But to the extent that these crops were something that gave

9. Governor Lewis [to Board of Trade], July 25, 1766, in Kings MSS, 300, f. 27.

10. Agent at Cape Coast Castle to Royal African Company, July 2, 1722, in Chancery Papers, 113/36, Part I, 1541, ff. 18–19, 5.

the new African a sense of the familiar, that reminded him of his homeland, his new environment was less strange and his adjustment, perhaps, less traumatic.

Slaves from the Windward Coast and Senegambia regions were better prepared for their New World experience than has been commonly assumed, especially if they came to South Carolina. For rice not only grew there but was cultivated, and not only by freemen but by slaves, many of whom later came to America. A slave trader resident two years on the coast of Sierra Leone estimated that three-fourths of the population where he stayed was in some form of indigenous servitude. Many of these people were employed in cultivating land and were entirely subject to their master's will. He reported that slaves brought from the interior before the beginning of the rainy season were employed on the "plantations" of coastal peoples before being sold to Europeans or transferred locally from one master to another after rice was planted. Although caution must be taken in making facile analogies between indigenous African practices and apparently similar institutions elsewhere, and despite the obvious distinction that slavery in sub-Saharan Africa was not racial in the way that it became in North America, there are striking similarities as well as differences between the situation in Upper Guinea and in North America. The trader wrote that:

The Slaves are of 2 Classes
 1. House
 2. & Plantation
The 1st is considered as part of ye family, & is educated. The Plantⁿ Slaves live in Towns separate from ye Master, and whatever they have is considered as their Master's property. Each has ground to cultivate sufficient for ye Subsistence of himself & Family. They marry & have many Children, but they [have] only one wife; tho' polygamy is allowed in ye Country it is practised only by the rich.

. . . .

The plantation Slaves are employed in cultivating Rice, which they sell to ye Ships, & Cotton for their own Consumption. The Rice is cultivated with great labour, according to their manner, as they have new ground to clear every Season. The Slaves go into ye field at Sunrise and work to about 11, but they reckon time only by ye Sun. They have their Meal which consists of Rice cooked in ye fields. After they have finished their meal they return to their labour till Sunset & then get a 2d Meal. They work he believes willing & industriously; at least never heard compulsion was necessary. Have no Instruments of husbandry but a Hoe made of an Iron Barr, & owing to their imperfect manner of clearing the ground, the proportion of produce is very small.[11]

The dichotomy between the house and plantation slave in Upper Guinea was probably greater than that between the house and field slave in North America (if, as John Blassingame avers, both of the latter were part of the same slave community), and the situation of the house slave in the two regions is not really comparable.[12] In Africa, for instance, the former was not usually sold. Under the best of North American conditions, the plantation slave may have discovered his new lot to be somewhat similar to his old, though he would not likely have profited by the change. This analogy ought not to be pressed too far, though Gerald Mullin has suggested the extent to which the patriarchal nature of plantation

11. "Extracts from the Evidence of Jno. Matthews Esqr. given to ye Committe of Privy Council," March 4, 1788, in Long's Collections, Add. MSS 18272, ff. 1–6. This description coincides with modern studies of traditional African servitude in this region. Eric Pollet and Grace Winter in *La Société Soninke (Dyahunu, Mali)* (Brussels, 1972), 240–65, describe three types of slaves. The first was a body of slaves whose services were only at the disposition of a village chief and whose essential task was to secure the execution of duties required for the good of the village. They represented a privileged servile class, lived apart, cultivated land only for their own use and were not, in the later years of the institution, subject to endogamy, though in the case of marriages of inequality, the child followed the condition of the mother. There were the domestic slaves (*captifs de case*) who were also privileged, could not be sold, had many rights, and were essentially members of the family, though subject to endogamy. The third group were trade slaves (*esclaves de traite*), who could be bought and sold. Though allowed to cultivate patches of land for their own use and to sell certain goods for their own benefit, they possessed no real rights of separate ownership. They were also endogamous. *Captifs de traite* became *captifs de case* after they had stayed with the same master for a long period of time or when they had children. There were liberal methods of manumission. In "Extracts," Add. MSS 18272, ff. 1–6.

The Pollet-Winter study focused on one group of Mande-speaking peoples in the Upper Guinea region, but J. Suret Canale writes that the social and political structures of the whole area were deeply influenced by the Mande civilization. See J. F. Ajaye and Michael Crowder (eds.), *A History of West Africa* (New York, 1972), I, 392. Also see Curtin's discussion of African slavery in the same work, pp. 241–43.

12. John W. Blassingame, *The Slave Community: Plantation Life in the Antebellum South* (New York, 1972), 154–83.

society in eighteenth-century Virginia recalled a comparable social structure in traditional Africa.[13] The argument here is twofold. First, without a doubt the African background gave the African immigrant the capability to contribute more than just brawn to the development of the plantation society in North America. (The governor of South Carolina told the Board of Trade in 1753 that the only tobacco grown in the province was by Negroes for their own use.)[14] Second, the new environment was not so strange and their new experiences not so shocking that Africans virtually ceased to be autonomous, functioning human beings, as suggested by the "extended metaphor" of Stanley Elkins—a situation that, in any event, would have rendered them psychologically incapable of tendering knowledgeable service.[15]

Although Africans were knowledgeable about practically all of the major North American staple crops, our concern in this instance is with the mainstay of South Carolina's colonial economy, rice. In order to gauge the extent to which an African contribution to the development of rice cultivation in the colony was possible, it will be necessary to look in some detail at the varieties of rice and the ways in which this crop was produced in Africa and South Carolina.

II

Scattered throughout Africa are various indigenous varieties of wild rice. The most common form, *Oryza Barthii* (after the German explorer Barth, who "discovered" it in 1853), is found in an area stretching from the River Senegal in West Africa to the White Nile in the East and southward as far as Angola and Tanzania.[16] Two other common species, *O. Breviligulata* and *O. Brachyanta*, appear to be more closely limited to West Africa, especially the

13. Gerald W. Mullin, "Religion and Slave Resistance."

14. John Glen to the Board of Trade, March 1753, in Colonial Office Papers, 5/374, f. 147.

15. Elkins, *Slavery*, 89–103. The Elkins thesis has been largely discredited by historians. See Ann J. Lane (ed.), *The Debate Over Slavery: Stanley Elkins and His Critics* (Chicago, 1971).

16. Roland Portères, "Le Riz Vivace de l'Afrique," *L'Agronomie Tropicale*, IV (January–February, 1949), 12.

latter, which is not widespread at all.[17] These plants often grow as intrusive weeds among cultivated varieties of rice (though in contrast to *O. Breviligulata, O. Barthii* also grows alone) and are very difficult to detect before they reach the budding stage. They are sometimes, perhaps frequently, used for food (particularly *O. Barthii*, which is prized as a luxury item) and are useful when natural disasters decrease the cultivated crop.[18] But their yield is low, harvesting is laborious, and they are a threat to the cultivated crop if not checked in time. The appearance of *O. Breviligulata* is taken as a sign that the fertility of the soil has decreased, and African cultivators conventionally let any plot of ground in which it appears lie fallow.[19]

Rice was cultivated in West Africa from an early period. Roland Portères, an authority on African food crops, suggests that as early as 1500 B.C. two important centers of rice cultivation emerged in Africa, the first (circa 1500 B.C.) just west of the bend of the Niger in the Western Sudan—in the Central Niger Delta—and the second (between 1500–1800 B.C.) in Senegambia in the area of the Casemance River. These cultures were based on an indigenous rice, *Oryza glaberrima*, thought to have been ennobled from the wild variety *O. Breviligulata*. He suggests further that the invention of rice cultivation in Africa was an independent development, unrelated to rice cultivation in Asia, though this view is not universally accepted.[20] The Africanist R. Mauny theorizes that rice cultivation came into Africa from the Mediterranean, introduced by the Arabs between the eighth and fifteenth centuries, but it is uncertain that the Asian variety of rice, *Oryza sativa*, had pen-

17. Pierre Viguier, "La riziculture indigène au Sudan français," *Annales agricoles de l'Afrique occidentale française et étrangères* (January–March, 1938), 34–46.
18. Aug. Chevalier, "Le Riz Sauvage de l'Afrique Tropicale," *Journal d'Agriculture Tropicale*, XI (January, 1911), 3.
19. Viguier, "Riziculture indigène," 35.
20. See Roland Portères, "Vieilles Agricultures de l'Afrique Intertropicale: Centres d'origine et de diversifications varietale primaire et berceaux d'agriculture antérieurs au XVIe siècle," *L'Agronomie Tropicale*, V (September–October, 1950), 489–507, and Tadeusz Lewicki, *West African Foods in the Middle Ages, According to Arabic Sources* (Cambridge, 1974), 33. See also J. Desmond Clark, "The Spread of Food Production in Sub-Saharan Africa," *Journal of African History*, III, 2 (1962), 219, and Philip Curtin, "African Civilization and World Civilization: The Problem of 'Lag,'" in Melvin Drimmer (ed.), *Black History: A Reappraisal* (Garden City: Doubleday, 1968), 20–27.

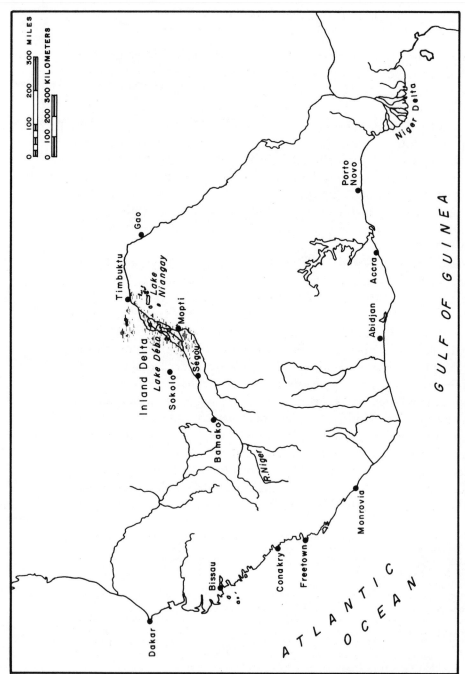

West Africa, showing inland delta of rice cultivation

Map by Dean L. Pendleton

etrated the Western Sudan by that period.[21] Arab travelers, who journeyed in the Sudan from the eighth century, made numerous references to the presence and use of rice in the Sudan but without making clear whether the crop was cultivated or merely collected from wild varieties.[22] Not until the sixteenth century does Mahmoud Kati in his *Tarikh el-Fettash* make clear reference to cultivated rice in the empire of Songhai. Speaking of the reign of Askia Daoud (1549–83), he noted that the emperor possessed royal property in all the territory bordering the Niger, from Lake Debo in the west to Dendi in the east. In every village along this route the emperor owned slaves organized in groups numbering from twenty to one hundred, each under the authority of a royal official known as a *fanfa* (pl. *fanafi*). Many of these estates were devoted to the cultivation of rice. The seeds were dispensed to the *fanafi* each year from a central location, and every estate was responsible for furnishing the king with a predetermined number of bags of grain at the end of the harvest. The Venetian explorer Cada Mosta mentioned a similar structure of crop production in the fifteenth century under the kingdom of Mali, and although he does not specifically mention rice, it is not too much to assume that the crop was under cultivation by then.[23]

The rice being cultivated at this period was most likely the African *Oryza glaberrima* rather than the Asian *Oryza sativa*. The Polish scholar Tadeusz Lewicki, for example, notes that the Greek geographer Strabo mentioned the cultivation of rice at Augila or Aujila in Cyrenaica in A.D. 12 but made no mention of it in Egypt at the same time and concludes that this was the African variety obtained from the Western Sudan.[24] Michal Tymowski (in support of R. Mauny) argues that the rice dispensed by the Songhai monarchs was the variety *O. sativa* because it has a higher yield than the local variety, but if this were true it would seem that *O. glaber-*

21. R. Mauny, "Notes historiques autour des principales plantes cultivées d'Afrique occidentales," *Bulletin de l'IFAN*, IV, 2 (1953), 718, and Lewicki, *West African Foods*, 34.

22. Lewicki, *West African Foods*, 34.

23. See Michal Tymowski, "Les domaines des princes de Songhay (Soudan occidental): Comparaison avec la grande propriété foncière en Europe au début de l'époque féodale," *Annales*, XV (1971), 1637–58, esp. 1637–43.

24. Lewicki, *West African Foods*, 34.

rima should have been displaced to a much larger extent than is actually the case, especially if the introduction occurred under the auspices of a central administration. In fact, *O. sativa* is much more common along the Atlantic seaboard, where it was introduced by the Portuguese in the sixteenth century, than in the Middle Niger, where it was allegedly introduced earlier.

According to Portères, *O. glaberrima* had spread from its original centers of domestication to the Atlantic littoral, between the River Senegal in the north to Axim on the Gold Coast in the south, by the sixteenth century. When *O. sativa* was introduced from the Atlantic, it took root in those areas where the cultivation of rice was already known. The most important centers of introduction were, first, in the region between the Rivers Casamance and Nunez (the area from southern Senegal and Guinea-Conakry to northern Guinea-Conakry), and, second, between the River Sherbro and Grand Bassa (Buchanan) in current Sierra Leone and Liberia, regions heavily frequented by slave ships in the eighteenth century.[25]

Since the introduction of *O. sativa*, there have been generally three broad categories of cultivated rice in western Africa. The first group, characterized by leaning (hanging or bent) and rather loose panicles with white grains of rice, is associated with *O. sativa*. The second group, recognized by erect and compact panicles with red grains of rice, is associated with *O. glaberrima*. The third, possessing slightly leaning panicles with red grains of rice, is considered to be a hybrid of the Asian and African varieties. This is a simplification, because *O. sativa* has proven so adaptable to African conditions and developed so many different varieties, either by natural selection, mutation, or hybridization, that it is often difficult, if not impossible, to follow precise lines of evolution. The third category, for example, subsumes plants with panicles at various degrees of bent and in other characteristics is not distinct from the first group (itself not free of hybrids), except that the caryopsis is red or rose colored. The greater adaptability of *O. sativa* has contributed to regression of *O. glaberrima*, and the profusion

25. Portères, "Vieilles Agricultures," 492, 493.

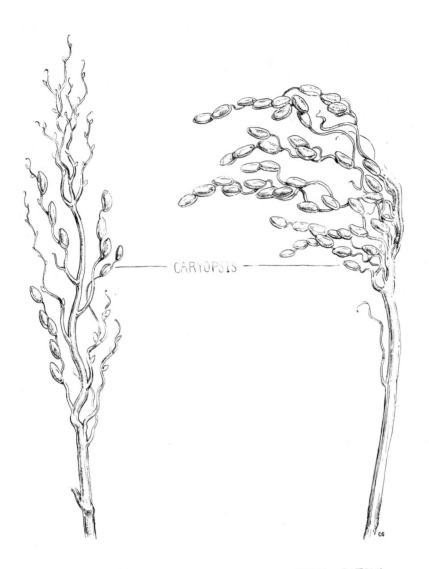

CARYOPSIS

ORYZA GLABERRIMA

ORYZA SATIVA

The rice panicle
Drawing by Cheryl Grenier

of varieties that have developed in West Africa has made it a principal center of rice (meaning *O. sativa*) diversification equal to the more-noted Madagascar. Indeed, there are more varied systems and practices of rice cultivation in West Africa than in all of Asia.[26]

The distinguishing fact about traditional rice cultivation in Africa (in particular contrast to South Carolina) was that it was a culture utilizing floodplains rather than extensive irrigation. Africans modified their agricultural practices to suit the environment, rather than vice versa, though minor alterations were sometimes made. In the region of the Middle Niger obstructions, embankments or palisades were put up to keep predator fish from getting into the rice paddies, or (in the Bamba region, between Timbuktu and the bend of the Niger) dikes were used to improve the retention of water. In some cases, small canals were dug to admit and control the flow of water into lowland areas, and, in the Senegambia region, some tribes did practice irrigation. All of these practices had analogues in South Carolina. This background would have been useful in the province, but these examples are exceptions to a general rule of accepting rather than changing the setting. West Africans were consequently dependent upon the vagaries of the weather and terrain as crucial determinants of what crops they grew and how they grew them. In terms of rice, this meant preeminently the availability of water, which, in the Western Sudan, determined that the great regions of rice cultivation were (and are) along the Niger River.[27]

From its headwaters in the Fouta-Djalon to Macina in Mali, the floodplains of the Niger River form a slight valley that, during the rainy season, the waters completely overflow but not very deeply. Here rice forms a principal crop but is accompanied by various millets and other produce, dependent on the rainfall and the proximity of the cultivated areas to the riverbed. At the outer reaches

26. Viguier, "Riziculture indigène," 31–33; Portères, "Vieilles Agriculture," 493, and "Le système de Riziculture par franges univerietales et l'occupation des fonds par les Riz flottants dans l'Ouestafricain," *Revue internationale de Botanique Appliquée et d'Agriculture Tropicale*, XXXIX (November–December, 1949), 563.

27. Pierre Viguier, "La riziculture indigène au Soudan français," *Annales agricoles de l'Afrique occidentales française et étrangères*, I (1937), 288, and Aug. Chevalier, "L'Importance de la Riziculture dans le domaine colonial française et l'orientation à donner aux recherches rizicoles," *Revue de Botanique Appliquée et d'Agriculture Tropicale*, XVI (January, 1936), 27.

of the floodplain, rice may be either a principal or a supplementary crop, depending on the terrain, the extent of the overflow, the amount of rain, and various other factors. At Mopti the Niger is enlarged by its confluence with the River Bani, and beginning at Macina the alluvial floodplain spreads out, rising gently by stages to form an inland delta. Millions of hectares of land are inundated by the floodwaters of the wet season and villages become "veritable islets" in a tract crisscrossed by rivulets and spotted with dunes, but mostly underwater. The amount of land not subject to inundation is insufficient to support a feasible alternative, and rice is of necessity the major agricultural concern. This region, especially a triangle formed by Mopti, Macina, and Djenne, is the largest rice-producing region in the Western Sudan (and perhaps in all of Africa). The network of rivers and streams from this inland delta pour into Lake Debo, the approximate center of the area, whence the Niger divides to form two lake series before it unites again south of Timbuktu. The interlacustrine region is cut by rivers and dune formations and dotted with depressions that become still and stagnant lakes when the waters recede. The variant depths and divergent rates of evaporation of these ponds provide for the production of myriad sorts of rice, though not every village, particularly at the far reaches of the floodplain, is obliged to grow it. (But this ability to relate different rice types to various soil conditions may have proven quite useful in Carolina.) From Timbuktu, the floodplain once again assumes a more even character, and peoples in its reach have greater leeway in crop production. Rice is a principal commodity, but it shares the land with millet and other staples.[28]

Because West Africans did little to alter the environment, they manipulated crops instead. Consequently, ecological and typological conditions had a determining effect on the type of rice used and the method of growth. In the delta region, where a supply of water is assured and most of the land is submerged, the rice grown is *O. glaberrima*, particularly its various floating varieties, which are able to grow fast enough to keep their heads above water as

28. This paragraph follows R. Clérin, "La Riziculture au Soudan français," *L'Agronomie Tropicale*, VI (July–August, 1951), 400; Viguier, "Riziculture indigène," 291–92.

floodwaters rise. The local people distinguish two classes of rice (of which there are many varieties) in terms of speed of maturation. Fast rice (*riz hatif*), possessing a maturation period of between four and four and one-half months (or 115–140 days, from about June to September), is planted in the more shallow places and is usually consumed locally, whereas slow rice (*riz tardif*), possessing a maturation period of about six months (July to December), is planted in the deeper areas and is usually exported. The interlacustrine region also has two distinct categories of *O. glaberrima*, suited to variant conditions. The first is "river rice," of many types, planted on relatively flat lands subject to inundation. The taste of this rice is preferred to that of "pond rice" (*riz de mare*), which is capable of growing in the stagnant water to which the topology of the region gives rise, though it must be transplanted. To the east of Timbuktu, in the postdeltic region, the people recognize three classes of *O. glaberrima*, two of which are floating varieties and one of which is more properly paddy rice. The latter is a fast rice with a maturation period of about five months (June or July to November). Cultivated in the shallower areas, its yield is not so good as its companion floating rice. The first of the latter is a slow rice (maturation period of six months, from about June or July to November or December) with a better yield than the fast varieties but not so good as the other floating type, a very slow rice with a longer maturation period of six and one-half to seven months. Because of these various types of rice, peoples in this region have a harvest season stretching over two months while different crops reach maturity.[29]

The method of clearing the land differs with the region.[30] In the delta country, northwestward from Diafarabé, where the land is habitually underwater and the shrubbery is scarce, the task of clearing is easier than elsewhere. When the fields are submerged, at the beginning of the wet season, the weeds are cut off just below the waterline so that they suffocate. It is a laborious task because it must be accomplished in waist- and sometimes neck-deep water.

29. See Viguier, "Riziculture indigène," 34–46; Clérin, "Riziculture au Sudan français," 400–401. Viguier gives the local African names of the various types.
30. The following section is based on Viguier, "Riziculture indigène," 72–81.

At Macina, on the delta fringes, the weeds are cut, gathered, left to dry and be burned during the dry season. Outside the delta the most usual method of clearing land is through the use of fire. In the basin southwest from Macina, for example, the underbrush is burned and then the roots of the weeds are pulled up with the use of a small hoe called a *daba*—not unlike a comparable tool used in the New World. Trees are cut down but the stumps are not removed since they do not hinder the planting and the job would cost more labor than it is worth.

In general, land is prepared for cultivation at the end rather than at the beginning of the growing season and is done as quickly as possible after the water recedes, while the ground is still wet. In the case of land already under cultivation, the ground is worked as soon as the harvest is over. Only in areas where the job is not completed before the ground dries does preparation take place at the new rains. The ground is broken up into clods or clumps of earth with the *daba* and allowed to remain until the rainy season begins. When the rains come, the seed is sown broadcast and then (in some cases) is covered by breaking up the clumps of earth with the *daba* or (in others) by allowing the seed to be covered naturally by the action of the rain on the clumps of earth. In the latter instance, much grain is lost to birds. The decision when to plant is always a gamble. The grain should be sown soon enough after the rains commence so that the plant has sufficient maturity to withstand the flood and the assaults of phytophagous fish and to be able to continue its growth as the water mounts. But if it is sown too soon it might die before the next rain, and the sowing will have to be repeated. Account has to be taken also of the periodic locust flights. The rice fields are usually weeded twice, once at the beginning of the season just before or just after the land is inundated and once again later in the season.

There are regional divergences from this general sketch. Some ethnic groups are more conscientious in the cultivation of their crop than others. The Bambara and Marka in the Macina region prepare the ground very carefully, turning the soil well and laboriously removing the roots and rhizomes of wild rice and other weeds, while the Fula or Fulbe (Peul-Rimaibe) of the same region are not nearly so thorough. The Malinke, southwest of Macina, break the soil, but because much of it is not turned under, many of the weeds are not destroyed. The Songhai (Songhai-Gabibi) east of Timbuktu scarcely bother to break the soil at all. They simply scrape the topsoil with the *daba* and cover over the seeds; or, if the ground has cracked in drying, the seeds are pushed into the crevices with branches. Mande-speaking peoples west and southwest of Bamako, by contrast, often plant the rice in ridges, turning the soil completely as the rainy season commences, though this practice usually occurs when they have been unable to prepare the land at the end of the previous season.

In the lacustrine region, between Lake Debo and Timbuktu, transplanting is practiced. The rice is first planted on high ground in a light clay soil prepared by the *daba* at the end of April or May. These nursery plants are not dependent on the rains but rather are watered from calabashes two or three times a week. When the plants have attained two or three months' growth, they are removed to fields where inundation is just beginning. In some cases, if the waters are not yet sufficiently high to flood the fields completely, canals are dug to irrigate the plants with water brought in calabashes until the fields are submerged. Transplanting is practiced at various other locations but on a much smaller scale.

Finally, in some places in the Sudan, rice is planted utilizing seed holes. Two or three grains of rice are dropped in holes dug five or twelve centimeters apart and are covered over. It is an excellent agricultural technique, yielding larger returns and facilitating weeding, which can be accomplished with the *daba* and not by hand as is usual in other cases. But the practice is not very common and where it occurs is left to the women, and to older women at that, so that despite its advantages it is not highly regarded. As a general rule, wherever rice cultivation is a major concern, it is the primary responsibility of the men and, wherever and to the extent that it has a supplementary character, it is the responsibility of the women.

The harvest season stretches from October to December or January, depending on the region. In some places (the delta area) the crop ripens before the waters have receded and the rice is collected in pirogues. In others (southwest of Macina) the rice comes to maturity when the water is low and can be collected on foot. The tops of the plants are cut off with a sickle or special reaping knife, tied in bunches, and left to dry in or near the fields to await threshing and winnowing. Those varieties whose grain is more loosely attached to the rachis or axis are harvested before those whose grain is more secure. Rice straw in the Niger Valley is not commonly used to feed cattle; indeed, in the basin upstream from Macina it is burned in the fields as soon as it is dry. Then the process of preparing for the next season's crop begins anew.

In the *sahel* outside the Niger Valley various types of *O. sativa* and its hybrids are cultivated. The varieties of rice depend upon the temporal extent and depth of the floodwaters, if within the reaches of a floodplain, and, outside of that, on the amount and frequency of rainfall. On these considerations rice is divided into three kinds. The first is mountain (or dry) rice, which can be cultivated in the same way as other crops—millet, for example—but does better on moister ground. The cultivation of this type was reported in 1938 not to extend beyond thirteen degrees north latitude in the Western Sudan and not to be very extensive. The second, a wet rice, is cultivated in very humid or miry soils but is not immersed. The third is swamp rice, cultivated on land that has been inundated, but not to a great depth. For all these types of rice there are numerous varieties.[31]

In the tropical rain forests of the Guinea Coast rice also holds sway. Its domain stretches from as far north as Cape Verde in Senegal and to the south and eastward as far as the Bandama River on the Ivory Coast, where yam cultivation becomes the primary pursuit.[32] In an area known as the Southern Rivers (from the River Saloum in central Senegal to Sierra Leone), rice cultivation in traditional Africa reaches its height. On the coast as a whole, the

31. *Ibid.*, 5.
32. The Bandama River is the traditional dividing line between rice and yam cultivation; but this boundary may not reflect modern conditions, nor is it certain that this line has remained constant in the past. W. B. Morgan, "The Forest and Agriculture in West Africa," *Journal of African History*, III, 12 (1961), 235–39.

same general types of rice exist as in the Sudan, though the use of mountain (upland or dry) rice is much more important and wide-spread than in the Niger Valley, while the Baga around the Rio Nunez (in Guinea-Conakry) utilize floating rice.[33] Various kinds of swamp rice are also cultivated, under similar conditions as exist in the Sudan, on floodplains or in stagnant ponds left by the over-flow of the rainy season.

Because the common methods of rice production are more or less the same throughout West Africa, a description of cultivation in the forest region does not vary greatly from that in the savanna, and important distinctions are easy to note. Upland rice can be cultivated wherever there is more than 1100 millimeters of annual rainfall and, in the forest zone, is commonly (though not always) intercropped with other produce such as maize, pumpkins, okra, tomatoes, millet, peanuts, and even cotton. The task of clear-ing the fields begins in April or May. The ground is cleared of bushes, weeds, and (if new) of trees, the debris being stacked into piles, allowed to dry, and then burned. In some places (among the Mende and Temne of Sierra Leone, for example), the burnt patches are worked with the hoe; in others, where it would be dangerous in terms of erosion (among the Kisi of Guinea-Co-nakry) the soil is not disturbed. When the rains begin, in May or June, the seeds are sown broadcast and are sometimes but not al-ways covered over with soil. This wasteful and inefficient practice is occasionally replaced by one in which the seed is planted in rows, but in some places where this change occurs, it may be a more recent rather than a traditional practice. The hard work of clearing the fields is carried out by the men; the women and chil-dren take care of the weeding. Fields are weeded only once in some areas, twice or more in others. The harvest commences in September and is the work of the whole family. As the crop ripens, the children are put into the fields to frighten away the rice birds (a pest and a practice also common in the Carolina region);

---

33. R. Portères, "Un problème d'Ethnobotanique: Relations entre le Riz flottant du Rio Nunez et l'origine medinigerienne des Baga de la Guinée Française," *Journal d'Agriculture Tropicale et de Botanique appliquée*, II (October–November, 1955), 538–42.

then men and women set out to gather the crop. Handfuls of rice are cut off near the top of the stalk, tied into bundles that in turn are stacked into piles, covered over to protect them from rice birds and other predators, and left to dry in the fields.

At the end of a period of years, ranging from two to five, the fields are allowed to lie fallow, and new ones are cleared. The fallow period is roughly equivalent to the period of use if rice alone is cultivated, extending from three to five years, but is much longer if the production of rice is coupled with that of other crops, particularly manioc, which exhaust the soil. The varieties of dry rice in this region—fast, medium, and slow—are numerous, more than thirty-seven being classified in one zone alone. The drawback of dry rice is that its yield is relatively low, averaging no more than between 500–800 kilograms per hectare (or about 450–700 pounds per acre), and its quality is generally inferior to that of rice grown by submergence.[34]

In the region of the Southern Rivers, rice was cultivated by irrigation—one of the few places where Africans engaged in significant alteration of the landscape for purposes of crop production. A slave-ship captain who visited the area of Guinea-Conakry at the end of the eighteenth century described one group and their method of cultivation.

> The Bagos are very expert in Cultivating rice and in quite a Different manner to any of the Nations on the Windward Coast. The country they inhabit is chiefly loam and swampy. The rice they first sew on their dunghills and rising spots about their towns; when 8 or 10 Inches high [they] transplant it into Lugars made for that purpose which are flat low swamps, at one side . . . they have a reservoir that they can let in what water they please, [on the] other side . . . is a drain out so they can let off what they please. The Instrument they use much resembles a Turf spade with which they turn the grass under in ridges just above the water which by being confined Stagnates and nourishes the root of the plant. Women & Girls transplant the rice and are so dextrous as to

---

34. See Jean Dresch, "La riziculture en Afrique occidentale," *Annales de géographie*, LVIII (1949), 304–306; Frederick R. Irvine, *A Textbook of West African Agriculture: Soils and Crops* (London, 1944), 94–95; Denise Paulme, *Les Gens du Riz: Kissi de Haute-Guinée Française* (Paris, 1954), 24–49.

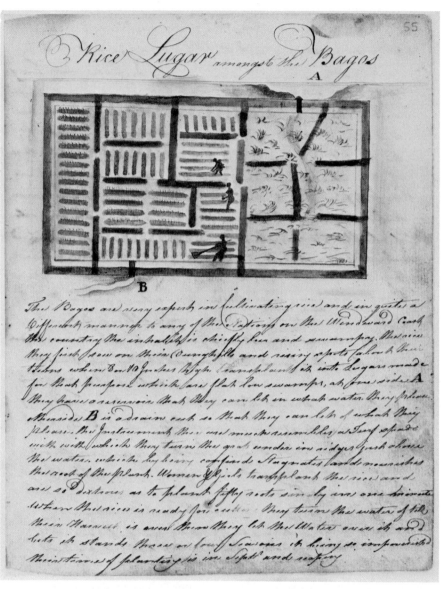

Illustration and description of Baga rice cultivation, in Captain Samuel Gamble's journal, *ca.* 1793.

plant fifty roots singly in one minute. When the rice is ready for cutting they turn the water off till their Harvest is over then they let the Water over it and lets it stands three or four Seasons it being so impoverished. Their time of planting is in Sept.[35]

The Bagas represented the southern limit of the most advanced practice of rice cultivation in traditional Africa, and many of their methods are analogous to those in South Carolina. Not until 1885 was a modification of their method of agriculture introduced into the Great and Little Scarcies and Port Logo regions of Sierra Leone.[36] Part of the captain's statement is not entirely clear. Philip Curtin notes that in the eighteenth century English captains usually considered the Windward Coast, from a Gold Coast point of reference, as stretching from Cape Mount (in Liberia) to Assini (on the Ivory Coast), while in the nineteenth century the term was sometimes used for the area on either side of Sierra Leone.[37] If the former usage is adopted, the statement is understandable, though the limits of what he considers the Windward Coast are much farther north than usual. If the latter usage is adopted, however, his meaning is less clear, or perhaps he is simply incorrect, for the method he describes, or variants of it, is common along the littoral from the region south of Cape Verde to the area north of Sierra Leone.[38] Moreover, this type of agriculture has been practiced in parts of this region from at least the fifteenth century. The Baga, who moved into the area from the Niger Valley in the sixteenth and seventeenth centuries, were relative latecomers and borrowed these methods from peoples farther north.[39]

Although it has sometimes been asserted that the form of irrigation current in the region was adopted under the influence of the Portuguese, Paul Pélissier argues convincingly for the African ori-

35. Journal kept by Samuel Gamble, 1793–1794, in *Sandown* MS, p. 55, National Maritime Museum.

36. Irvine, *Textbook*, 90.

37. Curtin, *Atlantic Slave Trade*, 128.

38. The voyage took place in 1793 and slaving was conducted largely in the region to the north of Sierra Leone. Journal kept by Samuel Gamble, 1793–1794, in *Sandown* MS, *passim*.

39. Portères, "Un problème d'Ethnobotanique," and "Les Appelations des Céréales en Afrique," *Journal d'Agriculture Tropicale et de Botanique Appliquée*, VI (April–May, 1959), 205.

gins of this cultivation. First, new crops introduced into Africa made headway only in those places where the techniques of agricultural populations were sufficiently advanced to receive them; second, from the sixteenth century, Portuguese and other voyagers reported utilization of dikes, levees, causeways, and transplanting in the area; third, the characteristic and unique agricultural implement used in the locale is admirably suited to the peculiar conditions in which it is found and cannot have been introduced from anywhere else. Finally, it does not appear that the Portuguese were initially prepared for the introduction of improved methods of rice cultivation even had they possessed them. They may have introduced Asian rice, but the agricultural techniques appear to be purely African.[40]

The extraordinary topography of this region dictated the development of unusual technology. Instead of the cliffs and sand dunes that characterize other portions of the coast, the area of the Southern Rivers is a lowland, marked by numerous estuaries where rivers flowing from the Fouta Djalon meet the sea. Heavy silt and other detritus carried by the waters form deltas along the coast, and islands and islets in zones where the coastline is uneven. The littoral is swept by strong currents of wind and sea, and the tides here reach a height three to six times as great at Conakry, Bissau, and other points as they do at Dakar to the north or Abidjan to the south. These conditions mean that the rivers are tidal for considerable distances from their mouths, and for meters inland the terrain is periodically covered with brackish water which gives rise to mangroves, whose network of aerial roots and pneumatophores clutch the soil and hold the alluvium deposited by the floods. The deltas, often partially submerged, are crisscrossed by interconnecting streams or river branches called *bolongs* (or other, similar terms depending on the locale), which help enclose swamps and distribute sediment. It is a region containing some of the richest soil in West Africa, admirably suited to rice culture but so difficult to work that, in the words of one scholar, one would think that it might be abandoned to "the fish, the crocodiles, the crabs, the

---

40. Paul Pélissier, *Les Paysans du Sénégal: Les Civilisations agraires du Cayor à la Casamance* (Saint-Yrieix, 1966), 710–16.

mosquitoes and the birds" were it not inhabited by some of the most industrious agriculturalists in Africa.[41]

There are minor differences in the way the land is claimed for cultivation, but the general outline is common. The usual area of culture is a mangrove swamp, which is cleared of underbrush and set aside by the construction of a dike at the edge of a river branch, or *marigot*. Designed to keep out salt water and stop predator fish, the levee is furnished with sluice gates of hollowed tree trunks or old canoes, which are closed at high or opened at low tide to provide for the washing of the saline soil by the fresh waters of rain and river. The field is subdivided by a series of canals and causeways that ensure the flow of water and aid in irrigation and can be drained when necessary. It is allowed to sit for a period of two or three years while the alluvium is gradually desalinated. Then, in those sections closest to the sea, or most susceptible to salination, cultivation takes place on ridges. These the men form using a long shovel-like instrument called a *kayondo* in the north among the Joola of the Casamance, a *kofi* or *kopi* among the Bagas in the south. The action of the *kayondo* serves to aerate the soil, provide for its continuing desalination, and bury noxious weeds. The earth is first turned in March and April and again after the first rains. Meanwhile, the women use a small hoe (the *kayondo* to them is forbidden) to prepare other fields on higher ground, near the village, where the rice is sown broadcast to begin its growth. Beginning in August, when it has attained a certain maturity, it is transplanted in the fields prepared by the men.

These fields are permanent and require neither crop rotation nor fallowing. After the harvest, the cattle are allowed to feed on the straw and fertilize the fields. The manure thus obtained is supplemented by cinders and other waste materials from the village, which the women spread over the soil. The harvest, between November and January, is largely the task of the men and is carried on in basically the same way as described for dry rice, except that while the women cut the stalks one at a time, the men gather

41. This follows Dresch, "La riziculture," 306–307; and Irvine, *Textbook*, 90. Also see A. Aubreville, "La Casamance," *L'Agronomie Tropicale*, III (January–February, 1948), 25–30.

handfuls. The yield is much better than with dry rice. Not only do many varieties of rice grow in the same region but there are many kinds of fields, varying with the condition of the land. Where the soil is not so saline, ridges might not be constructed, though all other aspects of cultivation remain the same. Again, the rice might or might not be transplanted. Where the *kayondo* is not used, the women assume a greater responsibility for the crop.

Rice fields in the Southern Rivers run the gamut from those utilizing irrigation to those, in typical Sudanese fashion, dependent entirely on the natural formation of swamps and ponds during the rainy season as well as those geared to the rainfall. Both *O. glaberrima* and *O. sativa* are grown here, and although the latter requires more care, it continues to expand at the expense of the former. There are also many hybrids.[42]

It is clear, then, that various African groups—Malinke, Soninke, Serer, Joola, Balante, Kisi, Papel, Baga, Mende, Temne, and others—were conversant with numerous varieties of rice, both African and Asian, and with various methods of rice cultivation, some of them quite advanced. It is also evident that knowledge of rice production was widespread in West Africa, centering along the Niger in the interior and along the littoral in the tropical rain forest. Even when West Africans made little attempt to alter the environment, their agricultural practices required a sophisticated knowledge of the terrain, soil types, and properties of different kinds of rice. In agricultural terms, therefore, the African was anything but an ignorant savage. But the questions remain, how much of this knowledge, and how many of these people, traversed the ocean.

III

There has been a great deal of speculation about the beginnings of rice cultivation in South Carolina, where the first rice came from, when it made its first appearance, and who was most responsible

---

42. The foregoing is based on Dresch, "La riziculture," 307–12; Pélissier, *Les Paysans du Sénégal*, 716–59, and J. A. Massibot and Louis Carles, "Mise en Valeur des 'tannes' Rizicultivable du Sine (Sénégal)," *L'Agronomie Tropicale*, I (September–October, 1946), 451–66.

for its successful culture.[43] The theory that it was introduced by chance has been discredited for some years, and it is clear that the crop was one among many others that the lords proprietors envisioned as a "vendible commodity" for the province at its inception. It is also clear that many Africans were experienced rice producers and conversely that English colonists in South Carolina had some difficulty in cultivating the crop successfully. Recent historians have been highly conscious of the fact that the period in which rice became an important export commodity coincided with that in which Africans were imported in significant and eventually overwhelming numbers. In view of the ignorance of Englishmen there, the African contribution to the development of rice cultivation in South Carolina undoubtedly could have been more important than commonly realized, particularly because many of the practices of early production paralleled those in Africa. If, however, English colonists were willing to take advantage of their servants' knowledge, it would have been necessary for them to possess an early awareness that Africans commanded the requisite information.

It is often forgotten that rice was successfully grown (though apparently not for export) by English colonists in Virginia.[44] As early as 1609 a promotional pamphlet listed rice among the staples proposed to be raised there. Noting the similarity between the climate of this region of the New World and that of the Mediterranean, the writer thought that rice and other crops would "there grow and increase, as well in *Italy* or any other part of the streights, whence we fetch them now."[45] A Virginia pamphleteer

43. See, most recently, Wood, *Black Majority*, 55–62, and L. C. Gray, *History of Agriculture in the Southern United States to 1860* (Washington, D.C., 1933), I, 277–93; A. S. Salley, Jr., *The Introduction of Rice Culture into South Carolina*, Bulletins of the Historical Commission of South Carolina, No. 6 (Columbia, S.C., 1919). For traditional accounts see Edward McGrady, *The History of South Carolina Under the Proprietary Government, 1670–1719* (New York, 1897), 348–49, and B. R. Carroll, *Historical Collections of South Carolina* (New York, 1836), I, 140–42.

44. Not to any great extent, anyway, though rice is mentioned along with wheat and maize as possible export staples to New England and the West Indies. *Calendar of State Papers, Colonial Series, 1696–97* (London, 1905), XV, 642.

45. Samvel Macham, "Nova Britannia: Offering Most Excellent fruits by Planting in Virginia," in Peter Force, *Tracts and Other Papers Relating Principally to the Origin, Settlement, and Progress of the Colonies in North America, from the Discovery of the Country to the Year 1776* (Washington, 1838), Vol. I, No. 6, p. 22.

in 1648 praised the "great Plains, fine and thick Grasse, Marshes
. . . [and] rich black mounded countries for Tobacco, Flaxe, Rice
choice Trees and Timber for Shipping." More important, letters
sent to England from the colony in the same year contained reports similar to the following:

> The Governor *Sir William* [Berkeley], caused half a bushel of Rice
> (which he had procured) to be sowen, and it prospered gallantly and
> he had fifteen bushels of it, excellent good Rice, so that all those fifteen
> bushels will be sowen again this year; and we doubt not in a short time
> to have Rice so plentiful as to afford it at 2d a pound if not cheaper, for
> we perceive the ground and Climate is very proper for it as our
> *Negroes* affirme, which in their Country is most of their food, and
> very healthful for our bodies.[46]

Unfortunately, there is no indication whence Berkeley had "pro-
cured" his half-bushel of rice, nor any description of local rice
cultivation; but at the end of the seventeenth century it was still a
serviceable crop, for a report informed the Board of Trade in 1697
that "Wheat, rice, Indian corn and other kinds of grain grow in
great plenty and are very useful for supply of the West Indies and
New England."[47]

The success of tobacco rendered the pursuit of rice as an important export staple unnecessary in the Chesapeake region, but the
fact that it was grown there is significant because it indicates that
the association of Englishmen with rice cultivation is somewhat
longer than is commonly noted and evinces an awareness that Africans were knowledgeable about the crop. The lords proprietors
surely knew of the Virginia experience; one of them had even been
involved in it. Indeed, it is possible that the first rice grown in
South Carolina had come from the Chesapeake rather than from
some foreign source. The crop in North Carolina described by
John Lawson at the beginning of the eighteenth century quite possibly could have been the same as, or derived from, that cultivated
by its northern neighbor, because most of its early settlers had
come from Virginia. It would not be unreasonable to assume, in

46. In Force, *Tracts*, II: Beauchamp Plantagenet, "A Description of the Province of New
Albion," No. 7, p. 8, and Plantagenet, "A Perfect Description of Virginia," No. 8, p. 14.
47. *Calendar of State Papers, Colonial Series, 1696–97* (London, 1905), XV, 642.

view of the existing interest, that the plant would continue its southern migration. But the evidence adduced by early historians of South Carolina is contradictory and makes what might seem a logical explanation more speculative. The rice grown in Virginia and North Carolina would appear to have been of an "upland," or dry, variety. Lawson's description seems to suggest this; and Alexander Hewatt's comment that before South Carolinians learned how to cultivate rice in the lowlands, they "long went on with this article, and exhausted their strength in raising it on higher lands," would tend circumstantially to sustain the theory of a southward diffusion.[48] Such a practice would have been commensurate with their prior experience. As Rowland Ernle has shown, Englishmen were notoriously slow in changing their agricultural methods, even when new procedures had been proven more effective.[49]

In a work published forty years earlier than that of Hewatt, Mark Catesby suggests that rice was first cultivated in the lowlands of South Carolina, and that it "requires to grow wholly in water." If true, this statement would mean that the grain was a different type than that cultivated in the Chesapeake, especially because, he says, a new grain introduced from Madagascar in 1696 could be raised by either wet or dry culture, indicating a definite contrast with the earlier grain.[50] Because rice is such an adaptable crop, it is difficult to distinguish varieties from casual descriptions of the way in which it is cultivated, and Catesby's story of its introduction is no more dependable than any other.[51] But letters written by John Stewart from South Carolina in 1690 indicate that

48. John Lawson, *History of North Carolina* (London, 1714), 77–78; Alexander Hewatt, *An Historical Account of the Rise and Progress of the Colonies of South Carolina and Georgia* (London, 1779), I, 159.

49. Rowland Ernle, *Pioneers and Progress of English Farming* (London, 1888), 29–47; and *English Farming, Past and Present* (Chicago, 1961), 110–12.

50. Mark Catesby, *The Natural History of Carolina, Florida and the Bahama Islands etc.* (London, 1771), I, xvii. This is a later edition of a work first published in 1731. M. Y. Nuttonson, *Rice Culture and Rice-Climate Relationships with Special Reference to the United States Rice Areas and their Latitudinal and Thermal Analogues in Other Countries* (Washington, D.C., 1965), 16.

51. The descriptions of Lawson and Catesby are similar in terms of what the grain looked like but quite different in how it was cultivated in the two regions, and they may not have been talking about the same type of rice. Lawson, *History of North Carolina*, 77, and Catesby, *Natural History*, xvii.

settlers there were already experimenting with cultivating rice in swamplands, though the tenor of his letters suggests variety in the ways the crop was grown. For example, he recommended sowing rice "as barley," that is, broadcast, a habitual way of sowing dry rice, but mentioned that others planted it in rows.[52] It is probable, as Gray and Wood both aver, that rice had various introductions into South Carolina from divergent sources, from among which the Chesapeake should not be excluded.[53]

It might seem strange that Englishmen in South Carolina should have had such a relatively difficult time in producing rice in view of the Virginia background. On the other hand, somewhat dissimilar circumstances or a different motivation—a desire for a different type of grain suitable for the European market and suited to Carolina conditions, for example—could explain the lag in production. Certainly Carolina rice had a distinctive reputation, is obviously a hybrid, and doubtless took time and effort to develop.[54] Lest this task appear to have been beyond those who were relatively ignorant about rice and lacking in contemporary agricultural technology, a climatologist has recently pointed out that most crops have been introduced into new areas not by scientists or other specialists but by practical men who tackled and solved agrarian conundrums before the problems were properly appreciated by authorities.[55] The need to find or develop such a plant could mean that the connection between African imports and successful rice culture came about by design rather than by chance.

52. John Stewart, "Letters from John Stewart to William Dunlop," *South Carolina Historical and Genealogical Magazine*, XXXII (January, 1931), 1–33, 81–114.

53. Gray, *History of Agriculture*, 279; Wood, *Black Majority*, 36.

54. Of the Asian variety of rice, which is most commonly in use, there are generally two types: *Oryza sativa indica* and *Oryza sativa japonica*. The former is traditionally grown in tropical areas and is a tall, weak-stemmed plant, light sensitive, whose yield is not particularly responsive to improved agricultural practices, especially to nitrogen fertilizer applications. The latter is shorter stemmed, has a higher yield, and is more responsive to nitrogen applications and other improved agricultural practices. It is traditionally associated with temperate zones, and its transfer to tropical regions has been frustrated by high temperatures and day length. There is a third type that is regarded as *indica* but resembles *japonica* and is grown in subtropical areas such as South Carolina. It is short-stemmed, erect, and has a high yield response to nitrogen applications. See M. Y. Nuttonson, *Rice Culture*, 8–20.

55. Juan Papadakis, *Climates of the World: Their Classification, Similitudes, Differences and Geographic Distribution* (Buenos Aires, 1970), 8.

That is, Englishmen, from the beginning, could have made a conscious effort to import slaves from those regions known to produce rice.

Unfortunately, this theory is easier to advance than to substantiate. Peter Wood has gone far in suggesting the circumstances that support a larger and perhaps determinant role by Africans in the development of rice cultivation in South Carolina, and it is difficult to push the argument further. Slave imports are not available for the crucial first years, which would permit us to see how soon particular regions were favored, though as early as 1700 ships from Carolina were reported in the Gambia River.[56] Moreover, as one scholar has written, similarities between preindustrial African and European patterns of culture make it sometimes difficult to gauge the precise extent of the respective contributions of each to any particular New World institution or creation.[57] Agriculture is no exception in this respect. The annual routine of neither group may have been altered drastically in South Carolina, though semi-tropical conditions in the region may have been more familiar to Africans than to Europeans.[58] Some agricultural practices appear also to have been closer to those used in Africa than in Europe, or at least in England. Frontier conditions characterized by a relative abundance of land, permitting longer fallow periods and necessitating replacement of the plow with the hoe as the prime agricultural implement, created a situation more nearly approaching that in West Africa than in Great Britain. The regular use of fire as a tool of clearing was also closer to African practice than to English.[59] These circumstances are not adduced to allege an African influence but only to suggest that Africans are much more likely

56. Donnan (ed.), *Documents*, IV, 225*n*. D'Avenant, *Political and Commercial Works*, V, 175–76.

57. William R. Bascom, "Acculturation Among the Gullah Negroes," *American Anthropologist*, New Series, XLIII (January–March, 1941), 43.

58. Peter Wood, for example, discusses epidemiological and other considerations that better suited Africans than Europeans to South Carolina's environment, in *Black Majority*, 63–91, 116–25.

59. Descriptions of English farming methods can be found in a number of works, notably in Ernle. He points out, for example, that paring and burning were not introduced into England until the middle of the seventeenth century, by Walloon emigrants. See his *Pioneers and Progress*, 36, or *English Farming*, 115. A largely statistical, multivolume work is James E. Thorold Rogers, *A History of Agriculture and Prices in England From the Year After the Oxford*

to have made a contribution if the environment was not entirely new to them. The fact that Englishmen, by contrast, very often worked under conditions and with crops that were unfamiliar to them—the fact that maize and rice frequently displaced the familiar wheat as a food staple—doubtless heightened English perceptions of those who used the environment more easily.[60]

Before this line of argument is pursued further, it is worth considering where else Englishmen might have learned about rice cultivation. They knew, of course, that the cereal was grown in Italy, and from that example a pamphleteer even suggested in 1650 that it might be produced in England. He remarked that rice "groweth in the Fenny places of *Milan*, and why may it not grow in our Fens?"[61] This statement is significant, among other reasons, because it signifies a recognition that swamplands or other inundated terrain was suitable for rice cultivation, but it also highlights a need for some knowledge of hydraulic control. The fens had only recently started to be drained when the pamphleteer wrote, and the English had to appropriate Dutch technology to do it. But fenmen had for years modified their environment and brought marshes under cultivation by using drains, dikes, and embankments.[62] The knowledge may not have been widespread, but it was available. It certainly ought to have been sufficient to enable Englishmen to cope with inland swamplands in Carolina, though perhaps not so advanced as to permit them to use the tide flow.

<hr />

Parliament (1259) to the Commencement of the Continental War (1793) (Oxford, 1866). For a very readable, succinct account of the open-field, three-course rotation system of farming, which typified English agriculture in the seventeenth and early eighteenth centuries, see C. S. Orwin, *A History of English Farming* (London, 1949), 1–24.

60. For an illustration see J. Norris, *Profitable Advice for Rich and Poor* (London, 1712), 23–27.

61. Samuel Hartlib, *Samuel Hartlib His Legacie: Or an Enlargement of the Discourse of Husbandry Used in Brabant and Flaunders; Wherein are Bequeathed to the Commonwealth of England More Outlandish and Domestick Experiments and Secrets in Reference to Universall Husbandry* (London, 1651), 82.

62. Joan Thirsk, "Fenland Farming in the Sixteenth Century," in Leicester, England, University College, Department of English Local History, *Occasional Papers No. 3* (1953), 24–25. Ernle remarks that large amounts of land lay waste in seventeenth-century England for lack of drainage. Although reclamation of marsh and fenlands was begun as early as the reign of Henry VIII, the major work of reclaiming the fens was undertaken from 1626 under the direction of the Dutch engineer Cornelius Vermuyden. See *English Farming*, 112–30, and *Pioneers and Progress*, 34–36. Also see Orwin, *History of English Farming*, 42–44.

A knowledge of drainage from England and of rice from Italy would have obviated the necessity to borrow from Africa, though knowledgeable workers would still have been desirable. But this theory is less satisfactory than the Wood thesis because it can be supported by no evidence at all. If Englishmen brought in a Dutchman to help drain their fens, they could have imported an Italian to teach them to cultivate rice. But there is nothing to indicate that they did so. The systems of cultivation in Italy and South Carolina were significantly different.[63] Even had they been similar nothing would be proven by this fact alone. Of course, a like objection could be advanced with regard to the African evidence, except that Africans were on the scene—a fact that makes the case for their influence more tenable. The technology of drainage may (or may not) have come from England, but it would still have had to be correctly applied to obtain a suitable crop. Nor could this information have been secured from native Americans. Amerindians did collect the seeds of a river grass called variously wild, or Indian, rice; Indian, water, or wild, oats; or sometimes marsh rye; but this is not a true rice, being classified as *zizania aquatica* rather than as any kind of *sativa*, and it was not cultivated. Moreover, English colonials (in South Carolina anyway) did not adopt the Indian method of husking the grain, though some modification of that process would presumably work as well on true rice; they adopted, rather, the mortar and pestle—in the African way.[64]

So one is brought back to the African connection, to the inter-

63. Rice was introduced into Italy in the fifteenth century, either from Spain, where it was brought in by the Arabs, or from Egypt. Its culture depends there on an extensive and intensive canal system, and much of the crop is grown on land suitable for other cereals, with which it is often rotated. Relatively little of the crop is grown in swamplands. In South Carolina, by contrast, rice was grown on land largely unsuitable for anything else. These distinctions do not entirely obviate the possibility of borrowing, but it is interesting to note that the conditions which led to the development of an intricate canal system in Italy caused abandonment of the first method of cultivation in South Carolina. See Duncan Clinch Heyward, *Seed from Madagascar* (Chapel Hill, 1937), 14; Henry L. de Vilmorin *et al.*, *Les Plantes de Grande Culture: Céréales, Plantes Fourragères, Industrielles et Economiques* (Paris, 1892), 29–30; Pierre Poirier, "Le Riz Italien," *Journal des Economistes, Revue Mensuelle de la Science Economique et de la Statistique*, LVI (October–December, 1917), 79–85; René Musset, "Le Riz dans le Monde," *Revue de botanique appliquée*, XXII (1942), 162–67, 275–77.

64. See Charles C. Willoughby, "The Virginia Indians in the Seventeenth Century," *American Anthropologist*, New Series, IX (January–March, 1907), 57–87, and Gardner P. Stickney, "Indian Use of Wild Rice," *American Anthropologist*, IX (April, 1896), 115–22,

action between Africans and Englishmen. It was, perhaps, a certain racialistic blindness (characteristic of a later, though not the colonial, period), together with an honest ignorance of African cultures, that prevented an earlier concern with the question of what, besides labor, Africans might have contributed to rice production. This kind of mental block is evidenced by an early twentieth-century rice planter who, having studied pictures of Chinese methods of cultivation, concluded from no other evidence that the Carolina system was an adaptation of the Chinese.[65] If, however, he had looked at the Baga system, he might have come to a similar conclusion in regard to their manner of cultivation, and with more justice. They operated under conditions more closely approximating the Carolina situation than did the Chinese. They knew how to clear swamps and prepare them for culture; they made drains, using hollowed-out tree trunks in a way similar to that adopted by early Carolinians;[66] they used tools analogous to those used in South Carolina.[67]

On the other hand, this reference to China recalls the Madagascar tradition. Rice came into the "Grande Ile" from southern Asia

---

which describes the Indian manner of husking. Albert E. Jenks, *The Wild Rice Gatherers of the Upper Lakes: A Study in American Primitive Economy* (Washington, D.C., 1905), 1066–70, reports that other methods were also used. Also see Albert B. Reagan, "Wild or Indian Rice," *Indiana Academy of Science Proceedings*, VIII (1919), 241–42.

65. Heyward, *Seed from Madagascar*, 8–10.

66. David Doar, *Rice and Rice Planting in the South Carolina Low Country* (Charleston, S.C., 1936), 12, 29. This is a case in which one is struck by a similarity with Africa, though the practice may not have come from there. Another is in the use of fertilizers. If South Carolinians had used fertilizers more commonly than was apparently the case, they might have adopted—or arrived independently at—the Africans' habit of spreading cinders over the fields to increase fertility.

Doar goes on to relate a practice that was almost certainly an African carry-over. Speaking of rats which inhabited the rice fields, he says, "It will be news to some people to know that these Middle Island rice-negroes ate these rats and thought them a delicacy. The last negro old man that would eat one came from there and died two years ago." Denise Paulme, *Gens du riz*, 27, describes a comparable situation in the rice fields of Guinea-Conakry. G. T. Surface, "Rice in the United States," *American Geographical Society Bulletin*, XLIII (July, 1911), 509, comments on the chemical requirements of the rice plant, which a practice such as the use of cinders, as well as the African custom of using straw as a fertilizer, might have answered.

67. Compare, for example, Heyward's description of inland rice cultivation in *Seed from Madagascar*, 12–14, to that of the Baga. For descriptions of rice cultivation in South Carolina other than those already cited see R. Russell, "Culture of Carolina Rice," in a binder of pamphlets entitled *Rural Economy*, Library of Congress.

via Indonesia, and though there may be local variations in cultivation, the general outlines of traditional modes appear to have been largely the same throughout the region.[68] Similarities between rice cultivation on the island and in South Carolina are indeed impressive, and the theory that rice culture came into Carolina from there would seem to be entirely plausible. The planter referred to above discussed the portrayal he had seen of the Chinese system, as follows:

> The first of these Chinese pictures shows the plowing and harrowing of the soil of the seed-beds, both processes being done under water, the Chinaman and his black 'water buffalo' nearly up to their knees, and the latter looking as if he did not trust his footing and was anxious to turn back. Then follows the sowing of the seed broadcast on the water, the transplanting of the growing crop, the harvesting, until finally the rice is carried to the barnyard, where it is threshed and pounded. Anyone at all familiar with the methods used by the early planters in South Carolina cannot fail to be struck by their similarity to the methods shown in the old Chinese pictures, and especially is this true of the implements used.[69]

In fact, the early Carolina means of clearing the fields did not utilize the plow, and in the use of the hoe and other circumstances of cultivation was much closer to the Madagascar (or West African) system than to the Chinese. The rest of what he describes, with the exception of the manner of threshing, is equally applicable to Madagascar. Moreover, the early modes of production in South Carolina had already developed before any presumed interaction with China occurred. On the contrary, there was ample opportunity for contact between Madagascar and South Carolina.

68. For rice cultivation in Madagascar and the relationship between Madagascar, Indonesia, and other parts of Asia, see Hubert Deschamps, *Histoire de Madagascar* (Paris, 1960), 13–59; Marius-Ary Leblond, *La Grande Ile de Madagascar* (Paris, 1946), 242–51; J. Cardot, *Le Riz dans le Monde et en Indochine* (Paris, 1928); M. Tran-Van-Hun, *La Riziculture en Cochinchine* (Paris, 1927); Roland Portères, "Les Appellations des Céréales en Afrique," 189–233; Cecil Yampolsky, "Rice: The Plant and Its Cultivation," *Wallerstein Laboratories Communications*, VI (1943), 83–94; René Musset, "Le riz dans le monde," *Revue de botanique appliquée*, XXIV (1944), 71–83, 221–82; XXII (1942), 151–80, 263–306.

69. Heyward, *Seed from Madagascar*, 9–10. The only contact with China that he mentions would have occurred sometime after 1738, probably around 1758, when South Carolinians had been raising rice for years.

Not only is the traditional story, that rice came from Madagascar, relevant, but there were two periods in the late seventeenth and early eighteenth centuries (from the 1670s to 1698 and between 1716 and 1721) when a slave trade existed between the island and British America.[70] Although there is no evidence of direct importation into South Carolina during these periods, Malagasy slaves could have been transshipped from the West Indies. Certainly there were Madagascar slaves in South Carolina, and in Virginia too.[71] One historian suggests that Madagascar slaves and rice may have been brought into Charleston by privateers between 1693 and 1696.[72]

It would not be especially useful to present a detailed comparison of cultivation in South Carolina and Madagascar, because little could be indicated beyond what has been suggested already.[73] Yet it might be worthwhile to make some general observations relating South Carolina to both of these African regions of production. First, in terms of the type of rice grown in South Carolina, it is definitely an Asian variety (the indigenous African variety grows only in West Africa), and a French scholar comments that the rices grown in Madagascar and South Carolina appear to be related.[74] The irrigation methods utilized in Madagascar, generally more sophisticated than those in West Africa, reinforce the theory of its association with South Carolina, but this assertion is vitiated by the fact that there were peoples along the West African littoral whose systems were just as well-developed, despite more taxing conditions. Third, the procedure for threshing rice adopted in

---

70. Virginia Bever Platt, "The East India Company and the Madagascar Slave Trade," *William and Mary Quarterly*, Third Series, XXVI (1969), 548–77. Malagasy slaves were carried to New York, Massachusetts, and the West Indies. In an earlier period, the English tried to establish a settlement on Madagascar, but attempts proved abortive and there is no indication that anyone involved in the endeavor learned anything about rice cultivation or came to the New World. See W. Foster, "An English Settlement in Madagascar in 1645–46," *English Historical Review*, XXVII (1912), 239–50.

71. Curtin, *Atlantic Slave Trade*, 157.

72. Wood, *Black Majority*, 57n.

73. The best descriptions of rice cultivation are provided in James Sibree, *Madagascar Before the Conquest: The Island, the Country, and the People* (London, 1896), 52–81; J. Delpon, *L'Agriculture à Madagascar: Les Principales Productions* (Paris, 1930), 6–14; Samuel Copland, *A History of Madagascar*, (London, 1839), I, 294–303.

74. J. Delpon, *L'Agriculture*, 6.

South Carolina, using flails, is not practiced in Madagascar at all but is characteristic of West Africa.[75] Hence, while it is entirely possible that rice came into South Carolina from Madagascar, among myriad other places, and that rice cultivation in South Carolina was an adaptation of the Malagasy system, it is probable that West Africans had something to do with its evolution, and possibly a great deal.

Again, an attention to the slave trade is instructive. When Richard Oswald sent wives from Bence Island in Sierra Leone to the slaves on his plantation in East Florida during 1767, he remarked, "Besides these I have directed the Agents in Africa to send a few, full grown Men (not exceeding 10 in Number) in case they can light of such as have been used to the Trades of that Country, believing they will soon become usefull & handy in a New Plantation." Although the evidence is not conclusive, he could well have been following a precedent set decades earlier in South Carolina. And when Henry Laurens dispatched a newly imported slave to the governor of East Florida in 1765, he noted that the man was reputed to be a blacksmith, and he continued ethnocentrically, "He is a stout Young fellow & if he has wrought any time in his [own] country he will soon be improved in his knowledge by practice under a White Man."[76] But in an earlier period, when Englishmen could not afford such arrogance, they might have been willing pupils.

IV

If it can be assumed that part of the reason that South Carolinians preferred slaves from the Gambia region was because of their familiarity with rice cultivation, what is responsible for more Angolas being imported? Despite intimations to the contrary, rice culture does not appear to have been significant in that region.[77]

75. William Ellis, *History of Madagascar* (London, 1839), 300, describes the method of threshing, a variant of which was used in South Carolina to obtain seed rice.

76. Richard Oswald to Grant, May 20, 1767, and Laurens to Grant, July 22, 1765, in Grant of Ballindalloch MSS, 0771/295 and 0771/359, respectively.

77. It is difficult to find a great deal of information about the history of rice in the Congo-Angola region. Although the crop is an important staple in parts of the region in the

This phenomenon could be partially explained in terms of volume—by the relative ease in securing larger numbers of slaves in the latter than in the former region.[78] Cargoes of Angola slaves were usually larger than those from Gambia, though ships sent to the more southerly region were not unusually large. Of twenty-five vessels recorded in the naval office lists as having come into Carolina from Angola in the span between 1717 and 1767, the average size was 111 tons, while twelve from Gambia averaged 81 tons, with the number of slaves averaging 255 and 134 respectively (see Table 1). Yet if these (and other) Angola ships are compared in size with those dispatched to other regions, it can be seen that the largest ships were sent to the heart of the trade region in the Gulf of Guinea. Of seventy-two ships sent out from Liverpool to engage in the slave trade in 1787 the average tonnage was 179. The typical vessel increased in size in virtual mathematical progression outward from a central point located at Bonny in the Niger Delta, where the average ship weighed 363 tons (see Table 2). By contrast, the common vessel ordered to Gambia was 72 tons and to Angola was 123. Hence the general area where slaving was greatest received larger ships than either of the two peripheral regions with which South Carolina was so closely identified. Nor does the suggestion of one scholar that larger ships went to the Congo-Angola region because of a longer sailing time appear to be valid.[79] A slave trader reported that the passage was longer from the Gulfs of Benin or Biafra than from anywhere else on the

---

modern period, rice cultivation seems to have been introduced relatively late—with the advent of the Europeans—and, in some areas, long after colonization. See Marvin Miracle, *Agriculture in the Congo Basin* (Madison, 1967), 257–58; Gabriel Lefebvre, *L'Angola, Son Histoire Son Économie* (Liège, 1947), 151. D. S. Whittlesley, "Geographic Provinces of Angola: An Outline Based on Recent Sources," *Geographical Review*, XIV (January, 1924), 113–26, does not mention rice at all, though he talks about the crops that characterized each geographical province.

Lydia Parrish, in *Slave Songs of the Georgia Sea Islands* (New York, 1942), 227, states that "one explorer mentioned that rice was so plentiful in Kongo and Angola that it hardly bears any price," though she gives no authority for her statement. It is possible, however, that this was a reference to wild rather than to cultivated rice.

78. African traders left no doubt of this. Joseph Debat and Council to the Company of Merchants, James Fort, August 20, 1761, in Treasury Papers, 70/30, f. 420. Tyndall and Ahseton to Isaac Hobhouse, July 18, 1721, in Jefferies Collection, XIII, f. 106.

79. Peter Wood, "'More Like a Negro Country: Demographic Patterns in Colonial South Carolina, 1700–1740," in Engerman and Genovese, *Race and Slavery*, 151.

Table 1   Ships and Slaves in South Carolina from African Regions, 1717–1767

Region	Ships	(%)	Slaves	(%)	Tonnage	(Average)	Ratio Slaves to Tonnage
Africa*	88	(58)	17,819	(61)	8,564	(97.3)	2.02
Angola	25	(16)	6,373	(22)	2,780	(111.2)	2.34
Calabar	3	(2)	434	(1)	305	(101.6)	1.42
Gambia	12	(8)	1,606	(5)	970	(80.8)	1.65
Guinea	20	(13)	2,436	(8)	1,435	(71.75)	1.69
Senegal	2		90		175	(87.5)	.514
Total:	150		28,758		15,229	(94.8)	2.02

*One vessel with tonnage missing was omitted.
SOURCE: Naval Office Lists, in Colonial Office Papers, 5/508, 509, 510, 511, Public Record Office, London.

Table 2   DESTINATION OF SLAVE SHIPS
               SENT FROM LIVERPOOL, 1787

Site*	(Ships)	Tons	(Average)	Slaves†	Slaves per ton
Gambia	(3)	215	(71.66)	390	1.81
Windward Coast	(25)	3,012	(120.48)	5,950	1.97
Anamaboo	(10)	1,782	(178.20)	3,970	2.22
Lagos	(2)	560	(280.00)	1,130	2.01
Benin	(1)	190	(190.00)	400	2.10
New Calabar	(6)	1,184	(197.33)	2,260	1.90
Bonny	(10)	3,631	(363.10)	7,050	1.94
Old Calabar	(7)	1,323	(189.00)	2,590	1.95
Cameroons	(4)	506	(126.50)	900	1.77
Angola	(4)	490	(122.50)	960	1.95
Total	(72)	12,893	(179.06)	25,600	1.98

*The sites are arranged in order of geographical location on the coast from north to south.
†These were the numbers of slaves the vessels were ordered to collect, not numbers actually brought in.
SOURCE: Liverpool Papers, v. CCXXVII, Add. MSS 38416, ff. 1, 2, British Museum.

coast and stated that "the Passage from Angola is quick."[80] It would seem, then, that the volume of trade was the prime determinant of ship size.

The fewer slaves collected in the Gambia region is reflected in the ratio carried per ton. The vessels from Angola, during the period of record, transported an average cargo of 2.02 bondsmen per ton while those from Gambia managed only 1.65. The smallest vessel sent to Gambia was twenty-five tons while the smallest sent to Angola was eighty tons, the mean size of Gambia ships. These distinctions help explain why Herbert Klein in his study of the Virginia slave trade should have found a lower average of slaves per vessel carried to South Carolina than to Virginia, a variance doubtless due to their divergent slave sources.[81]

80. Testimony of Archibald Dalzell, *Report to the House of Lords, 1789*, in Bristol Archives Office.
81. Klein, "Slaves and Shipping," 392–94.

If the theory associating South Carolina with rice-growing regions has any validity, though, one would have to include not just Gambia but the rest of the Windward Coast, including Sierra Leone. By that measure, 43 percent of the Africans brought into South Carolina during the eighteenth century came from regions where rice was an important crop—a larger percentage than from any other region. But this still leaves the 40 percent from the Congo-Angola region to be explained.[82] Indeed, in the five years between 1735 and 1740, this southernmost part of Africa accounted for 70 percent of South Carolina's involuntary labor.[83] If, as suggested earlier, there was a prevailing consensus about the value of particular ethnic groups with these southern Africans at the lower end of the scale, West India colonies, as the more highly prized, would get the better product with the continent getting what was left over. Curtin's figures show that a larger number of Angola slaves entered British America during the 1730s than in any period up to that time, so it would not seem strange that a great percentage should have come to South Carolina. A smaller number but larger percentage of Angola slaves had been carried by the English in the decade of the 1720s, but records of Carolina imports in that decade are incomplete, and for most of the 1740s the slave trade to South Carolina was prohibited. Curtin's estimates indicate that South Carolina received a larger percentage of Gambia and Windward Coast slaves than was characteristic of the English slave trade as a whole, and this can be said to have been a matter of preference. The high percentage of Angolas can be assigned to a combination of acceptability and availability.

It is clear, then, that South Carolinians did place a positive emphasis on slaves from rice-growing regions. It has also been established that before Carolina was settled, Englishmen were aware that Africans possessed the technical knowledge to produce this crop and that from the earliest period of successful rice production

---

82. These and other figures from Curtin, *Atlantic Slave Trade*, 150, 157. Some of Curtin's original findings have been modified by later studies. See Roger Anstey, "The Volume and Profitability of the British Slave Trade, 1761–1807," pp. 3–31, and Philip Curtin, "Measuring the Atlantic Slave Trade," in Engerman and Genovese, *Race and Slavery*, 107–28.

83. Wood, "More Like a Negro Country," 150, and *Black Majority*, 340.

in South Carolina a relationship developed between this region and rice-growing regions in Africa. Finally, it has been shown that while Englishmen in Carolina had no prior experience with rice cultivation and had some difficulty inducing rice to grow, they evinced a willingness to avail themselves of the African skills of their bondsmen. The evidence is circumstantial but leads to the suggestion that the early connection between South Carolina and Gambia was a purposeful one, related to the production of rice. In this regard, Englishmen had everything to learn and Africans much to teach. Common sense would have dictated a continued desire for laborers familiar with the crop to be produced. In the early years, however, Carolinians may well have gone to Gambia as students and brought Africans back as teachers, making the African influence on the development of rice cultivation in Carolina a decisive one.

Chapter **5**

Perceptions and Social Relations

I

The cosmopolitan nature of colonial South Carolina is painted in advertisements for slave runaways. "Lately run away from my plantation at Ashepoo," James Parsons wrote in the *South Carolina Gazette* in 1761, "two tall likely young new Bambara negro fellows, name *Abram* and *Lymat*. . . . Also run away . . . about two years ago, a short chubby hairy *Angola* fellow named *March*, and about two months since a very black slip shod fellow, this country born, called *Harry*. . . . Likewise went away about this time twelve month . . . a new negro lad of the Pappa country named *Arrow*."[1] A similar diversity is reflected in a roll call of those who had been recaptured and confined to the workhouse in September, 1774: a new Negro fellow of the Guinea country, named Anthony; a new Negro man of the Limba country, named Primus; a new Negro man of the Timmene country, named Tallar; a new Negro boy of the Guinea country, named Bob.[2] The exotic character of this scene is portrayed by descriptions of some of these folk: a Gambia fellow, who called himself Woolaw, with "several long cuts about his Face, one on each side of his Nose and some on his Forehead in the Manner of their Country";[3] a man of "yellow complexion" with "two black stripes down each side of his face, his ears bored, his upper teeth filed";[4] a Kisi woman with "her country marks from neck down to her waist, pitted with the small-pox";[5] Tobey who "hath no cloths but an old piece of quilt

1. South Carolina *Gazette* (hereinafter cited as *SCG*), October 24, 1761.
2. South Carolina *Gazette and Country Journal* (hereinafter cited as *SCGCJ*), September 20, 1774.
3. *SCG*, February 5, 1737.
4. *SCGCJ*, May 2, 1769.
5. *Ibid.*, July 13, 1773.

115

round his middle, his hair . . . twisted up like twine,"[6] and several who ran away naked. The force of this scene is increased when one considers that the majority of the population was black. The white population was early outnumbered. Of 17,048 people in South Carolina in 1720, 12,000 were black and 5,048 were white; in 1730, a population of 30,000 was two-thirds black, and between 1735 and 1740, 12,589 more blacks were imported. Only 1,562 Africans were brought in between 1741 and 1750, but at the beginning of that decade only 15,000 of 45,000 people were white. Between 1751 and 1760, 18,889 Africans were imported; from 1761 to 1770, 18,687 slaves were imported and in the five years between 1771 and 1775, 19,215 Africans survived the passage to Charleston.[7] In 1720, blacks outnumbered whites two to one in the colony, and the ratio probably climbed steadily through the 1750s. Only after the massive immigration of whites into the backcountry beginning in the late 1750s did this gap begin to narrow. By 1770 whites constituted almost half of the population. Prior to 1760, however, as a Swiss immigrant remarked in 1737, Carolina indeed looked "more like a negro country than a country settled by white people."[8]

Nowhere else in British North America was this setting replicated on a comparable scale, and the massive presence of blacks could not help but affect the thoughts and perceptions of white South Carolinians. Indeed, in building or maintaining plantations requiring the acquisition of slaves from overseas, their need to distinguish various African ethnic groups may have been only slightly less than that of agents in Africa, and one has to doubt Donnan's theories about the declining importance of ethnic considerations in planter calculations.[9] Slaves who absconded continued to be identified in terms of their origin as well as by reference to skills, appearance, habits, or raiment.

6. *SCG*, October 27, 1759.
7. The colonial population figures are obtained from United States Bureau of the Census, *Historical Statistics of the United States: Colonial Times to 1957* (Washington, D.C., 1960), 756; importation figures are from W. Robert Higgins, "The Geographical Origins of Negro Slaves in Colonial South Carolina," *South Atlantic Quarterly*, LXX (Winter, 1971), 40–45.
8. Quoted in Wood, *Black Majority*, 132.
9. See p. 27, herein.

II

Runaway notices in South Carolina newspapers between 1732 and 1775 strongly reflect a continuing awareness of the ethnic origins of the slaves (see Table 3).[10] Not only is the range of ethnic groups referred to great but the precision in their identification is remarkable. Moreover, South Carolinians' knowledge of African ethnology apparently grew as the century advanced, for the number of tribal labels appearing in the newspapers increased dramatically. Whether this increasing specificity was the result of a growing number of immigrants from an ever larger area of Africa, a more sophisticated and detailed acquaintance with ethnic differences, or, as is more likely, some combination of the two, however, is unclear. What is unquestionable is the increased awareness of ethnic differences. Distinctions based on cultural peculiarities were convenient handles of description, hence the emphasis upon various tribal markings, or "country marks." They were the most common trait recorded, aside from skin color and other differentia such as types of clothes (Table 4). Sometimes planters attempted to represent these cultural signatures schematically, as was done in the case of Pawly, a "new negro" who spoke no English and was "marked down his temples and cheeks thus)))"; other markings were more difficult to depict with typescript.[11] Of course, as in this case, not all markings were directly associated with a particular region, but they were clearly associated in the minds of South Carolina whites—advertisers and readers—with ethnic designations. With so many ethnic groups confronting them, whites seized upon whatever features might help them make crucial distinctions.

Occasionally, they supplied their own means of identification through branding. Brands were second only to country marks as

10. Because my research was carried out at various locations at different times, I used the South Carolina *Gazette* of February, 1732, to December, 1768, and September to December, 1775, and the South Carolina *Gazette and Country Journal* of January, 1769, to July, 1775. A spot check indicated an identicalness in the ads run.

11. *SCG*, November 18, 1756.

Table 3   Ethnic and Geographical Origins of Runaway Slaves in South Carolina, 1732–1775

Region	30s No.	(%)	40s No.	(%)	50s No.	(%)	60s No.	(%)	70s No.	(%)	Total No.	(%)
Windward Coast and Hinterland												
Gambia	13	(14.1)	5	(5.2)	26	(14.1)	14	(3.3)	2	(.38)	60	(4.5)
Mandingo (Malinke)			1	(1.0)	9	(5.1)	44	(10.4)	29	(5.4)	83	(6.3)
Jalonka (Joola?—Senegambia)							6	(1.4)			6	(.46)
Bambara (Mali)	1	(1.0)			2	(1.1)	16	(3.7)	5	(.90)	24	(1.8)
Fullah/Fuiler (Fulbe—Senegambia)									10	(1.9)	10	(.76)
Araba									1	(.19)	1	(.07)
Sierra Leone									1	(.19)	1	(.07)
Limbo (Limba—Sierra Leone)							1	(.23)	3	(.57)	4	(.22)
Temna/Timmene (Temne—Sierra Leone)									5	(.90)	5	(.38)
Windward Coast					4	(2.2)					4	(.30)
Boler (Bola—Guinea-Bissau)									2	(.38)	2	(.15)
Kishee (Kisi—Guinea-Conakry)							7	(1.6)	65	(12.1)	72	(5.4)

Grain Coast					3 (.57)	3 (.22)
Total	14 (15.2)	6 (6.2)	41 (23.1)	90 (21.2)	126 (23.5)	277 (20.9)
Leeward Coast and Hinterland						
Gold Coast	1 (1.0)		3 (1.6)	2 (.50)	5 (.90)	11 (.8)
Coromantee (Akan—Gold Coast)		1 (1.0)	1 (.56)	11 (2.6)	14 (2.6)	27 (2.0)
Cromttey (Coromantee?)					2 (.38)	2 (.15)
Fantee (Akan—Gold Coast)				2 (.47)		2 (.15)
Yaney (Fantee?)					1 (.19)	1 (.07)
PawPaw/Papa (Popo—Dahomey-Togo)	1 (1.0)	1 (1.0)		7 (1.6)	6 (1.1)	14 (1.1)
Whydah (Dahomey)					2 (.38)	2 (.15)
Nego (Nago—Oyo-Yoruba)					1 (.19)	1 (.07)
Carbady (Gbari—Bight of Benin)					3 (.57)	3 (.22)
Simbey (Somba—Bight of Benin)					1 (.19)	1 (.07)
Total	2 (2.1)	1 (1.0)	4 (2.2)	22 (5.2)	35 (6.5)	64 (4.8)

Table 3—Continued

Region	30s No.	(%)	40s No.	(%)	50s No.	(%)	60s No.	(%)	70s No.	(%)	Total No.	(%)
Niger Delta												
Ibo	8	(8.6)	9	(9.3)	19	(10.7)	15	(3.5)	20	(3.7)	71	(5.4)
Calabar	1	(1.0)	1	(1.0)	3	(1.6)	4	(.94)	9	(1.7)	18	(1.4)
Total	9	(9.7)	10	(10.4)	22	(12.4)	19	(4.5)	29	(5.4)	89	(6.7)
Congo-Angola												
Congo							5	(1.1)	28	(5.2)	33	(2.5)
Angola	36	(39.1)	30	(31.2)	25	(14.1)	75	(17.6)	68	(12.7)	234	(17.6)
Malimbo (Malimbe)							2	(.47)	1	(.19)	3	(.22)
Wollonga									1	(.19)	1	(.07)
Bambo (Bambona?—Congo)									4	(.75)	4	(.30)
Patango (Badongo?—Congo)									1	(.19)	1	(.07)
Total	36	(39.1)	30	(31.2)	25	(14.1)	82	(19.3)	103	(19.1)	276	(20.8)
Guinea			2	(2.0)	7	(4.0)	58	(13.6)	121	(21.4)	188	(14.2)
Unidentified												
Cheraz	1	(1.0)							1	(.19)	1	(.07)
Bossue (Basa?)											1	(.07)
Anonda									1	(.38)	1	(.15)

	A	B	C	D	E	Total
Surago				5 (1.1)		5 (.37)
Lorca					2 (.38)	2 (.15)
Malagoscow (Madagascar?)	1 (1.0)					1 (.07)
Serrecea					1 (.19)	1 (.07)
Beesaw (Bissau?)					1 (.19)	1 (.07)
Total	2 (2.1)			5 (1.1)	6 (1.3)	13 (1.0)
West Indies and elsewhere						
Spanish	3 (3.3)	2 (2.1)	1 (.23)	1 (.19)		7 (.53)
Bermuda		3 (3.1)	3 (1.7)	6 (1.4)		12 (.90)
Anguilla		1 (1.0)				1 (.07)
Barbados	2 (2.1)	1 (1.0)	2 (1.1)	2 (.47)		6 (.45)
West Indies	2 (2.1)	1 (1.0)	5 (2.8)	4 (.94)	1 (.19)	13 (.98)
Jamaica			1 (.56)	12 (2.8)	5 (.94)	19 (1.4)
Saint Croix			1 (.56)			1 (.07)
Antigua					2 (.38)	2 (.15)
French		1 (1.0)	1 (.56)			2 (.15)
Cuba			1 (.23)		1 (.19)	2 (.15)
Montserrat			1 (.56)			1 (.07)
Saint Kitts					1 (.18)	1 (.07)
Portuguese			1 (.56)			1 (.07)
Total	7 (7.6)	9 (9.3)	15 (8.4)	26 (6.1)	11 (2.2)	68 (5.1)

Table 3—*Continued*

Region / Decade:	30s No.	(%)	40s No.	(%)	50s No.	(%)	60s No.	(%)	70s No.	(%)	Total No.	(%)
North America												
Cape Fear									1	(.19)	1	(.07)
Virginia					1	(.56)					1	(.07)
New York/Staten Island									2	(.38)	2	(.15)
North Carolina									1	(.19)	1	(.07)
Country born (South Carolina)	22	(23.9)	38	(39.5)	62	(35.0)	123	(28.9)	102	(19.0)	347	(26.1)
Total	22	(23.9)	38	(39.5)	63	(35.6)	123	(28.9)	106	(19.7)	352	(26.5)
Grand Total	92		96		177		425		537		1327	
Row Percentage	(6.9)		(7.2)		(13.3)		(32.0)		(40.5)			

Table 4   DESCRIPTION OF SLAVE RUNAWAYS IN
                 COLONIAL SOUTH CAROLINA

Description	Number	Total Percentage	Adjusted Percentage
Country marks	463	12.0	44.0
Teeth filed	34	.9	3.0
Branded	138	3.6	13.0
Pock marks	119	3.1	11.0
Other	310	8.0	29.0
(Sub-total)	(1064)		(100.0)
Unrecorded	2806	72.5	
Total	3870	100.0	

features of distinction and were fairly common.[12] John Mullryne, for example, advertised that he had taken up "two lusty Negro Men . . . branded on the breast IC." "Two Negro Fellows, named *Cuffee*, marked HB, and *Abraham*" were lodged in jail in August, 1735, and in the same month in 1738 the *Gazette* reported that a "new Negro Man Slave . . . branded behind the left Shoulder" with two circles, one above the other, had run away from the ship *Princess Carolina*. Some of these markings could have been applied before the slave arrived in South Carolina, particularly, for example, the double circle, which appears to have been a common marking on the African coast. The teenaged Hector, "branded with a Blotch on each Breast, and upon the left Buttock IR," could have been marked in Africa, as could "a tall *Angola* Negro Fellow, mark'd with a Cross on the left Shoulder." In most cases, however, the brands suggest a local application because of the association between the mark and the name of the advertiser. Thus, Thomas Wright notified the *Gazette* that "Trampous . . . mark'd

12. This measure, by which brands come first and country marks second, excludes the category *other*, which included such individual characteristics as missing limbs and so forth. (The extent of branding was greater than the figures indicate because the computer program did not provide for the listing of more than one distinguishing feature, and such ethnic characteristics as country marks and filed teeth seemed to be more important to this study.)

either upon the shoulder or Breask [*sic*] with a W" had absconded. James Bulloch advertised for three slaves "branded upon their right Breasts just above the nipple B." Alexander Frissel desired the return of Cesar, "branded on the left Thigh A.F.," and Alexander Godin was missing three men "branded BG. on the right or left Breast."[13] Branding seemed to decrease in frequency as the century advanced, though it did not disappear. James Williams and Primus, advertised in the workhouse during January and April, 1769, respectively, were both branded but had been born in Jamaica and may have been marked there. William Oswald, who advertised in September, 1769, for Abraham, Stephen, and Neptune, "branded on the back of their jackets WO, with blue negro cloth,"[14] may have represented a change in feeling regarding branding in the province, some evidence to the contrary, especially in 1772 and 1773, notwithstanding.[15]

But Tables 3 and 4 reveal far more than an awareness of ethnic differences or the prevalence of branding. Table 3, in particular, shows as well the prominence of regions and groups associated with rice cultivation in Africa; one-fifth of all the runaway slaves were identified with the Windward Coast area and another fifth with Congo-Angola. From these regions came the largest number of slave imports and runaways. This point is more clearly made in Table 5, in which slaves born in America, who constituted one-fourth of the total runaways, are eliminated. In this table, however, Senegambia is separated from the Windward Coast, and so to equal the listing in Table 3 the figures for these two regions must be added. To the extent that the proportion of runaways is an accurate reflection of the proportion of slaves imported from the various regions, the early years reflect the dominance of peoples from Congo-Angola. Fifty-seven percent of runaways in the 1730s and 61 percent in the 1740s had come from that part of the coast. Accounting for the variation in time, these proportions do not differ greatly from Peter Wood's calculations of imports for

13. *SCG*, June 15, 1754, August 9, 1735, August 24, 1738, September 21, 1738, June 11, 1741, December 7, 1738, December 13, 1735, March 23, 1738.

14. *SCGCJ*, January 1, 1769, April 4, 1769, and September 19, 1768.

15. See, for example, *ibid.*, January 28, 1772, May 5, 1772, July 7, 1772, August 4, 1772, January 5, 1773, July 6, 1773, February 14, 1775.

Table 5 GEOGRAPHICAL ORIGINS
of AFRICA-BORN RUNAWAY SLAVES

Region	30s No.	(%)	40s No.	(%)	50s No.	(%)	60s No.	(%)	70s No.	(%)	Total No.	(%)
Senegambia	14	(22.2)	6	(12.2)	37	(37.4)	80	(29.0)	46	(11.0)	184	(20.2)
Windward Coast (includes Sierra Leone)					4	(4.0)	10	(3.6)	79	(18.9)	93	(10.3)
Gold Coast	1	(1.6)	1	(2.0)	4	(4.0)	15	(5.4)	22	(5.3)	43	(4.7)
Slave Coast (Dahomey–Togo)	1	(1.6)					7	(2.5)	13	(3.1)	21	(2.3)
Niger Delta	9	(14.3)	10	(20.4)	22	(22.2)	19	(6.9)	29	(6.9)	89	(9.8)
Congo–Angola	36	(57.1)	30	(61.2)	25	(25.3)	82	(29.7)	103	(24.6)	276	(30.4)
Guinea			2	(4.1)	7	(7.1)	58	(21.0)	121	(28.9)	188	(20.7)
Unidentified	2	(3.2)					5	(1.8)	6	(1.4)	13	(1.4)
Total	63		49		99		276		419		907	

the half-decade from 1735. But the same is not true for slaves from other regions, for Gambias, as measured against Wood's figures, are overrepresented among runaways.[16]

The preponderance of Angolas among their slaves was a fact of which South Carolinians were very much aware, even before the Stono Rebellion hammered the point home. Isaac Porcher, for example, who owned a plantation at Wassamsaw, desired the return in 1737 of "a new *Angola* Negro Man named Clawss." "As there is abundance of Negroes in this Province of that Nation," Porcher noted, "he may chance to be harbour'd among some of them, therefore all Masters are desired to give notice to their Slaves who shall receive the same reward, if they will take up said Runaway."[17] Porcher's advertisement indicated a recognition both that a large contingent from one area made it easier for runaways of that nation to find shelter and succor but also that the best way for the planters to handle such a situation was to attempt to divide these people against each other, a practice common in other parts of the Americas.

Before proceeding with the analysis, we should attempt to measure the relationship between imports and runaways more precisely. If adjustments are made in my figures to make them comparable to Curtin's (Table 6), it can be seen that Gambias were more highly represented among runaways than among imports, a fact which should have vitiated their desirability and which strongly suggests that their agricultural skills were sufficiently desirable to counterbalance the tendency to run. On the other hand, slaves from other parts of Upper Guinea were represented less among runaways than among imports, and because the two regions were often combined in the minds of South Carolinians, they should probably be treated together, in which case the relationship between runaways and imports is almost the same. Figures for runaways and imports of Angolas are practically identical. It is probable, therefore, that the incidence of runaways

16. Wood, *Black Majority*, 341. Wood calculated that 69.6 percent of the slaves imported into South Carolina between 1735 and 1740 were from the Congo-Angola region, while 6.1 percent were from the Gambia.
17. *SCG*, August 6, 1737.

Table 6   COMPARISON OF RUNAWAYS WITH IMPORTS IN
SOUTH CAROLINA

Region	Runaways* S. C. Gazette[†] 1732–75	Imports Curtin 1733–1807	Imports Naval Office Lists* 1717–67
Senegambia	26.1	19.5	19.9
Windward Coast	13.2	23.1[‡]	——
Gold Coast	6.1	13.3	——
Bight of Benin[§]	3.0	1.6	——
Bight of Biafra[§]	12.6	2.1	5.1
Angola	39.1	39.6	75.0[11]
Senegambia & Windward Coast Combined	39.2	42.6	

*Excludes listing of *Guinea* and *Africa* in Table 1 and *Guinea* and *Unidentified* in Table 5 to make my figures equable with Curtin, *Atlantic Slave Trade.*
[†]Runaways are from the South Carolina *Gazette* and the South Carolina *Gazette and Country Journal.*
[‡]Curtin's separate listings of Sierra Leone and Windward Coast were combined to equal my figures.
[§]Curtin's *Bight of Benin* is roughly equable to my *Slave Coast* and his *Bight of Biafra* to my *Niger Delta* in Table 5.
[11]This figure is doubtless too high but can be compared to Peter Wood's calculations in *Black Majority,* 340, which show that about 80 percent of the slaves imported between 1735 and 1740 were Angolas.

among peoples from Congo-Angola and Upper Guinea correlated roughly with their importation. This was not true with other groups. Peoples from the Bight of Benin and the Bight of Biafra (Calabars and Ibos) were more highly represented among runaways than among imports; in the case of the latter region, the divergence was quite large. This propensity for absconding might have been a contributing factor to the ill repute in which they were held by South Carolinians and others (though some peoples from the Bight of Benin were held in high esteem). By contrast, the Gold Coast is less prominent among runaways than among imports, coinciding with the superior reputation they maintained and vindicating Laurens' advice to James Grant that they were "less inclined to wander." These statistics give further evidence that the assessments made of various African groups were not simple stereotypes. Alternatively, they suggest the extent to which stereotypes, being so often based on elements of truth, are difficult to eradicate.

When U. B. Phillips wrote his history of American slavery in 1918, he considered the ethnic background of fugitives in Jamaica. He found that in the workhouses of that island in 1803 there were 1,046 recaptured Africans distributed as follows: "284 Eboes and Mocoes, 185 Congos and 259 Angolas as compared with 101 Mandingoes, 60 Chambas (from Sierra Leone), 70 Coromantees, 57 Nagoes and Pawpaws, and 30 scattering, along with a total of 488 American-born negroes and mulattoes, and 187 unclassified." He concluded that Congos, Angolas, and Ibos "were especially prone to run away, or perhaps particularly easy to capture when fugitive."[18] He does not compare these numbers with import and population statistics, but he does bring up the contrast between running away and success at evading recapture. If a distinction is made between these two conditions in South Carolina (Table 7),

18. Phillips, *American Negro Slavery*, 44. In British plantation colonies a workhouse was a repository for runaway slaves. A South Carolina law enacted in May, 1740, provided that persons who took up fugitive slaves should "send such slave to the master or other person having the care or government of such slave" if known, or otherwise he was to "be sent, carried or delivered into the custody of the warden of the work-house in Charleston." The law required the warden to "publish in the weekly gazette, such slave, with the best descriptions he shall be able to give, first carefully viewing and examining such slave, naked to the waist, for any mark or brand, which he shall also publish." It may be assumed, then, that most slaves advertised as brought to the workhouse were runaway slaves, though some may have been there for other reasons. Slaves that were guilty of other crimes need not have been described in the same way unless they were also fugitives. Charleston built a workhouse in 1736, but advertisements for runaways indicate that before the law of 1740 they were taken to jail. Some may have been taken who were simply out without permission but their numbers might help to balance those runaways who were returned without ever seeing either workhouse or jail. How many there were of the latter one can only guess. In any case, all else being equal, a reasonably large sample should render reasonably dependable suggestions about the capabilities of various ethnic groups.

The workhouse received fugitive seamen and others as well as the poor and runaway slaves. In 1768, a Poor House was constructed to better "accommodate the . . . poor . . . and to relieve them from the company and noise of disorderly offenders." The workhouse was to be "wholly applied for the reception of runaway slaves and disorderly persons." See David J. McCord, *The Statutes at Large of South Carolina* (Columbia, S.C., 1840), VII, 90.

Table 7   Contrast of Escaped and Recaptured Slaves
in Colonial South Carolina

			Runaway		Workhouse/Jail		Other	
	No.	(%)	No.	(%)	No.	(%)	No.	(%)
Senegambia	184	(100)	68	(37.0)	115	(62.5)	1	(1.5)
Gambia			56	(93.3)	4	(6.7)		
Mandingo			7	(8.4)	75	(90.4)	1	(1.2)
Jalonka					6	(100)		
Bambara			5	(20.8)	19	(79.2)		
Fullah/Fuiler (Fulbe)					10	(100)		
Araba					1	(100)		
Windward Coast	93	(100)	11	(11.8)	81	(87.1)	1	(1.0)
Sierra Leone					1	(100)		
Limbo (Limba)					4	(100)		
Boler (Bola)					2	(100)		
Temna/Timmene			1	(20.0)	4	(80.0)		
Windward Coast			4	(100)				
Kishee (Kisi)			3	(4.2)	69	(95.9)		
Rice Coast					1	(50.0)	1	(50.0)
Grain Coast			3	(100)				
Gold Coast	43	(100)	25	(58.1)	17	(39.5)	1	(2.3)

Table 7—Continued

	Runaway		Workhouse/Jail		Other	
	No.	(%)	No.	(%)	No.	(%)
Gold Coast	10	(90.9)	1	(9.1)		
Coromantee	12	(44.4)	14	(51.9)	1	(3.7)
Cromttey	1	(50.0)	1	(50.0)		
Fantee	2	(100)				
Yaney			1	(100)		
Slave Coast						
(Bight of Benin)	9	(41.6)	12	(58.3)		
Pawpaw/Papa	9	(64.3)	5	(35.7)		
Whydah			2	(100)		
Nego (Nago)			1	(100)		
Carbady (Gbari)			3	(100)		
Simbey (Somba)			1	(100)		
Niger Delta						
(Bight of Biafra)	35	(39.3)	53	(59.6)	1	(1.1)
Ibo	29	(40.8)	41	(57.7)	1	(1.4)
Calabar	6	(33.3)	11	(66.7)		
Congo-Angola	129	(46.7)	139	(50.4)	9	(2.9)
Congo	2	(6.1)	31	(93.9)		

Slave Coast total: 21 (100)
Niger Delta total: 89 (100)
Congo-Angola total: 276 (100)

Angola			127	(54.3)	99	(42.3)	8	(3.4)
Malimbo (Malimbe)					3	(100)		
Wollonga					1	(100)		
Bambo (Bambona)					4	(100)		
Patango (Babongo)					1	(100)		
Guinea	188	(100)	67	(35.6)	121	(64.4)		
Unidentified	13	(100)	7	(53.8)	6	(46.2)		
West Indies	58	(100)	46	(79.3)	11	(19.0)	1	(1.7)
North America	354	(100)	281	(79.4)	70	(19.8)	3	(.8)
Country born (South Carolina)			279	(80.4)	65	(18.7)	3	(.9)
Elsewhere	10	(100)	9	(90.0)	1	(10.0)		
Origin unknown	2536	(100)	1558	(61.4)	941	(37.1)	37	(1.5)
Invalid	6							
Total	3868	(100)	2245	(58.0)	1570	(40.6)	53	(1.4)

Senegambians and those from the Windward Coast were more susceptible to recapture than peoples from Congo-Angola by a considerable margin. Indeed, relatively more of the former were advertised as confined to the workhouse or jail than from any other region except "Guinea," a generic designation. Why this should be so is not apparent. The greater facility of Angolas in avoiding capture might be explained by their larger numbers, making concealment easier, except that if Upper Guinea is taken as a whole, the two groups were about equal. But it is possible that the Angolan population in South Carolina was more homogeneous than that from Senegambia and its environs. This conclusion is suggested by the larger number of ethnic listings for the latter. The question of numbers assumes greater importance when it is noted that relatively more Angolas ran away in the 1730s and 1740s when they were heavily predominant and when the colony was less settled (Tables 3 and 5). There was also the attraction of the Spanish at Saint Augustine, where Angolas who had some knowledge of Portuguese would have had little difficulty in understanding Spanish. Probably many had this ability. Thus, it was reported of one Angolan who had been recaptured that "by what can be discovered in his speech [he] is either *Spanish* or *Italian*," but he was more likely Portuguese.[19]

Comparatively more slaves from the area in and around Senegambia escaped capture during the latter half of the period when the province was more settled and the slave population more heterogeneous. Still, if particular groups are singled out, Mandingos, who composed the majority of unfortunates from Senegambia, were disastrously inept at evading capture. Fully 90 percent were advertised as being confined rather than as fugitives. Moreover, in whole numbers they composed one of the larger groups. They were exceeded in their propensity to recapture, among groups for whom the sample is sufficiently large to be comparable, only by the Kisi of Guinea-Conakry, on the Windward Coast—*i.e.*, from the same general region. The relatively few escapees from the Gold Coast were more successful than not in maintaining their

19. *SCG*, July 11, 1759.

tenuous freedom, while runaways from the Bights of Benin and Biafra were more often noted from confinement.

While African-born slaves were more likely to be fugitives, American-born slaves, whether native to the West Indies or North America, were less likely to be caught if they did stray. Less than one-fifth of this group was listed in the workhouse or jail. Their greater success is doubtless due to their acculturation and to their understanding of the language, manners, and sensibilities of their masters. Doubtless, too, they were aided by the gullibility of white South Carolinians, by the unstable plantation setting, and by the heterogeneous nature of both African and European settlement. Finally, there must have been an even greater degree in South Carolina than in Virginia of what Gerald Mullin classifies as unwitting acknowledgment and approval of the fact "that at last among the strange and threatening plantation slaves a significant [or in this case, any] number had come to learn white ways and could now play their social games with artistry." [20]

Artistry there was aplenty. Thus, *Gazette* readers were advised to beware of Chelsea, known also as Wilson, who was "a cunning, sly, talkative fellow, and apt to impose on people that are not apprized of his artfulness"; of Josiah Saunders, described as "extremely artful and sensible . . . very likely active and mannerly; he generally takes Snuff and is remarkably clean and neat in his Dress . . . and speaks English extremely well"; of a woman "between the *Indian* and *Mulatto* breed" who with malice aforethought had obviously planned ahead, her master noting: "As she frequently told sundry persons that she was an apprentice to my wife, may now very likely say she is free"; of "a short, well-sett, fat Wench" who "may be taken to be a Free Wench, and has her Tongue at Pleasure" though her "Back will shew the marks of her former misdeeds." The adroitness of some of these people is indicated by the distances they had traveled and the length of time they had been away. Josiah Saunders escaped from Saint Eustasius in November, 1756, and was seen in Bermuda in July, 1757, before his master advertised for him in South Carolina in November, 1758.

20. Mullin, *Flight and Rebellion*, 92.

George, a slave taken up in Savannah, Georgia, had been absent four years from his master on the Potomac in Virginia. Hercules had been away seven years when he was claimed at the workhouse in 1745.[21]

The varied background of African immigrants, many of whom had traveled widely, increased the social complexity of South Carolina. This variation was reflected among the slaves in a way that extended beyond African ethnic divergence and abetted the escapades of fugitives. Boston, of John's Island, was born in Guinea but spoke excellent English, Spanish, and Portuguese. Obviously a leader, he was "a cunning, artful fellow," had been in "different parts of the world," and had convinced two others, who could not even speak English, to join in his escape.[22] Five blacks who absconded from a plantation in Purrysburgh all spoke good English, French, and German, their master Abraham Ehrhardt warned. Pierro, who called himself Peter, spoke English, French, and Dutch. A woman who escaped with her husband from Point Comfort on the Savannah spoke "good *English, Chickesaw,* and perhaps *French,* the *Chickesaws* having taken her over from the *French* Settlements on [the] *Mississippi.*"[23] There was a notable population of Spanish speakers. Most of these blacks probably had not been, like Luke, born in Spain,[24] but they were frequently mentioned as absent from their master's service.[25] When not actively involved in running away, they were sometimes suspected of aiding others; thus the owner of Steven, an elderly piragua keeper, "supposed he keeps amongst Mr. *Welshuysen's* or Mr. *Porter's* Spanish Negroes."[26] This babel must have been perplexing to anyone seeking to establish unalterable verities of racial, linguistic, and servile classification. Generalizations surely were made, but conceivable exceptions were so many and alternatives to English language and culture so numerous that able slaves were permitted

21. *SCG,* February 16, 1767, November 10, 1758, May 18, 1755, May 26, 1733, October 6, 1758, March 4, 1745.
22. *SCGCJ,* August 8, 1769.
23. *SCG,* March 4, 1756, June 7, 1740, September 22, 1746.
24. *SCGCJ,* September 1, 1772.
25. See, for example, *SCG,* January 3, 1733, February 21, 1736, July 25, 1740.
26. *Ibid.,* September 10, 1737.

to play upon the credibility of the masters at the same time they sowed suspicion.

III

Racial assumptions were also mitigated by the variety of slave capabilities. "In established Plantations," James Grant wrote the duke of Athole in 1768, "the Planter has Tradesmen of all kinds in his Gang of Slaves, and 'tis a Rule with them, never to pay Money for what can be made upon their Estates, not a Lock, a Hing or a Nail if they can avoid it."[27] The shortage of white labor, the undependability of white indentured servants, the unquestioned "suitability" of blacks for labor in warm climes, and the popular belief that slave labor was more economical than white labor—all made planters eager to use slaves in a variety of trades, both skilled and unskilled. Consequently, slaves who knew a trade or who were capable of learning one were very much in demand. Henry Laurens once bought a couple who could speak fairly good English, the man a sailor (who could "in a Sailor like fashion wait in a House well enough") and the woman able to sew, wash, and cook, simply because they were cheap, considering their skills. He did not think it wise to pass up the bargain. He lauded the perspicacity of James Grant in placing a number of young slaves under the tutelage of a white craftsman—an example, he felt, of good management.[28] Planters in South Carolina generally desired slaves with knowledge either of a crop or of a craft. This desire fueled the demand for slaves from rice-growing regions, and it may have been a partial explanation for the eminent acceptability of slaves from Congo-Angola.

We have established that Angolas had a reputation for being peculiarly adept at acquiring mechanical skills.[29] To the extent that runaways are an accurate index of the situation in South Carolina, this characterization would appear to be valid. (See Tables 8 and

27. Grant to Duke of Athole, February 12, 1768, in Grant of Ballindalloch MSS, 0771/Letterbook.

28. Laurens to Grant, December 13, 1764, and November 24, 1767, in *ibid.*, 1771/359.

29. See p. 13, herein.

Table 8   Skills of Runaway Slaves
               in Colonial South Carolina

Trade	Number	Percentage
Cooper	52	15.3
Carpenter	40	11.5
Sawyer	31	8.8
Sailor	19	5.9
Bricklayer	16	4.7
Waitingman	14	4.1
Boatman	14	4.1
Shoemaker	12	3.5
Housework	10	2.9
Patron of a pettiauger	10	2.9
Ship carpenter	10	2.9
Blacksmith	9	2.7
Washer	7	2.1
Fisherman	7	2.1
Seamstress	6	1.8
Tailor	6	1.8
Market tender	6	1.8
Wheelwright	5	1.5
Cowpen tender	5	1.5
Fiddler	4	1.2
Fieldhand	4	1.2
A kind of doctor	3	.9
Tanner	3	.9
Saddler	3	.9
Painter	3	.9
Hired out in town	3	.9
Driver	3	.9
Butcher	3	.9
Fruit and vegetable seller	3	.9
Servant	2	.6
Plowman	2	.6

Trade	Number	Percentage
Needleworker	2	.6
Patron of a schooner	2	.6
Wagon driver	2	.6
Boat pilot	2	.6
Porter	2	.6
Cattle hunter	1	.3
Gardener	1	.3
Cook	1	.3
Barber	1	.3
Waiter	1	.3
Silversmith	1	.3
Newspaper seller	1	.3
Charm bell ringer (?)	1	.3
Used to stock (?)	1	.3
Coasting business	1	.3
Shipwright	1	.3
Jeweler	1	.3
Total	337	

9). Not only were Angola-born slaves more prominent than any other African group among fugitives who were listed with trades, but their skills were among the most useful or most called for, if the extent to which they were noted among runaways paralleled their actual utility. This stereotype of Angolas could have been self-fulfilling in the way that many beliefs seem to be. If colonials thought that these people had such a predisposition, then they would most likely single them out to be trained; once the cycle started, it would be self-perpetuating. Still, it is interesting that the findings bear out the credo. There does not seem to have been any public statement of this assumption in South Carolina. But if this belief permeated other sections of the South Atlantic System,

Table 9   CORRELATION OF SKILLS AND AFRICAN ETHNIC GROUPS IN COLONIAL SOUTH CAROLINA

	Angola	Ibo	Country born	Mandingo	West Indies	Guinea	Malagoacow	Gambia	Cuba	Cromttey	Jamaica	Coromantee	Spanish	Bermuda	French	Montserrat	Bossue	Kisi	Total Number	Percent of Slaves with Skills	Percent of Trade
Cooper	2	3	7	1	1														14	15.1	26.9
Blacksmith						1	1												2	2.2	22.2
Tailor			1																1	1.1	16.6
Wheelwright			1																1	1.1	20.0
Market tender								1											1	1.1	16.7
Cattle hunter			1																1	1.1	100.0
Shoemaker			1																1	1.1	8.3
Sawyer	8		4																12	12.9	40.0
Houseworker			3																3	3.2	30.0
Waitingman			4																5	5.4	35.7
Carpenter	1		6		1	2			1	1									12	12.9	30.8
Ship carpenter			1																1	1.1	100.0
Washer	1		1																2	2.2	28.6
A kind of doctor		1																	1	1.1	33.3
Saddler			1																1	1.1	33.3
Cowpen																					

Table Cut III

Occupation																			Total number	Percent of slaves with skills	Percent of origin
town			1																1	1.1	33.3
Butcher	1		1																2	2.2	66.6
Bricklayer	2					1													3	5.2	18.8
Tanner	1		1																2	2.2	66.6
Sailor	3	1	2		2	1				1				1	1				12	12.9	60.0
Painter		1	1																1	1.1	66.6
Plowman	2																		2	2.2	100.0
Boatman	2																		2	2.2	100.0
Wagon driver	1								1										2	2.2	100.0
Fieldhand	2																		2	2.2	50.0
Porter				1															1	1.1	100.0
Used to stock																1			1	1.1	100.0
Shipwright										1									1	1.1	100.0
Patron of schooner	1																	1	1	1.1	50.0
Total number	15	4	50	1	4	4	1	1	1	3	1	1	1	2	1	1	1	1	93	100	
Percent of slaves with skills	16.1	4.3	53.8	1.1	4.3	4.3	1.1	1.1	1.1	3.2	1.1	1.1	1.1	2.2	1.1	1.1	1.1	1.1	100.0	1.4	
Percent of origin	6.7	5.7	14.4	1.2	30.8	2.2	100.0	1.7	50.0	16.7	3.7	14.3	15.4	50.0	100.0	100.0	1.4				
Asterisk if sample of origin 50+	*	*	*	*		*		*		*											

NOTE: The category *Percent of slaves with skills* in the row at the bottom refers to the proportion that that ethnic group represents of all the slaves with skills. In the column at the right it refers to the proportion that that skill represents among the slaves with skills. The category *Percent of origin* refers to the proportion of skilled slaves among the particular ethnic group.

and it appears that it did, then it probably existed in Carolina as well.[30]

This assumption notwithstanding, the comparative ranking in terms of desirability of Gambias and Angolas would remain unchanged because with Gambias colonials would be purchasing a known quality and with Angolas only a predilection. Moreover, I have already adduced evidence of planters acknowledging that West Africans possessed indigenous skills useful on New World plantations. The blacksmith that Henry Laurens sent to James Grant was a Gambian; Richard Oswald dispatched his ship for artisans to Sierra Leone.[31] If prior experience permitted peoples from Senegambia and circumjacent regions to perform other tasks as well as cultivate rice, their value to South Carolina could hardly be surpassed. Yet the representation of this area among skilled runaways is remarkably small. Angolas accounted for 16 percent of the skills identified with an ethnic group; Upper Guineans (the listings for Gambia, Mandingo, and Kisi), only 3.2 percent. The two regions were almost equal in imports and fugitives, with this distinction: more Angolas had come in earlier. This difference might have been crucial both because those slaves who had been longer in the colony were most likely to be taught crafts and because the prior experience of Senegambians with rice cultivation might have automatically consigned them to the fields. Despite the fact that they had been in the colony longer, the ethnic background of Angolas would not cease to be identified if they ran away. Even in more favorable circumstances the ethnic association remained strong, so that when twenty-eight blacks were offered for sale at Beaufort, Port Royal in April, 1739, they were said to be the "Remainder of those that were landed at the said Place in May, 1736, by Mr. Delas out of the *Susannah*, Capt. *Mallortie* from *Angola*; therefore they are Season'd to this Country."[32] Both their origin and the fact that they were seasoned appeared to be important.

The most proficient group among skilled fugitives was, as one

---

30. Gonzalo Beltrán, in fact, attributes this reputation to an English source, in *La población negra de México*, 141.
31. See p. 109, herein.
32. *SCG*, March 17, 1739.

might expect, native- or country-born slaves. They composed over half of those listed as artisans. Moreover, these craftsmen amounted to 14 percent of all identifiable Carolina-born slaves who absconded (whereas, by contrast, Angola tradesmen were only 7 percent of their fugitives). Hence, both relatively and absolutely, local-born slaves led in the possession of plantation skills, though, again, this is hardly surprising.

The range of tasks performed by slaves (Table 8) is noteworthy but not extraordinary in a situation wherein the ideal was to have slaves as versatile as possible. The occupations extend, in degree of skill, all the way from a silversmith and jeweler down to a stockman. But this fact has already been established by Peter Wood, who adds such trades as gunsmith to the list. He notes that "the demand for experienced craftsmen of all sorts was intense enough so that such questions as whether workers were free, indentured, or slave, or whether they were red, white, or black, often mattered less than their availability and aptitude."[33] This was especially true when new plantations were being formed and where white labor was scarce and undependable.

Other scholars have also commented on the unusual degree of responsibility exercised by servitors in the area. Black foremen (or drivers), for example, according to Mullin, are found during the antebellum period only in South Carolina.[34] That statement ought (and perhaps is meant) to include contiguous regions to the south which were closely related in economy and outlook. But the amount of authority slaves exercised, and the extent to which masters were dependent upon them, was clearly far greater than has been commonly assumed. A Georgia merchant bought several bondsmen from a Carolina planter for service in East Florida. "The two fellows with the families," he explained to his correspondent, "have been born on his plantation, are likely young people, well acquainted with Rice & every kind of plantation business, and in short [are] capable of the Management of a plantation themselves." He also dispatched four young, single blacks who

33. Wood, *Black Majority*, 196–200.
34. Mullin, "Religion and Slave Resistance."

were "excellent Sawyers, having been rented out for that purpose for two years at £18 Stlg. each" and were "as good as any in the two Provinces [of Georgia and South Carolina]." Finally, he advised that, although he had "sent all over Carolina almost, for Overseers" on behalf of another planter, he had not succeeded in getting one. Therefore the planter would have to make do with slaves: "The Negro I send him is capable to manage all his planting business very well, especially for this year. There is no such thing to be mett with as a good Overseer & Carpenter at the same time[;] he must have a Negro Carpenter."[35] South Carolina newspapers were full of notices offering to sell or requesting to buy a variety of slave artisans. Hence, attitudes and circumstances that would have permitted Europeans to learn from and depend upon Africans in the early period did not change materially as the century went on.

There was more than one pursuit in South Carolina for which an African background would have been adequate preparation. Africans in scattered parts of the continent were used to tending cattle, fishing, and boating, among other things, and Wood has presented an extended discussion of the degree to which these folk were better suited to Carolina's environment than Englishmen.[36] Of the skills listed in Table 8, 25 percent were related in some way to fishing or boating. But whether any of these tasks were related in the minds of Carolinians with particular African regions cannot be asserted. Except in one case, in which the term "used to stock" (which presumably relates to herding) was associated with a "Bossue," all the fugitives who had been involved with cattle, boats, or the sea were American born. This fact establishes nothing, however, because there were numerous runaways whose origins were not recorded, and many others may have been relatively content at a task they had performed at home. Thus many of the "fishing Negroes at the Markett place" in Charleston in 1737, among whom Kennedy O'Brien's Peter had been seen, may well have been Africans.[37] A fugitive listed as "tending market" was a Gambia.

35. John Graham to Grant, March 1, 1768, in Grant of Ballindalloch MSS, 0771/401.
36. Wood, *Black Majority*, 95–130.
37. *SCG*, October 29, 1737.

Not all prior experience was recommendable. Africans were often assumed to be knowledgeable about poisons, an assumption well established in South Carolina by the middle of the eighteenth century.[38] In 1751, the *Gazette* reprinted "the *Negro* CAESAR's Cure for Poison," which had also been published the previous year.[39] Other cultural carry-overs, some of a mysterious nature, were exhibited occasionally, as in the case of an Ibo, who "pretends to be a sort of a doctor." This epithet could have had both positive and negative connotations. If positive, it could have modified or, if negative, accentuated the derogation of peoples from the Niger Delta, if Ibos were its usual exponent.

IV

In one of the minor ironies with which life is rife, women were most available in that region of Africa whose men were universally disparaged. We have seen that women were not equally accessible for purchase everywhere along the coast. I have suggested, too, that more African women were imported into North America than anywhere else around the South Atlantic.[40] If these facts are true, then one would expect to find more Ibo women in North America than those of any other African ethnic group. Insofar as fugitives roughly reflected their proportion of importation, groups with a significant sample (fifty or more) could be used to gauge the validity of this expectation. Under most circumstances, women do not seem to have taken to flight so often as men in South Carolina; there was a heavy disproportion of males (Table 10). Other things being equal, however, it is reasonable to assume that a greater percentage of women in any group would mean that more women of that group had been imported. This assumption would seem to be justified, for relatively more Ibo women (28.2 percent) ran away than women from any other African group, and more from the Bight of Biafra (22.5 percent) than from any other African region (Table 11). Next to Ibos were

38. See Wood, *Black Majority*, 289–92.
39. *SCG*, February 25, 1751.
40. See pp. 56–72, herein.

Table 10   SEX OF SLAVE RUNAWAYS

Sex	Number		Percentage	
Male, black	2810		72.6	
Male, mulatto	55		1.4	
Male, yellow	181		4.7	
Male, mustee	101		2.6	
Total men		3147		82.4
Female, black	584		15.1	
Female, mulatto	11		.3	
Female, yellow	44		1.2	
Female, mustee	32		.8	
Total women		671		17.6
Sub-total		3818		100.0
Missing	52		1.3	
Total	3870		100.0	

the Kisi (15.3 percent) from the Windward Coast, whose region (with 14 percent) was second to the Bight of Biafra. It should be stressed that these figures are not meant as a measure of the sex ratio of the various groupings but as a potential index to total numbers. That is to say, Ibos might have been more disposed to abscond than members of other ethnic groups, but there is no reason to suppose that the sexual distribution among runaway Ibos would diverge from that of other absentee Africans unless it were already different in the population as a whole. Thus we can conclude with some confidence what has already been suggested from other evidence: that comparatively more Ibo women were imported.

It is remarkable that Ibos as a group and the Bight of Biafra as an area had a greater proportional representation of women among runaways than was produced by the native black populace of South Carolina. In this they differed from all other African entities. The forces acting upon Americans and Africans were not the same. Peter Wood has suggested, for example, that women were more inclined than men to absent themselves temporarily to visit a friend or relative and to return voluntarily; this practice may have been more common among country-born than foreign-born slaves insofar as their web of interrelationships was more extensive.[41] More such women may therefore have been away at some time than the ads reflected. But as a general rule, even without this consideration, African women were less inclined to run away than country-born women if the African total of female runaways (10 percent) is taken as the norm. There were a number of ethnic and regional compilations that approached or exceeded this norm— Congo-Angola (9 percent), Guinea (12 percent), Windward Coast (14 percent), and Kisi (15 percent)—but none to the measure of the Ibos, who surpassed the norm by 142 percent. So in their identity both as Ibos and as women, Ibos stood out among runaways.

It is interesting to consider what effects these demographic facts had on the survival and evolution of facets of African culture in South Carolina. If any one group was numerically dominant, as Angolas were in the early years, the consequences of the Ibo's sexual disproportion may have been minimal insofar as maintaining aspects of culture that were peculiarly Ibo, though significant in terms of perpetuating elements of commonality among Bantu-speaking peoples. For although Ibo is not strictly a Bantu language, it is closely related—to such an extent, in fact, that it has been called "semi-Bantu"—and the Ibo people are located in an African region of cultural transition. During periods when no one culture predominated, the presence of large numbers of Ibo women might have given them an influence disproportionate to their numbers, particularly since they might have been able to play something of a bridging role between ethnic groups. In any case, statistics of importation together with descriptions of fugitives cannot help but make one wonder. There is the case of "*Cudjo* a sensible *Coromantee* Negro Fellow, about 45 Years old, stutters, and his wife *Dinah*, an Ebo wench that speaks very good English, with her two Children, a Boy about 8 Years old, and a Girl of about 18 months." The woman in this situation already ap-

41. Wood, *Black Majority*, 241.

Table 11   ORIGINS OF RUNAWAYS IN COLONIAL
SOUTH CAROLINA BY SEX

Region	Male black	Male mulatto	Male yellow	Male mustee	Female black	Female mulatto	Female yellow	Female mustee	Missing	Total
Senegambia	163 (88.6)		8 (4.3)		10 (5.4)				3 (1.6)	184
Gambia	55 (91.7)		3 (5.0)		1 (1.7)				1 (1.7)	60
Mandingo	73 (88.0)		3 (3.6)		5 (6.0)				2 (2.4)	83
Jalonka	6 (100.0)									6
Bambara	22 (91.7)		1 (4.2)		1 (4.2)					24
Fulbe	6 (60.0)		1 (10.0)		3 (30.0)					10
Araba	1 (100.0)									1
Windward Coast	71 (76.3)	1 (1.0)	8 (8.6)		13 (14.0)					93
Sierra Leone	1 (100.0)									1

Limba	4 (100.0)					4
Temne	5 (100.0)					5
Windward Coast	4 (100.0)					4
Bola	2 (100.0)					2
Kisi	52 (72.2)	1 (1.4)	8 (11.1)	11 (15.3)		72
Rice Coast	1 (50.0)			1 (50.0)		2
Grain Coast	2 (66.7)			1 (33.3)		3
Gold Coast	39 (92.9)		1 (2.4)	1 (2.4)	1 (2.4)	42
Gold Coast	10 (90.9)				1 (9.1)	11
Coromantee	28 (96.5)			1 (3.4)		29
Fantee	1 (50.0)		1 (50.0)			2

Table 11—Continued

Region	Male black	Male mulatto	Male yellow	Male mustee	Female black	Female mulatto	Female yellow	Female mustee	Missing	Total
Bight of Benin	19 (90.5)				2 (9.5)					21
Popo	13 (92.9)				1 (7.1)					14
Whydah	2 (100.0)									2
Nago	1 (100.0)									1
Gbari	2 (66.7)				1 (33.3)					3
Somba	1 (100.0)									1
Bight of Biafra	60 (67.4)		9 (10.1)		15 (16.9)		2 (2.2)		3 (3.4)	89
Ibo	46 (64.3)		5 (7.0)		15 (21.1)		2 (2.8)		3 (4.2)	71
Calabar	14 (77.8)		4 (22.2)							18

										Total
Congo-Angola	233 (84.4)		15 (5.4)	1 (0.4)	22 (8.0)		3 (1.1)		2 (0.7)	276
Congo	29 (87.9)				3 (9.1)		1 (3.0)			33
Angola	198 (84.6)		13 (5.6)	1 (0.4)	18 (7.7)		2 (0.9)		2 (0.9)	234
Malimbe	1 (33.3)		2 (67.7)							3
Wollonga	1 (100.0)									1
Bambona	4 (100.0)									4
Badongo					1 (100.0)					1
Guinea	153 (81.4)		12 (6.4)		18 (9.6)		4 (2.1)		1 (0.5)	188
South Carolina	229 (66.0)	2 (0.6)	39 (11.2)	9 (2.6)	58 (16.7)	1 (0.3)	5 (1.4)	3 (0.9)	1 (0.3)	347
Total	967 (78.0)	3 (0.2)	92 (7.4)	10 (0.8)	139 (11.2)	1 (0.1)	15 (1.2)	3 (0.2)	10 (0.8)	1240
African total	738 (82.6)	1 (0.1)	53 (5.9)	1 (0.1)	81 (9.1)		10 (1.1)		9 (1.0)	893
Total (all cases)	2810 (72.6)	55 (1.4)	181 (4.8)	101 (2.6)	584 (15.1)	11 (0.3)	44 (1.1)	32 (0.8)	52 (1.3)	3870

pears to be very well acculturated, and there might have been little or no attempt by either parent to preserve any of their heritage, though the children could not have failed to be aware of it. But if Dinah made contact with the likes of Lydia, another Ibo, who ran off at the same time as, and probably in the company of, Prince, an Angolan, or with Linda, also Ibo, married to Ben, "Guiney-born," and their child, recognizable traces of Ibo culture might remain, while whatever was peculiar to the Coromantee, Angola, or Guinea might have received less emphasis or disappeared.[42]

But statements relating to Africa in general are often so vague as to be vacuous, and it is well to attempt to go beyond such generalities even if immediate assessments can only be speculative. Bastide makes a distinction between ethnic origins and cultural patterns, pointing out that the predominance of an African culture in any New World region "bears no direct relationship to the preponderance of such-and-such an ethnic group in the slave-shipments to the area concerned."[43] Although some of Bastide's statements are suspect, especially as regards North America, this one rings true. It would require anthropological and linguistic studies to substantiate Ibo influence. Aside from that, it is difficult to decide just what, in a New World setting, the precise preconditions for the dominance of one African culture over another might be, and it is probable that there was no universal pattern. The overwhelming predominance of Angolas in the first decades of the eighteenth century may have given them an initial influence that was counteracted in the second half of the century by increasing importations of Senegambian and circumjacent peoples. Ibo importation tapered off in the fifteen years prior to the American Revolution but, though small, it was fairly constant, and the fact that most of these people were women could have given them an importance disproportionate to their numbers. Beyond the desirability of any woman in a situation of relative paucity, the ethnic character of Ibo women may have accentuated their attractiveness. The "constitutional timidity and despondency of mind" that

42. *SCG*, September 14, 1747, March 14, 1748, July 12, 1760.
43. Bastide, *African Civilizations*, 8–11.

made Ibo men so objectionable to white masters could have made their women more appealing among the slaves.[44] In addition, the women were described as better laborers than their men, an important consideration where slaves had to furnish a portion of their own livelihood. Finally, their propensity for absconding would have added an element of daring to their character, striking a responsive chord among more audacious males, whether the males' own exploits were of fact or fancy. All of these elements would have increased their stature and influence among the African population, either as Ibos in particular or as a Bantu-related group in general. But white masters preferred Senegambians.

V

On the contrary, there is a characteristic of Bantu culture, which the related Ibo culture seems to contain, that militated against its exercising a dominant role, namely, its capacity for assimilation. This feature was not determinative, as various American societies existed where, despite competition, Bantu culture was preeminent. But this factor complicates assessments based on demographic data alone. If evidence of English proficiency among runaway slaves in South Carolina is typical, however, this propensity for assimilation is validated (see Table 12). Among all African-born fugitives, a larger percentage of the peoples from the Bight of Biafra, among whom Ibos were numbered, possessed some English ability. If we consider the last two columns of Table 12, and combine the number of those fugitives whose language proficiency was not known with that of those who spoke no English, we find as follows: Bight of Benin, 92 percent; Windward Coast, 89 percent; Gold Coast, 89 percent; Senegambia, 85 percent; Guinea, 84 percent; Congo-Angola, 83 percent; Bight of Biafra, 81 percent. Therefore, Bantu and related peoples (the last two regions) showed a slightly greater capacity for assimilation, to the extent that language ability reflects this trend. But the variation, in most cases, is too slight to enable us to give this conclusion much

44. Edwards, *History of the British Colonies*, II, 281:

Table 12   COMPARISON OF ETHNIC GROUPS
BY ENGLISH PROFICIENCY

Region	Excellent	Very good	Good	Little	Very little	Bad	Poor	Very poor	Indifferent	No English	Unknown
Senegambia		5 (2.7)	3 (1.6)	9 (4.9)	4 (2.2)	2 (1.1)	2 (1.1)	3 (1.6)		29 (15.8)	126 (68.9)
Gambia		3 (5.0)	2 (3.3)	7 (11.7)		1 (1.7)	2 (3.3)			9 (15.0)	36 (60.0)
Mandingo		1 (1.2)	1 (1.2)	2 (2.4)		1 (1.2)		2 (2.4)		14 (17.1)	61 (74.4)
Jalonka										1 (16.7)	5 (83.3)
Bambara		1 (4.2)						1 (4.2)		5 (20.8)	17 (70.8)
Fulbe					4 (40.0)						6 (60.0)
Araba											1 (100.0)
Windward Coast				3 (3.3)	1 (1.1)			6 (6.5)		4 (4.3)	79 (84.9)
Sierra Leone											1 (100.0)
Limba				1 (25.0)							3 (75.0)

	I	II	III	IV	V	VI	VII
Temne	4 (80.0)			1 (20.0)			
Windward Coast	4 (100.0)						
Bola	2 (100.0)						
Kisi	60 (83.3)	4 (5.6)		5 (6.9)	2 (2.8)	1 (1.4)	
Rice Coast	2 (100.0)						
Grain Coast	3 (100.0)						
Gold Coast	26 (63.4)	10 (24.4)	1 (2.4)	1 (2.4)	1 (2.4)	1 (2.4)	1 (2.4)
Gold Coast	7 (63.6)	3 (27.3)	1 (9.1)				
Coromantee	16 (59.3)	7 (25.9)		1 (3.7)	1 (3.7)	1 (3.7)	1 (3.7)
Fantee	3 (100.0)						
Bight of Benin	17 (77.3)	3 (13.6)	1 (4.5)	1 (4.5)			
Popo	13 (92.9)			1 (7.1)			
Whydah		2 (100.0)					

Table 12—*Continued*

Region	Excellent	Very good	Good	Little	Very little	Bad	Poor	Very poor	Indifferent	No English	Unknown
Nago											1 (100.0)
Gbari											3 (100.0)
Somba										1 (100.0)	
Bight of Biafra	1 (1.1)	1 (1.1)	4 (4.5)	5 (5.6)	1 (1.1)	2 (2.2)	1 (1.1)	3 (3.4)		12 (13.5)	59 (66.3)
Ibo	1 (1.4)	1 (1.4)	3 (4.2)	4 (5.6)		1 (1.4)	1 (1.4)	2 (2.8)		10 (14.1)	48 (67.6)
Calabar			1 (5.6)	1 (5.6)	1 (5.6)	1 (5.6)		1 (5.6)		2 (11.1)	11 (61.1)
Congo-Angola	2 (0.7)	2 (0.7)	19 (6.9)	4 (1.5)	5 (1.8)	4 (1.5)		10 (3.6)	1 (0.4)	34 (12.4)	194 (70.5)
Congo								1 (3.0)		2 (6.2)	30 (90.9)
Angola	2 (0.9)	3 (1.3)	19 (8.1)	4 (1.7)	5 (2.1)	4 (1.7)		8 (3.4)	1 (0.4)	32 (13.7)	156 (66.7)

Malimbe										3 (100.0)
Wollonga										1 (100.0)
Bambona								1 (25.0)			3 (100.0)
Badongo								3 (75.0)			1 (100.0)
Guinea			6 (3.3)	8 (4.4)	6 (3.3)	1 (0.5)		11 (6.0)		10 (5.5)	146 (79.8)
North America	4 (1.1)	29 (8.2)	39 (11.0)		1 (0.3)			1 (0.3)	1 (0.3)	1 (0.3)	277 (78.5)
South Carolina	4 (1.2)	29 (8.4)	38 (11.0)		1 (0.3)				1 (0.3)	1 (0.3)	273 (78.7)
Elsewhere		1 (10.0)	2 (20.0)							2 (20.0)	5 (50.0)
West Indies	1 (1.7)	13 (22.4)	7 (12.1)						2 (3.4)		35 (60.3)
African Total	4 (0.1)	8 (0.9)	32 (3.6)	30 (3.4)	18 (2.0)	9 (1.0)	3 (0.3)	35 (3.9)	3 (0.3)	102 (11.4)	647 (72.6)
Unlisted	14 (0.6)	61 (2.4)	131 (5.2)	27 (1.1)	21 (0.8)	19 (0.7)	1 (0.0)	27 (1.1)	2 (0.1)	127 (5.0)	2104 (83.0)

NOTE: In this table language ability is listed as described in the South Carolina *Gazette*.

emphasis. Consequently, before we pursue this line further, we ought to determine how to evaluate these data.

Gerald Mullin has suggested that, on the whole, the language ability of South Carolina slaves was inferior to that of servitors in the Chesapeake, a proposition not difficult to accept in view of the higher proportion of native Africans in the former.[45] Indeed, he suggests that learning English was not expected of Africans in the more southerly region and that the process of acculturation was slower. So while in Virginia advertisements for fugitives commented on the linguistic competence of African-born slaves alone, in South Carolina the capabilities of African and country-born both elicited notice. Certainly, large numbers of blacks did not speak English. The newspapers abound in ads for the likes of "a new negro man named *Pompey*, speaks no English," or of a new Negro boy between twelve and fourteen, "lately purchased out of Capt. *Bostock*'s cargo, from *Gambia*, and cannot speak a word of English," or of Sampson, Nero, Plenty, and Jupiter, the first two Bambaras, the last two Mandingos, who could not speak English, though the warden of the workhouse commented, "By what I can inform myself by my negro fellow who can speak with and understand them, they all belong to one master whose name they cannot tell."[46]

The sense of bewilderment that newly imported Africans felt was perhaps somewhat tempered by the presence of other, more experienced of their countrymen with whom they could communicate. Additionally, Mullin is doubtless correct in supposing the extensive usage of a patois that whites could not understand— "Gullah (or its equivalent)"—making South Carolina essentially bilingual, if not multilingual.[47] Still, this situation must have done little immediately to reduce the apprehension and astonishment of "salt-water" slaves. One can only surmise the wonderment of a newcomer "very scarrified from one temple to the other, many marks of the whip on his back," whose inability to speak the master's tongue likely made it difficult, and sometimes impossible, for

---

45. Mullin, "Religion and Slave Resistance."
46. *SCG*, August 15, 1753, November 7, 1761, October 27, 1759.
47. Mullin, "Religion and Slave Resistance."

him to understand what he was required to do and why he was being punished. The same can be said for a Mandingo, who had "been much whipt about his belly, and is branded on the left buttock cR in one," and for others whose harsh introduction to the rigors of North American slavery must have surpassed their imagination, even if they had suffered a comparable lot in Africa. The social climate was such, therefore, that the least command of English was notable and significant. Thus a young fugitive named Amy was "very well known, but most remarkable for being more sensible and speaking better English than most negroes." Nor does Mullin err in his statement about the expectations of planters as to the speed with which the slaves would acquire English. One planter noted that Paul, absent two months, could not "speak any English having been only one Year in a Plantation."[48]

Under such circumstances, one would expect landowners to pay close attention to the English spoken by their servants and might conclude that where this ability was not mentioned, it was nonexistent. For almost 80 percent of the country-born slaves, though, it was not mentioned either (Table 12). However, this probably means that country-born slaves were assumed to know English. Only 20 percent of all runaways, from whatever source, had their language ability noted, a phenomenon doubtless explained by the lack of contact planters in South Carolina had with the vast majority of their laborers (see Table 13). Of those whose language abilities were noted, 45 percent were judged as speaking good to excellent English, 30 percent spoke no English at all, and the rest spoke some English. The top percentage probably represented artisans, body servants, and others with whom the planter came into close proximity. The second figure probably represented the other extreme—Africans who took flight immediately upon or soon after their arrival. The quarter whose ability was assessed as modest probably had made an impression in one way or another, maybe through possession of some skill acquired prior to their landing, whereas the great mass of the unnoticed may be an index of the lack of minute supervision that typified slavery in

48. *SCG*, May 7, 1754, October 27, 1759, January 14, 1764, October 29, 1737.

Table 13   ENGLISH PROFICIENCY OF RUNAWAY SLAVES
              IN COLONIAL SOUTH CAROLINA

English	Number	Total Percentage	Adjusted Percentage
Excellent	23	0.6	3.0
Very good	114	2.9	15.0
Good	211	5.5	27.0
Little*	97	2.5	12.4
Very little†	103	2.7	13.2
No English	232	6.0	30.0
(Sub-total)	(780)		(100.0)
Unknown	3090	80.0	
Total	3870	100.0	

*Includes listings of *Bad*, *Poor*, and *Indifferent* in Table 12.
†Includes listings of *Very poor* in Table 12.

South Carolina. Minor differences in numbers recorded, however, might be very important in effect.

If Table 12 is simplified and some of the categories consolidated (Table 14), it seems clear that most of the best English among native Africans was spoken by those of Bantu or related origin. Considering the first category in Table 14, the lead, proportionately, is held by Congo-Angola, followed by the Bight of Biafra; if the first two categories are taken together, the situation is reversed. But in either case, these two regions are in the forefront. Bastide writes that "the Bantus showed themselves more responsive than most to foreign influences. They realized, very clearly, that westernization and conversion to Christianity would (in a society where European standards provided the criterion for behaviour) offer them a chance for social self-betterment, whereas cultural resistance has precisely the opposite effect."[49] He goes on to point out that their less systematized religious structure, based on ancestor worship and attached to an African geographical locale, was easier to disrupt than that of some other groups. This fact fa-

49. Bastide, *African Civilizations*, 106.

Table 14   ENGLISH PROFICIENCY OF RUNAWAY SLAVES
IN COLONIAL SOUTH CAROLINA BY ORIGIN

Region	Total	Sub-total	Competent	Functional	Inadequate	None
Senegambia	183	57 (31.1)	8 (14.0)	13 (22.8)	7 (12.3)	29 (50.9)
Windward Coast	93	14 (15.2)		3 (21.4)	7 (50.0)	4 (28.6)
Gold Coast	41	15 (36.6)	1 (6.7)	2 (13.3)	2 (13.3)	10 (66.7)
Bight of Benin	22	5 (22.7)		1 (20.0)	1 (20.0)	3 (60.0)
Bight of Biafra	89	30 (33.7)	6 (20.0)	8 (26.7)	4 (13.3)	12 (40.0)
Congo–Angola	275	81 (29.5)	23 (28.4)	9 (11.1)	15 (18.5)	34 (42.0)
Guinea	188	42 (22.3)	6 (14.3)	9 (21.4)	13 (34.2)	10 (23.8)
North America	353	76 (21.5)	72 (94.7)	1 (1.3)	2 (2.6)	1 (1.3)
West Indies	58	23 (39.7)	21 (91.3)	2 (8.7)		
Africa together	891	244 (27.4)	44 (18.0)	45 (18.4)	53 (21.7)	102 (41.8)

NOTE: *Total* refers to total number of that group identified. *Sub-total* refers to the number whose language ability was noted, followed by the percentage of the total in parentheses. The other numbers in parentheses are percentages of the sub-totals. *Competent* consolidates the listings of *Excellent*, *Very good*, and *Good* in Table 12. *Functional* consolidates the listings of *Little*, *Bad*, *Poor*, and *Indifferent* in Table 12. *Inadequate* consolidates the listings of *Very poor* and *Very little* in Table 12.

Table 15   ANNUAL RUNAWAYS AS A PROPORTION OF THE BLACK
POPULATION IN COLONIAL SOUTH CAROLINA

Date	Blacks	Runaways For Decade	Annual Runaways	Annual Percentage
1739	27,000	512	64	.23
1749	35,000	619	62	.17
1759	51,267	847	85	.17
1769	67,661	1,037	104	.15
1775	43,650	844	141	.32

NOTE: Statistics on the black population are from the United States Census Bureau, *Historical Statistics*, 756. Since my runaway figures refer to decades from zero to nine and the population figures are given from zero to zero, I subtracted one-tenth from the figures of the Census Bureau to make the two equable. The figure for 1775 was derived by subtracting one-tenth from the 1780 figure and dividing it in half. The number of runaways over the decade was divided by the number of years counted to yield an approximate yearly average. The runaway figures for the 1730s begin in 1732.

cilitated their acculturation and gained the appreciation of whites. Assuming that Bastide's assessment is correct, therefore, this reasoning, together with circumstances mentioned above, would contribute further to the desirability of Angolas when Gambias could not be had, and even, perhaps, when they could. The way those of Bantu language and culture are pictured by Bastide also coincides with the earlier description of peoples from Congo-Angola, because the mechanical propensity they evinced could be no more than a sharpened willingness to learn and thus to succeed within the limits of possibility. In South Carolina, these peoples not only received greater relative notice, but when noticed, their English was notably better.

VI

In absolute terms, the number of runaways increased over the century, but the relative figure was remarkably small, never amounting, annually, to as much as 1 percent of the total black population (Table 15). Even that figure is significant, however, when compared to reported runaways in the nineteenth century. Larry Gara writes, based on census data, that "the South lost approximately a thousand slaves a year by running away." In 1850, for example, he counted approximately 1,011 fugitives, amounting to .03 percent of the southern black population.[50] If the number of fugitives remained fairly constant, the percentage of fugitives obviously decreased as the nation approached civil war. In fact, there may have been an absolute decrease as well. In 1860, only 803 runaways were reported.[51] Clearly, the mechanisms for slave control were more efficient in the nineteenth than in the eighteenth century.

In colonial South Carolina, the higher percentages of fugitives were at the beginning and end of the period of record. The first high period of runaways covered the interval of tension and unrest preceding the Stono Rebellion, and the second was during the season of uncertainty before the American Revolution. During such periods slaves who would not otherwise make the attempt were emboldened by the loosening of authority to leave the plantation. This seems the most likely explanation, because there does not appear to be any direct relationship between imports and fugitives (Table 16). The practical cessation of importation in the aftermath of the Stono Rebellion, for example, during the decade of the 1740s, had no significant effect on the proportion of runaways, which remained almost constant relative to population until the 1770s. Thus, the increase in the number of fugitives over the century was a primary function of population growth and not a concomitant of importation, except, of course, as importation contributed to growth. There may, indeed, have been other effects of importation; it may have been destabilizing, encouraging more runaways than would otherwise have been the case, but this effect is difficult to measure. Throughout the period of study, the number of runaways varied between 4 and 5 percent of the number of imports, except during the 1740s when it amounted to 40 percent. Domestic conditions, therefore, rather than changes in importation, were responsible for the unusual number of fugitives in the decades noted.

50. Larry Gara, *The Liberty Line: The Legend of the Underground Railroad* (Lexington, 1961), 30; U.S. Bureau of the Census, *Historical Statistics*, 12.
51. Gara, *Liberty Line*, 39.

Table 16   RUNAWAYS AS A PROPORTION OF IMPORTS
             IN COLONIAL SOUTH CAROLINA

Date	Imports	Runaways	Percentage
1735–39	11,849	512	4.32
1740–49	1,563	619	39.60
1750–59	15,912	847	5.32
1760–69	20,810	1,037	4.98
1770–75	20,808	844	4.05
Total	70,943	3,862	5.43

The new environment must have been intimidating and may have given newcomers pause, inhibiting runaways. Many would want to familiarize themselves somewhat with their surroundings before deciding to abscond, though the fact that some ran off almost immediately indicates that this consideration may have been of minimal importance. Probably a greater number ran away when they began to perceive some of the differences between servitude in North America and the parallel condition they had known in Africa, whether as master, slave, or commoner. The number of absentees who spoke no English and the fact that some of them had already been severely punished evokes a sharp picture of bewilderment. And this confusion may have been much more a function of the nature of their servitude than of servitude in the abstract.

Peter Wood has isolated three groups who commonly ran away: first, those who absconded to be with members of their family; second, those who had recently arrived; third, those who had been transferred to a new owner.[52] There is, however, a fourth category that ought to be considered—those who used the act to influence their master's behavior. Thus Henry Laurens refused to send a black cooper to Saint Augustine because he threatened to run away if dispatched out of the province. "I thought it best for your Interest," Laurens wrote Alexander Gray in 1768, "to in-

52. Wood, *Black Majority*, 248.

Table 17   AFRICAN RUNAWAYS AS A PROPORTION OF AFRICAN
            IMPORTS IN COLONIAL SOUTH CAROLINA

Date	Imports	Runaways	Percentage
1735–39	11,666	63	.54
1740–49	1,412	49	3.47
1750–59	13,024	99	.76
1760–69	17,266	276	1.59
1770–75	17,429	408	2.34
Total	60,797	895	1.47

NOTE: Importation statistics from Higgins, "Geographical Origins," 40–45. Runaway figures for the 1730s begin in 1732. Excepting the anomaly of the 1740s, these statistics
suggest increasing knowledge about Africans as the century advanced, since there is a
gradual increase in the percentage identified, though not in the proportion of slaves
running away.

dulge this fellow for fear of Accidents, as one bought for Doctor
Stork lately under the same declaration ran away & it cost me
much Trouble & expense to get him again & now I must endeav-
our to sell him to avoid a second Flight."[53] On the other hand,
some insisted on changing their master or locale, as did Abram,
whose owner wrote: "As I am insensible of any other cause of his
absenting himself from me than to be sold, any person inclinable
to purchase him, may treat with me." Or as did Jemmy and Athy,
whose master agreed that "if the above negroes will return home,
they will be pardoned and have tickets given them to look for a
new master." In other instances the threat or act was used to affect
conditions on the plantation. Peter, a black driver, probably did
not retain his position long if more than one of his underlings ran
away "when rice was planting last, on account of ill usage." Nor is
it unlikely that William Gordon, or Godard, curbed his sangui-
nary bent; his servant Caesar ran away when he was ordered to cut
off the head of a slave who had killed himself.[54]

53. Laurens to Alexander Gray, January 26, 1768, in Rogers *et al.* (eds.), *Papers of Henry Laurens*, V, 567–68.
54. *SCG*, March 4, 1751, October 31, 1761, November 18, 1756, December 15, 1758, May 5, 1759.

Naturally, planters did not like to have their authority questioned by their bondsmen; so there developed a tug-of-war between the two, the one to maintain his property and standing, the other to secure liberty or to expand the limits of freedom and maneuver. Landowners, therefore, were not always willing to accede to the wishes of their absentee workers. In an attempt to regain the allegiance of their servitors, however, they sometimes coupled threats with mercy and a hard line with concessions. Accordingly, after the disappearance of Wye, Thomas Stone gave "public notice to everyone whom it may concern, that I am determined not to sell him for any sum of money that can be offered by any person whatever for a negro." But if Wye would return within a week from the date of the *Gazette* notice, Stone promised to "overlook and forgive this offence." Stone was most determined that Wye should come back, or if he failed to do so, that his life in South Carolina would be made impossible. Consequently, he offered ten pounds current money to any person, black or white, who would deliver Wye to the workhouse within the week allowed for his voluntary return. After that time, fifty pounds would be paid for his head, should he die resisting arrest.[55]

Occasionally, planters used the threat of placing a price on the runaway's head simply as an inducement to get the errant servant to come in. David Brown gave Carolina ten days to return or, he said, he would advertise a bounty of fifty pounds. He was almost as good as his word. After the inducement had failed, he committed himself a few months later to paying thirty pounds for Carolina, dead or alive; but he then made a new offer: "*If the above negro will return to me, within a month after publication hereof, I will freely forgive him.*" James Michie also offered fifty pounds for Boston, Sue, and their child Sib, after an earlier appeal had failed. But he, too, promised "that if the said negroes will voluntarily come home and surrender themselves I will yet forgive them, notwithstanding their absence" of eight months. Thomas Tucker retreated from an earlier stance, acknowledging that "WHEREAS

55. *SCGCJ*, February 21, 1769.

the Reward I lately offered for the Head of my Negro CYRUS, had failed of the End proposed, that is of driving him Home," he offered twenty pounds to whomever would deliver him alive.[56]

The indomitable spirit of some slaves was such that planters appealed to the community, on whose support they depended anyway, for aid in humbling the bondsman. Lymus possessed such a spirit that many in Charleston had already complained of his "saucy and imprudent Tongue." Joshua Eden proclaimed, therefore, eight months before the Declaration of Independence: "I hereby give free Liberty, and will be also much obliged to any Person to flog him (so as not to take his Life) in such Manner as they shall think proper, whenever he is found out of my Habitation without a Ticket; for though he is my Property, he has the audacity to tell me, he will be free, that he will serve no Man, and that he will be conquered or governed by no Man." Noble sentiments, but not in a slave! After repeated exasperations, masters sometimes came to the end of their tether. So when London disappeared, William Caper declared: "Whoever will deliver the said fellow to me alive, shall receive a reward of 15 pounds, and 20 pounds for his head." For the return of Frank, Thomas Smith offered 10 pounds, "and 20 pounds for his head."[57]

Unsettled frontier conditions and the fact that Africans were more familiar than Europeans with the semitropical environment were two factors abetting Carolina fugitives. Another, however, no doubt became more important as the century advanced and the region became more thickly populated, namely, divisions within the white community. The pleading, threatening, and vindictive tone of the notices quoted above derived largely from the recognition or suspicion that the slave was encouraged or protected by whites. This practice evidently was widespread. Thomas Stone's Wye had been "seen in several different houses and kitchens" in Charleston before his master advertised for him. Thence was born the assertion that he would not be sold for any price. Francis God-

---

56. *SCG*, July 15, 1751, March 30, 1752, April 9, 1754, June 11, 1754, May 1, 1756.
57. *Ibid.*, November 7, 1775, August 4, 1758, November 20, 1755.

dard entertained the suspicion that his "Mustee Wench" Sarah was "kept by some person that has a mind to purchase her," and Stephen Hortley supposed the same concerning Kate.[58]

More commonly, white people simply utilized the skills of fugitives while (though not always) providing aid and shelter. Bristol, a wheelwright, had been formerly hired out by the month with a ticket from his master. But the latter complained in 1763 that "as [certain persons] have a good while past harboured, entertained and employed the said fellow without a ticket, by which I have lost above 300 l.," he offered to pay fifty pounds for information leading to conviction of the culprits. There were numerous ads to this effect, and obviously a lot of money was involved. Sometimes a fugitive split money earned elsewhere with his harborers. On other occasions, perhaps for a pecuniary consideration, whites would forge documents for fugitives. For example, John Chapman complained that his bricklayer and plasterer, Abraham, who had been away more than once, had "in some former elopements pretended to be free; for proof whereof he has produced a false certificate drawn up by some evil disposed person by which he has imposed on several people, who have employed him in the way of his trade." These practices became more frequent as the century advanced, if the stridency of the notices and the increase in reward for information on whites who harbored slaves are any index. Skilled slaves (and others as well) were thereby provided effective leverage to extend their autonomy and expand their freedom of action. The need for labor created rifts in the white population which enabled slaves to counteract some of the arbitrary power of the planter class. Slaves, though at a disadvantage, were not without their means and exacted contractual obligations they expected to be upheld. If masters reneged on their agreement, the slave, among other things, might simply run away again, and they sometimes stayed out for considerable lengths of time. So Kate, who had returned after an absence of "23 months together," presumably harbored in Charleston, left again when her situation displeased her.[59] These contingencies, while they did not mitigate the

58. *SCGCJ*, February 21, 1769; *SCG*, February 26, 1737, May 21, 1750.
59. *SCG*, December 10, 1763, October 12, 1767, October 13, 1757.

horror of slavery, helped to establish and maintain the personality and integrity of the human being who was enslaved.

VII

The plantation society portrayed in eighteenth-century runaway notices diverges profoundly from that so often evoked (usually erroneously) in the nineteenth century of supine laborers passively accepting whatever came their way. Proud and cunning, frightened and distraught, these people—Africans, new Negroes, and country born—coped with their situation as best they might with what they possessed, and what they possessed was sometimes greater than has commonly been acknowledged. But their very success in utilizing the leeway contained in the system rendered untenable the position of those who would evade the system altogether and be free and black in a society of masters and slaves. The situation of free blacks must have become increasingly tenuous as the century aged. It was no doubt easier for Johnny Holmes, wheelwright and carpenter, to be a "Free Negro Fellow" in 1736 than it was for Benjamin Walmsy in 1747, as the system became more rigid. The latter was, he said, born free in Rhode Island and "came to this Place in Capt. *Wanton* and was pressed on board his Majesty's Ship the *Aldborough* when she was commanded by Capt. *Robertson*." Unfortunately, he was "Taken up at Winyaw, and sent to the Work-House . . . to be secured as a runaway Slave."[60]

The situation was worse in 1756 for William Sanders, formerly Primus, who had been sold away to Pennsylvania twenty years earlier. He had the audacity to return when, he claimed, he was freed by his master. "For evidence of his being a freeman," wrote the warden of the workhouse, "he produces a pass, signed David Stuard, *Augusta* County [Va.], August the 18th, 1755, for *William Sanders*, a freeman, to pass and repass, which is indorsed by several other magistrates in *North Carolina*, which name of *William Sanders* he now assumes, and pretends he is the same identical per-

---

60. *Ibid.*, November 6, 1736, October 5, 1747.

son, and a freeman. But as there is great reason to suppose he is a slave, and escaped from some person in Virginia or *thereabouts*, any person that can claim their property in him within *six months*, may have him upon payment of charges to the warden of the workhouse."[61] One wonders what other evidence of freedom would have been necessary and, assuming his story to be true, whether he was ever free again. But, then, people did forge passes. A free black population continued to exist in South Carolina but not nearly so easily as in those regions, such as Jamaica, where a white minority was comparatively isolated and obliged to make greater accommodations.

Not all variations in Atlantic plantation societies can be explained with reference to geography alone. Gilberto Freyre notes that "for the English colonies the criterion for the importation of slaves from Africa was almost wholly an agricultural one. What was preferred was brute strength, animal energy, the Negro . . . with good powers of [physical] resistence. . . . In the case of Brazil there were other needs and interests to be taken into consideration: the lack of white women; and technical needs in connection with the working of metals as the mines were opened up."[62] The main thrust of this statement can be somewhat modified in the case of South Carolina, because there North American slavery, and perhaps, in some respects, slavery in all of English America, came closest to Brazil. Technological skills were important, but it was largely (though not exclusively) the ability to apply such skills to *agricultural* pursuits that was of primary concern. Interest in other indigenous skills was less systematic. That they existed was widely known, but whites were less preoccupied with them in choosing slaves. This very contrast highlights the association between South Carolina and Gambia and other rice-growing areas. But it also points to significant differences between British America and Brazil. For North America as a whole, Europe was the primary source of skilled laborers—even if for no other purpose than to teach the slaves. North of South Carolina, where whites were in the majority and where skilled and unskilled white

61. *Ibid.*, August 12, 1756, Supplement.
62. Freyre, *Masters and Slaves*, 308.

men eventually came in large numbers, the recognition of African talent, and even of the artisan capabilities of American blacks, was less necessary, though blacks obviously performed many artisan functions in the Chesapeake and elsewhere. Not until slavery was destroyed was this essentially northern predisposition (whether one speaks of North America as a whole or of the northern states) imposed in all those areas of the United States where the peculiar institution prevailed. The preconditions for this situation, however, were already laid in eighteenth-century America, and even in South Carolina, where it was most difficult to insist upon. Time and again the legislature attempted to discourage the training of servile labor, but the realities of demography and economic need demanded that such injunctions be ignored. South Carolina's strong tie to the South Atlantic was mitigated by its connection to the northern mainland, and the latter eventually held sway. Yet the mark of difference remained and helped to distinguish South Carolina from the rest of the colonies, especially prior to the great influx of whites into South Carolina after 1760.

Regarding other aspects of Freyre's statement, it is not clear what, if any, effect the sexual desires and composition of the white population in South Carolina had on the slave trade in terms of the kinds of slaves imported. This factor is difficult to measure, in part because miscegenation was frowned upon in British North America, though it came closer to being acceptable in South Carolina than anywhere else on the mainland. A contributor to the South Carolina *Gazette* in July, 1736, for example, took occasion to warn "Certain young Men" of Charleston to "frequent less with their Black Lovers the open Lots and the . . . House on the Green between old Church street and King street" lest steps be undertaken publicly "to coole their Courage and to expose them." He added, however, that they had "no need to be idle, since of their own Colour are lately arrived so many buxom Ladies, who are tenderhearted, and no doubt will comply easily with their request on small rewards." In defense of European women, he wrote that they were "full as capable for Service either night or day as any Africain Ladies whatsoever, unless their native Constitution is much alter'd." They had "always the praise for their Activity of Hipps and humoring a Jest to the Life in what Posture soever their Partners may fancy," which made him hope that they would "have the Preference before the black Ladies in the Esteem of the Widowers and Bachelors at C——Town." But the widowers and bachelors of Charleston were evidently not convinced. Accordingly, in April, 1737, Nicholas Burnham desired the return of a "Mustee Wench named *Lucy*," asking particular vigilance of ship captains to prevent her being taken off the province, noting that "if she is ship'd, she will be ship'd by the white Man that keeps her Company." In May, T. I. Ellery published a reward for the conviction of Richard Ratton who had "run off this Province, and carried with him a Negro Woman named *Flora*, and her child *Katey*" who did not belong to him. And the provincial grand jury in 1743 presented before the chief justice "THE TOO COMMON PRACTICE of CRIMINAL CONVERSATION with NEGRO and other SLAVE WENCHES IN THIS PROVINCE, as an Enormity and Evil of Ill-Consequence."[63]

Despite remonstrances, miscegenation continued, and a Charlestonian protested indignantly in 1772 that "to such a Pitch of Licentiousness have some Men arrived, that they cohabit, as Husband, with Negro Women, treating them as Wives even in public, and do not blush to own the Mongrel Breed . . . which is thus begotten; maintaining the spurious Progeny, as well as the Mother, in Splendor, whilst many virtuous and industrious white Women might be found, who, though in low Circumstances, would be a Credit to a Man, and much less expensive." He opined that "this *scandalous* Intimacy, which too much subsists between the Sexes of different Colours," was "a principal Reason why the Wenches are so insolent and useless to their Owners, as well as the Cause of their frequent Elopements, during which they are concealed and supported by their abject Paramours."[64] Josiah Quincy, Jr., who traveled through South Carolina in 1773, also disapproved of "the intercourse between the whites and blacks. The enjoyment of a negro or mulatto woman," he wrote, "is spoken of as quite a common thing: no reluctance, delicacy or shame is made about the matter. It is far

63. *SCG*, July 17, 1736, April 2, 1737, May 21, 1737, March 28, 1738.
64. *Ibid.*, August 27, 1772.

from being uncommon to see a gentleman at dinner, and his reputed offspring a slave to the master of the table. I myself saw two instances of this, and the company very facetiously would trace the lines, lineaments and features of the father and mother in the child, and very accurately point out the more characteristic resemblance. The fathers neither of them blushed or seem[ed] disconcerted."[65]

Table 10 possibly makes some suggestions about miscegenation, assuming runaway figures to be a rough reflection of the total slave population. One might suspect that during a period when large numbers of Africans were being constantly imported, the vast majority of the black population would be unmixed, both male and female. The extent of miscegenation, however, may have been greater than the percentage of mulattoes represented among fugitives indicates because they were less likely to abscond. Table 3, for example, supports the conclusion of Gerald Mullin that while most runaways in Virginia were acculturated slaves, most in South Carolina had been born in Africa.[66] Mulattoes were more likely to be acculturated and skilled. On the other hand, if the words of the indignant Charlestonian have merit, mulatto women, at least, may have been overrepresented.

It is possible that some of those called "yellow" were also mulattoes, in which case the degree of race mixture was considerably larger. But some Africans, particularly from the Niger Delta, were also perceived as "yellow," and it cannot therefore be assumed that this category referred to mulattoes, though it may reflect prior race mixture in Africa. The "mustee" category is significantly larger than the mulatto, which suggests various possibilities. There may have been more mustees than mulattoes because access to Indian women may have been easy for white and black alike (the term *mustee* in South Carolina referring to an Indian mixture with either African or European). Possibly, most of this group was a composite of red and black rather than red and white, because the former were more likely to come into contact as slaves or servants. Conceivably, mustees had it worse (or as

65. Josiah Quincy, Jr., "The Journal of Josiah Quincy, Junior, 1773," *Massachusetts Historical Society Proceedings*, XLIX (June, 1916), 463.
66. Mullin, "Religion and Slave Resistance."

concubines, better) than mulattoes, causing them to run away more often. Perhaps, the Amerindian heritage and connections of mustees made them more prone to escape. Their relative prominence among runaways, however, points strongly to the tripartite character of race relations in colonial South Carolina.

Despite the relative candor surrounding interracial sex, whether there were any assumptions about the superior sexuality of certain African groups over others is unclear. As has been illustrated, this uncertainty obviously does not mean that the British were essentially different from the Portuguese in restraining their sexuality. In the West Indies, slave concubinage was openly practiced and accepted. Moreover, one Britisher made his attitude and certain customs plain when he complained to James Grant in August, 1765, about his inability to perform physically as he had in his youth. "I cant walk anything like to what I did [even?] when you was last in England, and my Ankles Swell almost every night." Nor did he make love, he went on, using the graphic Anglo-Saxon expression, "half what I used to do" and "since I left London, wch was July 20th I have not Seen 3 women worth it, than they are so" misguided as to "misinterpritt the word Virtue." They would have sex with servants but not with masters and he could not "now go to the Woods, and fields & expose" himself to the elements as he had formerly. He must, he lamented, make love "betwixt Sheets or on a Carpett, The flying fucking is over w^t me." He then recalled with rapture, and in explicit and lurid detail, his amatory exploits in the West Indies with "the Black Desdimonas & Falimas." He noted that "Falima was the name of ye Negroe I lost my Madenhead w^t." Bulls, horses, asses, and goats, he thought, possessed so much greater ability while "we, the Lords of all, is born for other Amusements, however, Take a pearl." Lovemaking, he concluded, using the more succinct expression throughout, "is a pretty Diversion."[67] He might have written as much about South Carolina, but in general the colony was in an ambiguous position, in this regard as in others, in terms of the degree to which such practices were socially acceptable.

67. James Masterson to James Grant, August 20, 1765, in Grant of Ballindalloch MSS, 0771/553.

Clearly, however, the aspect of colonial settlement, needs of colonial society, and disposition of Carolina planters (whatever the amorous considerations of vibrant youth or jaded memory contributed to the equation) encouraged and reenforced an awareness of African ethnicity. Whether in close or casual association with blacks—working a plantation, managing a home, or observing or partaking of urban life in Charleston—colonials were always aware of individual and ethnic distinctiveness among slaves. The mere cognizance was not of itself unique, but the reasons for and extent of this recognition distinguished customs and attitudes in the colony.

Conclusion

South Carolina demonstrated a peculiar combination of mainland and tropical attributes. Its social structure represented a tense reconciliation of opposite tendencies brought about by a transitional climate, a unique geographical setting, an intermediate staple crop in terms of profits, and an exceptional demographic composition. These aspects created an unusual colony distinguished by idiosyncracies yet related in essence to a broad plantation tradition. The particularities of South Carolina were often ignored when generalizations were made about the mainland. Because of this disregard, important facets of the collaboration between African and European were overlooked in North America, though they were common knowledge farther south. From the vantage point of tropical America, the distinguishing characteristics of South Carolina were not always striking enough to be considered worth unusual attention. Nevertheless, South Carolina formed an essential link in a chain of English settlements and European plantations and illustrated how basically similar societies could be subtly modified by locale and outlook.

More important, comparing South Carolina's trade and structure with those of other plantation systems focuses attention on the African population. It becomes evident from such a study that many of the assumptions made about masters as well as about slaves are untrue, at least in South Carolina. Africans were not all the same and were not perceived as such, and many of the distinctions between one plantation society and another may be explained as much by the disparate origins of their servile populace as by other variables. Various scholars have raised this issue, and further study might help to substantiate or correct assertions that have already been made. Brazilian sociologist Gilberto Freyre, for example, has written that his country got the best Africans that the continent had to offer, whereas North American planters got a lesser breed. Aside from the value judgment involved, and some significant local differences, the total ethnic contrast between the two may not have been so great as he imagined. Or, at any rate, the divergence may not entirely support his conclusion. He says that the usual assumption has been that practically all Brazilian slaves came from the Angola and related regions, consisting primarily of Bantu peoples. But, he goes on, this picture is incomplete because large numbers of the so-called Sudanese, from the Slave and Gold Coast areas, also came.[1] He apparently thinks that the Sudanese have more to recommend them than do the Bantu. He does not give a statistical breakdown of these groups in Brazil, though because the trade to areas containing Bantu peoples went on for a much longer period of time and was larger than the trade to other parts of the coast, the majority of Africans in Brazil were probably of Bantu origin. If one looks at North America, one finds a similar situation: 46 percent came from regions containing Sudanese—that is, the Gold Coast, the Windward Coast, Senegambia, and Sierra Leone, and 54 percent came from the Niger Delta and the Congo-Angola-Mozambique region, containing Bantu-speaking peoples.[2] The likelihood, however, is that a greater percentage of Bantu speakers was to be found in Brazil than in North America. These terms—Bantu, Sudanese—are very general ones and are inadequate for any really dependable comparison; but, using Freyre's criteria, if a discrepancy existed between the attitudes and conduct of North American and Brazilian slaves, their ethnic background is, by itself, an insufficient explanation. He may have a point, but the case has yet to be proven and demands a much closer attention to the North American situation.

In this regard, the knowledge that colonial Americans had an awareness of the diverse backgrounds of their servile black population, and that for at least some of them it was a matter of intense concern, is important because it suggests that perhaps more can be known about this population, or its origins, than has been uncovered until now. It means, at least in theory, that if one were

1. Freyre, *Masters and Slaves*, 299–301.
2. Curtin, *Atlantic Slave Trade*, 157.

interested in the survival of Africanisms in a North American locale, one might begin by looking at the provenance of the populace under study and then going to a specific African area rather
than looking at Africa in general. More concrete African technical
skills and procedures, in particular, as opposed to abstract aspects
of African cultures, might be traced by this approach.

In another direction, a recognition that colonials were cog-
nizant, and willing to make use, of African know-how, together
with their consciousness of ethnic differences, suggests a recon-
sideration of the colonial outlook. The strength of their ethnocentrism permitted the English to assume superiority in face of
practically everybody they met, and Africans were certainly no
exception to this rule. Many have argued, in fact, that English culture had a peculiar predisposition towards a negative reaction to
black people. But if a distinction can be made between ethnocentrism and racism, then it might be safe to say that eighteenth-
century attitudes towards black labor partook more of the former
than the latter. This would be especially true in South Carolina,
where the contest was indeed more often between African and
European than between black and white. Clearly the posture
adopted towards blacks by white Americans in the nineteenth century—predicating their innate passivity and peculiar suitability to
slavery, their lack of ambition and intelligence, their inability to
handle or even to appreciate freedom—was not prevalent. Some
of these ideas existed in casual and inchoate form in the eighteenth
century, but they were not so widely and comfortably held as
would later be the case. Accordingly, a contemporary description
of the Stono Rebellion, the largest such event in British North
America, characterized it as a situation "wherein one [the blacks]
fought for Liberty and Life and the other [the whites] for their
Country and every thing that was Dear to them." This was certainly, as Winthrop Jordan states, "a revealing characterization of
an American slave rebellion" and serves to differentiate the at-
titudinal set of the colonial era from that of the national era.[3]

Finally, the questions of African ethnicity, cultural survivals,

3. Jordan, *White Over Black*, 120.

and technical expertise relate to the issue of African contributions to American civilization. The idea that Africans had nothing to offer but labor and rhythm has been firmly discredited, and it is now increasingly recognized that North American culture, like those elsewhere around the South Atlantic, is a composite of African and European elements. It is possible, indeed probable, that the full extent and significance of African influence has not yet been realized. A focus on the eighteenth century and earlier, when American culture began its development, should facilitate a better comprehension of the meshing of European and African attitudes and attributes. Africans were able to give technical advice and skill, which Europeans not only accepted but actually sought. Even more than is commonly assumed, the economic and social structures of American slave societies were, therefore, a mutual accomplishment.

Bibliography

Published Works

BOOKS

Adanson, M. *A Voyage to Senegal, the Isle of Goree and the River Gambia.* London, 1759.

Ajaye, J. F., and Michael Crowder, eds. *A History of West Africa.* New York: Columbia University Press, 1972.

Andrews, Evangeline W., and Charles M. Andrews, eds. *Journal of a Lady of Quality, Being the Narrative of a Journey from Scotland to the West Indies, North Carolina, and Portugal in the Years 1774 to 1776.* New Haven: Yale University Press, 1921.

Anstey, Roger. *The Atlantic Slave Trade and British Abolition.* London: MacMillan Press, 1975.

Bastide, Roger. *African Civilizations in the New World.* New York: Harper and Row, 1971.

Baumann, H., and D. Westermann. *Les Peuples et les Civilisations de L'Afrique; Les langues et L'Education.* Paris: Payot, 1970.

Beltrán, Gonzalo Aguirre. *La población negra de México: Estudio ethnohistórico.* México: Fondo de Cultura Economico, 1972.

Birmingham, David. *Trade and Conflict in Angola: The Mbundu and Their Neighbours Under the Influence of the Portuguese, 1483–1790.* Oxford: Clarendon Press, 1966.

Blassingame, John W. *The Slave Community: Plantation Life in the Ante-Bellum South.* New York: Oxford University Press, 1972.

Boxer, Charles R. *The Golden Age of Brazil, 1695–1750: Growing Pains of a Colonial Society.* Berkeley: University of California Press, 1969.

Cardot, J. *Le Riz dans le Monde et en Indochine.* Paris: Agence Economique de l'Indochine, 1928.

Carroll, B. R. *Historical Collections of South Carolina.* 3 vols. New York: Harper and Brothers, 1836.

Catesby, Mark. *The Natural History of Carolina, Florida and the Bahama Islands etc.* London, 1771.

179

Clowse, Converse D. *Economic Beginnings in Colonial South Carolina, 1670–1730*. Columbia: University of South Carolina Press, 1971.

Copland, Samuel. *A History of Madagascar*. London, 1822.

Craven, Wesley Frank. *White, Red and Black: The Seventeenth Century Virginian*. Charlottesville: University of Virginia Press, 1971.

Cruz, José Ribeiro da. *Geografia de Angola*. Lisbon, 1940.

Curtin, Philip D. *The Atlantic Slave Trade: A Census*. Madison: University of Wisconsin Press, 1969.

D'Avenant, Charles. *The Political and Commercial Works of That Celebrated Writer, Relating to the Trade and Revenue of England, the Plantation Trade, the East India Trade, and African Trade*. London, 1771.

Davies, K. G. *The Royal African Company*. New York: Atheneum, 1970.

DeBow, J. D. B. *The Industrial Resources etc. of the Southern and Western States*. New Orleans, 1852.

Delpon, J. *L'Agriculture à Madagascar: Les Principales Productions*. Paris: Agence Economique de Madagascar, 1930.

Deschamps, Hubert. *Histoire de la Traite des noirs de l'antiquité à nos jours*. Paris: Librairie Arthème Fayard, 1971.

———. *Histoire de Madagascar*. Paris: Éditions Berger-Levrault, 1960.

Dike, Kenneth Onwuka. *Trade and Politics in the Niger Delta 1830–1885: An Introduction to the Economic and Political History of Nigeria*. Oxford: Clarendon Press, 1956.

Doar, David. *Rice and Rice Planting in the South Carolina Low Country*. Charleston, S.C.: Charleston Museum, 1936.

Donnan, Elizabeth, ed. *Documents Illustrative of the History of the Slave Trade to America*. 4 vols. Washington, D.C.: Carnegie Institute, 1930.

Drimmer, Melvin, ed. *Black History: A Reappraisal*. Garden City, N.Y.: Doubleday, 1968.

Duffy, James. *Portuguese Africa*. Cambridge: Harvard University Press, 1961.

Dunn, Richard. *Sugar and Slaves: The Rise of the Planter Class in the English West Indies, 1624–1713*. Chapel Hill: University of North Carolina Press, 1972.

Edwards, Bryan. *The History Civil and Commercial of the British Colonies in the West Indies*. 4 vols. Charleston, S.C.: Morford, Willington, 1810.

———. *The History Civil and Commercial of the British Colonies in the West Indies to Which Is Added an Historical Survey of the French Colony in the Island of St. Domingo*. Abridged. London, 1798.

Elkins, Stanley. *Slavery: A Problem in American Institutional and Intellectual Life*. Chicago: University of Chicago Press, 1968.

Ellis, William. *History of Madagascar*. London, 1839.

Engerman, Stanley L., and Eugene D. Genovese, eds. *Race and Slavery in the Western Hemisphere: Quantitative Studies*. Princeton: Princeton University Press, 1975.

Ernle, Rowland. *English Farming, Past and Present*. Chicago: Quadrangle, 1961.

———. *Pioneers and Progress of English Farming*. London: Longmans, Green, 1888.

Fage, John D. *A History of West Africa: An Introductory Survey*. Cambridge: Cambridge University Press, 1969.

Foner, Laura, and Eugene D. Genovese, eds. *Slavery in the New World: A Reader in Comparative History*. Englewood Cliffs, N.J.: Prentice-Hall, 1969.

Force, Peter. *Tracts and Other Papers Relating Principally to the Origin, Settlement, and Progress of the Colonies in North America, from the Discovery of the Country to the Year 1776*. Washington, D.C., 1838.

Frazier, E. Franklin. *The Negro Family in the United States*. Chicago: University of Chicago Press, 1939.

Freyre, Gilberto. *The Masters and the Slaves: A Study in the Development of Brazilian Civilization*. New York: Alfred A. Knopf, 1966.

Fyfe, Christopher. *A History of Sierra Leone*. London: Oxford University Press, 1963.

Gailey, Harry A. *A History of the Gambia*. New York: Frederick A. Praeger, 1965.

Gara, Larry. *The Liberty Line: The Legend of the Underground Railroad*. Lexington: University of Kentucky Press, 1961.

Genovese, Eugene D. *The World the Slaveholders Made: Two Essays in Interpretation*. New York: Pantheon Books, 1969.

Goveia, Else M. *Slave Society in the British Leeward Islands at the End of the Eighteenth Century*. New Haven: Yale University Press, 1965.

Grant, Douglas. *The Fortunate Slave: An Illustration of African Slavery in the Early Eighteenth Century*. London: Oxford University Press, 1968.

Gray, J. M. *History of the Gambia*. London: Frank Cass, 1966.

Gray, L. C. *History of Agriculture in the Southern United States to 1860*. 2 vols. Washington, D.C.: Carnegie Institute, 1933.

Gray, Richard, and David Birmingham, eds. *Pre-Colonial African Trade: Essays on Trade in Central and Eastern Africa Before 1900*. London: Oxford University Press, 1970.

Gutman, Herbert G. *The Black Family in Slavery and Freedom, 1750–1925*. New York: Pantheon Books, 1976.

Hartlib, Samuel. *Samuel Hartlib His Legacie: Or an Enlargement of the Discourse of Husbandry Used in Brabant and Flaunders; Wherein Are Bequeathed to the Commonwealth of England More Outlandish and Domestick Experiments and Secrets in Reference to Universall Husbandry*. London, 1651.

Herskovits, Frances S., ed. *The New World Negro: Selected Essays in Afroamerican Studies*. Bloomington: University of Indiana Press, 1966.

Herskovits, Melville J. *The Myth of the Negro Past*. New York: Harper and Brothers, 1941.

Hewatt, Alexander. *An Historical Account of the Rise and Progress of the Colonies of South Carolina and Georgia*. 2 vols. London, 1779.

Heyward, Duncan Clinch. *Seed from Madagascar*. Chapel Hill: University of North Carolina Press, 1937.

Hippisley, John. *Essays*. London, 1764.

Huggins, Nathan, *et al.*, eds. *Key Issues in the Afro-American Experience*. New York: Harcourt, Brace Jovanovich, 1971.

Humphreys, R. A., and Elizabeth Humphreys, eds. *The Historian's Business and Other Essays*. Oxford: Oxford University Press, 1961.

Irvine, Frederick R. *A Textbook of West African Agriculture: Soils and Crops*. London: Oxford University Press, 1944.

Jenks, Albert E. *The Wild Rice Gatherers of the Upper Lakes: A Study in American Primitive Economy*. Washington, D.C.: Government Printing Office, 1905.

Johnston, Bruce F. *The Staple Food Economies of Western Tropical Africa*. Palo Alto: Stanford University Press, 1966.

Jones, William O. *Manioc in Africa*. Palo Alto: Stanford University Press, 1959.

Jordan, Winthrop D. *White Over Black: American Attitudes Toward the Negro, 1550–1812*. Chapel Hill: University of North Carolina Press, 1968.

Klein, Herbert S. *The Middle Passage: Comparative Studies in the Atlantic Slave Trade*. Princeton: Princeton University Press, 1978.

Knight, Franklin W. *Slave Society in Cuba During the Nineteenth Century*. Madison: University of Wisconsin Press, 1970.

Land, Aubrey C., *et al.*, eds., *Law, Society and Politics in Early Maryland*. Baltimore: Johns Hopkins University Press, 1977.

Lane, Ann J., ed. *The Debate Over Slavery: Stanley Elkins and His Critics*. Chicago: University of Chicago Press, 1971.

Lawson, John. *History of North Carolina*, London, 1714.

Leblond, Marius-Ary. *Le Grande Ile de Madagascar.* Paris: Editions de Flore, 1946.

Lefebvre, Gabriel. *L'Angola, Son Histoire, Son Économie.* Liège: George Thone, 1947.

Leung, Woot-Tsuen Wu, et al., *Composition of Foods Used in Far Eastern Countries.* Agricultural Handbook No. 34. Washington, D.C.: United States Department of Agriculture, 1952.

Lewicki, Tadeusz. *West African Foods in the Middle Ages, According to Arabic Sources.* Cambridge: University of Cambridge Press, 1974.

Long, Edward. *The History of Jamaica, or General Survey of the Ancient and Modern State of That Island with Reflections on Its Situations, Settlements, Inhabitants, Climate, Products, Commerce, Laws and Government.* New Edition. 3 vols. London: Frank Cass, 1970.

Malinverni, Alexis. *Le Riz de Verceil à l'Exposition de Vienna.* Turin: Imprimerie du Journal le Comte Cavour, 1872.

Martin, Phyllis M. *The External Trade of the Loango Coast, 1576–1870: The Effects of Changing Commercial Relations on the Vili Kingdom of Loango.* Oxford: Clarendon Press, 1972.

Mauro, Frédéric. *L'Expansion Européenne (1600–1870).* Paris: Presses Universitaire de France, 1964.

––––––. *Le Portugal et l'Atlantique au XVIIᵉ Siècle (1570–1670): Etude économique.* Paris: Ecole Pratique des Hautes Etudes, 1960.

McCrady, Edward. *The History of South Carolina Under the Proprietary Government, 1670–1719.* New York: MacMillan, 1897.

McGrath, Patrick. *Merchants and Merchandise in Seventeenth Century Bristol.* Bristol: Bristol Record Society, 1955.

Mello, A. Brandao de. *Angola, Monographie historique, géographique et économique de la Colonie destinée à l'Exposition Coloniale Internationale de Paris de 1931.* Loanda: Imprimerie Nationale, 1931.

Middleton, A. P. *Tobacco Coast: A Maritime History of the Chesapeake in the Colonial Era.* Newport News: Mariners' Museum, 1953.

Miracle, Marvin. *Agriculture in the Congo Basin.* Madison: University of Wisconsin Press, 1967.

––––––. *Maize in Tropical Africa.* Madison: University of Wisconsin Press, 1966.

Morgan, Edmund. *American Slavery, American Freedom: The Ordeal of Colonial Virginia.* New York: W. W. Norton, 1975.

Mullin, Gerald. *Flight and Rebellion: Slave Resistance in Eighteenth Century Virginia.* Oxford: Oxford University Press, 1972.

Mullin, Michael, ed. *American Negro Slavery: A Documentary History*. New York: Harper and Row, 1976.

Murchison, Carl A., ed. *A Handbook of Social Psychology*. New York: Russell and Russell, 1967.

Murdock, George Peter. *Africa: Its Peoples and Their Culture History*. New York: McGraw-Hill, 1959.

Nairne, Thomas. *A Letter from South Carolina, Giving an Account of the Soil, Air, Product, Trade, Government, Laws, Religion, People, Military Strength, etc. of That Province*. London, 1710.

Norris, J. *Profitable Advice for Rich and Poor*. London, 1712.

Nuttonson, M. Y. *Rice Culture and Rice-Climate Relationships with Special Reference to the United States Rice Areas and Their Latitudinal and Thermal Analogues in Other Countries*. Washington, D.C.: American Institute of Crop Ecology, 1965.

Orwin, C. S. *A History of English Farming*. London: Thomas Nelson and Sons, 1949.

Ottenberg, Simon, and Phoebe Ottenberg, eds. *Cultures and Societies of Africa*. New York: Random House, 1969.

Papadakis, Juan. *Climates of the World: Their Classification, Similitudes, Differences and Geographic Distribution*. Buenos Aires: Privately published, 1970.

Pares, Richard. *A West India Fortune*. London: Longmans, Green, 1950.

———. *Merchants and Planters*. Cambridge: Cambridge University Press, 1960.

———. *War and Trade in the West Indies, 1739–1763*. London: Frank Cass, 1963.

Parrish, Lydia. *Slave Songs of the Georgia Sea Islands*. New York: Creative Age Press, 1942.

Patterson, Orlando. *The Sociology of Slavery: An Analysis of the Origins, Development and Structure of Negro Slave Society in Jamaica*. Rutherford: Fairleigh Dickinson University Press, 1969.

Paulme, Denise. *Les Gens du Riz: Kissi de Haute-Guinée Française*. Paris: Librarie Plon, 1954.

Pélissier, Paul. *Les Paysans du Sénégal: Les Civilisations agraires du Cayor à la Casamance*. Saint-Yrieix: Imprimerie Fabreque, 1966.

Peytraud, Lucien. *L'Esclavage aux Antilles Françaises Avant 1789*. Paris: Librairie Hachette, 1897.

Phillips, Ulrich B. *American Negro Slavery: A Survey of the Supply, Employment, and Control of Negro Labor as Determined by the Plantation Regime*. Baton Rouge: Louisiana State University Press, 1966.

————. *Life and Labor in the Old South.* Boston: Little, Brown, 1929.

————. ed. *A Documentary History of American Industrial Society.* 4 vols. Cleveland: Arthur H. Clark, 1910.

Pitman, Frank W. *The Development of the British West Indies, 1700–1763.* London: Archon, 1967.

Polanyi, Karl. *Dahomey and the Slave Trade: The Study of an Archaic Economic Institution.* Seattle: University of Washington Press, 1966.

Pollet, Eric, and Grace Winter. *La Société Soninke (Dyahunu, Mali).* Brussels: University Libre de Bruxelles, 1972.

Pope-Hennessy, John. *Sins of the Fathers: A Study of the Atlantic Slave Traders, 1441–1807.* London: Weidenfelt and Nicolson, 1967.

Rodney, Walter. *A History of the Upper Guinea Coast, 1545–1800.* Oxford: Clarendon Press, 1970.

Rogers, George C., Jr., *et al.*, eds. *The Papers of Henry Laurens.* 7 vols. Columbia: University of South Carolina Press, 1968.

Roncière, Charles de la. *Nègres et Nègriers.* Paris: Éditions des Portiques, 1933.

Russell-Wood, A. J. R. *Fidalgos and Philanthropists: The Santa Casa da Misericordia of Bahia, 1550–1755.* Berkeley: University of California Press, 1968.

Saint-Méry, M. L. E. Moreau de. *Description Topographique, Physique, Civile, Politique et Historique de la Partie Française de l'Isle Saint-Dominique.* Philadelphia, 1797.

Salley, A. S., Jr. *The Introduction of Rice Culture into South Carolina.* Bulletins of the Historical Commission of South Carolina, No. 6. Columbia, S.C.: State Company, 1919.

Sellers, Leila. *Charleston Business on the Eve of the American Revolution.* Chapel Hill: University of North Carolina Press, 1934.

Sheridan, Richard. *Sugar and Slaves: An Economic History of the British West Indies.* Baltimore: Johns Hopkins University Press, 1974.

Sibree, James. *Madagascar Before the Conquest: The Island, the Country, and the People.* London: T. Fisher Unwin, 1896.

Smith, Raymond T. *The Negro Family in British Guiana: Family Structure and Social Status in the Villages.* New York: Grove Press, 1956.

Stevens, John. *A View of the Universe, or a New Collection of Voyages and Travels into All Parts of the World, with the Geography and History of Every Country.* London, 1710.

Studer, Elana F. Scheuss de. *La Trata de Negros en el Rio de la Plata durante el Siglo XVIII.* Buenos Aires: Universidad de Buenos Aires, 1958.

Tannenbaum, Frank. *Slave and Citizen: The Negro in the Americas.* New York: Alfred A. Knopf, 1947.

Taylor, G. R., ed. *The Turner Thesis Concerning the Role of the Frontier in American History*. Boston: D.C. Heath, 1956.

Tompkins, Daniel A. *Cotton and Cotton Oil*. Charlotte, N.C.: Privately published, 1901.

Tran-Van-Hun, M. *La Riziculture en Cochinchine*. Paris: Agence Economique de L'Indochine, 1927.

Vansina, Jan. *Kingdoms of the Savanna: A History of Central African States Until European Occupation*. Madison: University of Wisconsin Press, 1968.

Verger, Pierre. *Flux et Reflux de la Traite de Nègres entre le Golfe de Benin et Bahia de Todos os Santos du XVIIe au XIXe Siècle*. Paris: Mouton, 1968.

Vilmorin, Henry L. de, *et al.*, *Les Plantes de Grande Culture: Céréales, Plantes Fourragères, Industrielles et Economiques*. Paris: Vilmorin-Andrieux, 1892.

Wood, Peter H. *Black Majority: Negroes in Colonial South Carolina from 1670 Through the Stono Rebellion*. New York: Alfred A. Knopf, 1974.

ARTICLES

Allston, Robert. "Essay on Sea Coast Crops." *DeBow's Review*, XVI (June, 1854), 589–615.

———. "Memoir of the Introduction and Planting of Rice in South Carolina." *DeBow's Review*, I (April, 1846), 320–57.

Aubreville, A. "La Casamance." *L'Agronomie Tropicale*, III (January–February, 1948), 25–30.

Bailyn, Bernard. "Communications and Trade: The Atlantic in the Seventeenth Century." *Journal of Economic History*, XIII (Fall, 1953), 378–87.

Bascom, William R. "Acculturation Among the Gullah Negroes." *American Anthropologist*, New Series, XLIII (January–March, 1941), 43–50.

Bell, Herbert C. "The West India Trade Before the American Revolution." *American Historical Review*, XXII (January, 1917), 272–87.

Bennett, J. Harry, Jr. "The Problem of Slave Labor Supply at the Codrington Plantations." *Journal of Negro History*, XXXVI (October, 1951), 406–51, XXXVII (April, 1952), 115–41.

Chevalier, Aug. "Le Riz Sauvage de l'Afrique Tropicale." *Journal d'Agriculture Tropicale*, XX (January, 1911), 1–3.

———. "L'Importance de la Riziculture dans le domaine colonial français et l'orientation à donner aux recherches rizicoles." *Revue de Botanique Appliquée et d'Agriculture Tropicale*, XVI (January, 1936), 27–45.

Clark, J. Desmond. "The Spread of Food Production in Sub-Saharan Africa." *Journal of African History*, III, 2 (1962), 211–39.

Clérin, R. "La Riziculture au Soudan français." *L'Agronomie Tropicale*, VI (July–August, 1951), 400–406.

Curtin, Philip D., and Jan Vansina. "Sources of the Nineteenth Century Atlantic Slave Trade." *Journal of African History*, V, 2 (1964), 185–208.

Donnan, Elizabeth. "The Slave Trade into South Carolina Before the American Revolution." *American Historical Review*, XXXIII (July, 1928), 804–28.

Dresch, Jean. "La riziculture en Afrique occidentale." *Annales de géographie*, LVIII (October–December, 1949), 295–312.

Emerson, F. V. "Geographical Influences on the Development of American Slavery." *American Geographical Society Bulletin*, XLIII (January, 1911), 13–26, 106–18.

Foster, W. "An English Settlement in Madagascar in 1645–46." *English Historical Review*, XXVII (April, 1912), 239–50.

Frazier, E. Franklin. Review of *The American Negro: A Study in Racial Crossing*, by Melville J. Herskovits. *American Journal of Sociology*, XXXIII (May, 1928), 1010.

Fredrickson, George M., and Christopher Lasch. "Resistance to Slavery." *Civil War History*, XII (December, 1967), 315–29.

Genovese, Eugene D. "Rebelliousness and Docility in the Negro Slave: A Critique of the Elkins Thesis." *Civil War History*, XII (December, 1967), 293–314.

Greenberg, Joseph. "Linguistic Evidence Regarding Bantu Origins." *Journal of African History*, XIII, 2 (1972), 189–216.

Haley, Alex. "My Furtherest-Back Person—'The African.'" *New York Times Magazine*, July 16, 1972, pp. 13–16.

Handlin, Oscar, and Mary F. Handlin. "Origins of the Southern Labor System." *William and Mary Quarterly*, Third Series, VII (April, 1950), 199–222.

Herskovits, Melville J. "A Footnote to the History of Negro Slaving." *Opportunity*, XI (1933), 178–81.

———. "On the Provenience of New World Negroes." *Social Forces*, XII (December, 1933), 247–62.

———. "The Culture Areas of Africa." *Africa*, III (January, 1930), 59–76.

———. "The Significance of West Africa for Negro Research." *Journal of Negro History*, XXI (January, 1936), 15–30.

Higgins, W. Robert. "The Geographical Origins of Negro Slaves in

Colonial South Carolina." *South Atlantic Quarterly*, LXX (Winter, 1971), 34–47.

Jordan, Winthrop D. "American Chiaroscuro: The Status and Definition of Mulattoes in the British Colonies." *William and Mary Quarterly*, Third Series, XIX (April, 1962), 183–200.

————. "The Influence of the West Indies on the Origin of New England Slavery." *William and Mary Quarterly*, Third Series, XVIII (April, 1961), 243–50.

Klein, Herbert S. "North American Competition and the Characteristics of the African Slave Trade to Cuba, 1790 to 1794." *William and Mary Quarterly*, Third Series, XXVII (January, 1971), 86–102.

————. "Slaves and Shipping in Eighteenth-Century Virginia." *Journal of Interdisciplinary History*, V (Winter, 1975), 383–412.

————. "The Portuguese Slave Trade from Angola in the Eighteenth Century." *Journal of Economic History*, XXXIII (December, 1972), 894–918.

Kulikoff, Allan. "A 'Prolifick' People: Black Population Growth in the Chesapeake Colonies, 1700–1790." *Southern Studies*, XVI (Winter, 1977), 391–428.

————. "The Origins of Afro-American Society in Tidewater Maryland and Virginia, 1700 to 1790." *William and Mary Quarterly*, Third Series, XXXV (April, 1978), 226–59.

Land, Aubrey C. "Economic Behavior in a Planting Society: The Eighteenth Century Chesapeake." *Journal of Southern History*, XXXIII (November, 1967), 469–85.

MacInnes, C. M. "Bristol and the Slave Trade." University of Bristol, Bristol, England, Branch of the Historical Association. *Local History Pamphlets* No. 7, (1968).

Massibot, J. A., and Louis Carles. "Mise en Valeur des 'tannes' Rizicultivable du Sine (Sénégal)." *L'Agronomie Tropicale*, I (September–October, 1946), 451–56.

Mauny, R. "Notes historiques autour des principales plantes cultivées d'Afrique occidentales." *Bulletin de l'IFAN*, IV, 2 (1953).

McCrady, Edward. "Slavery in the Province of South Carolina, 1670–1770." *American Historical Association Report* (1895), 629–73.

Menard, Russell R. "The Maryland Slave Population, 1658 to 1730: A Demographic Profile of Blacks in Four Counties." *William and Mary Quarterly*, Third Series, XXXII (January, 1975), 29–54.

Merriam, Alan P. "The Concept of Culture Clusters Applied to the

Belgian Congo." *Southwestern Journal of Anthropology*, XV (Winter, 1959), 373–95.

Minchton, W. E. "Ship-building in Colonial Rhode Island." *Rhode Island History*, XX (October, 1961), 119–24.

Morgan, W. B. "The Forest and Agriculture in West Africa." *Journal of African History*, III, 2 (1962), 235–39.

Musset, René. "Le Riz dans le monde." *Revue de botanique appliquée*, XXII (1942), 162–67, 275–77.

Oliver, Roland. "The Problem of Bantu Expansion." *Journal of African History*, VII, 3 (1966), 361–76.

Pitman, Frank W. "Slavery on British West India Plantations in the Eighteenth Century." *Journal of Negro History*, XI (October, 1926), 584–650.

Platt, Virginia Bever. "The East India Company and the Madagascar Slave Trade." *William and Mary Quarterly*, Third Series, XXVI (October, 1969), 548–77.

Poirier, Pierre. "Le Riz Italien." *Journal des Economistes, Revue Mensuelle de la Science Economique et de la Statistique*, LVI (October–December, 1917), 79–85.

Polanyi, Karl. "Sortings and 'Ounce Trade' in the West African Slave Trade." *Journal of African History*, V, 3 (1964), 381–93.

Portères, Roland. "Le Riz Vivace de l'Afrique." *L'Agronomie Tropicale*, IV (January–February, 1949), 5–23.

———. "Le système de Riziculture par franges univerietales et l'occupation des fonds par les Riz flotants dans l'Ouest-africain." *Revue internationale de Botanique Appliquée et d'Agriculture Tropicale*, XXIX (November–December, 1949), 553–63.

———. "Les Appellations des Céréales en Afrique." *Journal d'Agriculture Tropicale et de Botanique Appliquée*, VI (April–May, 1959), 68–105, 189–233, 290–339.

———. "Un problème d'Ethnobotanique: relations entre le Riz flottant du Rio Nunez et l'origine medinigerienne des Baga de la Guinée Française." *Journal d'Agriculture Tropicale et de Botanique appliquée*, II (October–November, 1955), 538–42.

———. "Vieilles Agricultures de l'Afrique Intertropicale; Centres d'origine et de diversifications varietale primaire et berceaux d'agriculture antérieurs au XVIe siècle." *L'Agronomie Tropicale*, V (September–October, 1950), 489–504.

Quincy, Josiah, Jr. "The Journal of Josiah Quincy, Junior, 1773." *Mas-*

sachusetts Historical Society Proceedings, XLIX (June, 1916), 424–81.

Reagan, Albert B. "Wild or Indian Rice." *Indiana Academy of Science Proceedings*, VIII (1919), 241–42.

Rodney, Walter. "Upper Guinea and the Significance of the Origins of Africans Enslaved in the New World." *Journal of Negro History*, LIV (October, 1969), 327–45.

Rodriques, José Honório. "The Influence of Africa on Brazil and of Brazil on Africa." *Journal of African History*, III, 1 (1962), 49–67.

Rottenberg, Simon. "The Business of Slave Trading." *South Atlantic Quarterly*, LXVI (Summer, 1967), 409–23.

Rouse, Irving. "Culture Area and Co-Tradition." *Southwestern Journal of Anthropology*, XIII (Summer, 1957), 123–33.

Sheridan, Richard B. "Africa and the Caribbean in the Atlantic Slave Trade." *American Historical Review*, LXXXVII (February, 1972), 19–26.

———. "Commercial and Financial Organization of the British Slave Trade, 1750–1807." *Economic History Review*, Second Series, XI (December, 1958), 249–63.

Sirmans, M. Eugene. "The Legal Status of the Slave in South Carolina, 1670–1740." *Journal of Southern History*, XXVIII (November, 1962), 462–73.

Slattery, J. P. "The Carolina Open Trench System of Planting Rice." *Rice Journal*, XXX (February, 1927), 16, 23, 33.

Stewart, John. "Letters from John Stewart to William Dunlop." *South Carolina Historical and Genealogical Magazine*, XXXII (January, 1931), 1–33, (April, 1931), 81–114.

Stickney, Gardner P. "Indian Use of Wild Rice." *American Anthropologist*, IX (April, 1896), 115–22.

Surface, G. T. "Rice in the United States." *American Geographical Society Bulletin*, XLIII (July, 1911), 500–10.

Thirsk, Joan. "Fenland Farming in the Sixteenth Century." University of Leicester, Department of English Local History. *Occasional Papers No. 3*, 1953.

Thompson, Edgar T. "The Climatic Theory of the Plantation." *Agricultural History*, XV (January, 1941), 49–60.

Tymowski, Michal. "Les domaines des princes du Songhay (Soudan occidental): Comparaison avec la grande propriété foncière en Europe au début de l'époque féodale." *Annales*, XV (November–December, 1971), 1637–58.

Vansina, Jan. "Long-Distance Trade Routes in Central Africa." *Journal of African History*, III, 3 (1962), 375–90.

Viguier, Pierre. "La riziculture indigène au Soudan français." *Annales agricoles de l'Afrique occidentales française et étrangères*, I (1937), 287–326.

———. "La riziculture indigène au Sudan français." *Annales agricoles de l'Afrique occidentales française et étrangères*, II (January–March, 1938), 123–54.

Walton, Gary M. "New Evidence on Colonial Commerce." *Journal of Economic History*, XXVIII (September, 1968), 363–89.

Wax, Darold D. "Quaker Merchants and the Slave Trade in Colonial Pennsylvania." *Pennsylvania Magazine of History and Biography*, LXXXVI (April, 1962), 143–59.

———. "Negro Imports into Pennsylvania, 1720–1766." *Pennsylvania History*, XXXII (July, 1965), 254–87.

———. "Robert Ellis, Philadelphia Merchant and Slave Trader." *Pennsylvania Magazine of History and Biography*, LXXXVIII (January, 1964), 52–69.

———. "Preferences for Slaves in Colonial America." *Journal of Negro History*, LVIII (October, 1973), 371–401.

———. "Black Immigrants: The Slave Trade in Colonial Maryland." *Maryland Historical Magazine*, LXXIII (March, 1978), 30–45.

Whittlesley, D. S. "Geographic Provinces of Angola: An Outline Based on Recent Sources." *Geographical Review*, XIV (January, 1924), 113–26.

Willoughby, Charles C. "The Virginia Indians in the Seventeenth Century." *American Anthropologist*, New Series, IX (January–March, 1907), 57–87.

Yampolsky, Cecil. "Rice: The Plant and Its Cultivation." *Wallerstein Laboratories Communications*, VI (August, 1943), 83–94.

NEWSPAPERS

South Carolina *Gazette*, February, 1732–December, 1768; September–December, 1775.

South Carolina *Gazette and Country Journal*, January, 1769–July, 1775.

GOVERNMENT DOCUMENTS

Calendar of State Papers, Colonial Series: America and the West Indies. London: Public Record Office, 1860–.

Plantation Systems of the New World. Washington, D.C.: Pan American Union, 1959.

United States Bureau of the Census. *Historical Statistics of the United States: Colonial Times to 1957.* Washington, D.C.: Government Printing Office, 1960.

Unpublished Works

MANUSCRIPTS

Bristol Central Library, Bristol, England
  Black Prince Journal Manuscript
  Jefferies Collection
British Museum, London
  Additional Manuscripts
    Clarkson Papers
    Hamilton and Greville Papers
    Liverpool Papers
    Long's Collections for the History of Jamaica
    Papers of the Board of Trade and Plantations, 1710–1781
    Papers relating to the West Indies, America, Africa, and the Canaries, 1696–1786
    Egerton Manuscripts
    Papers relating to the commerce of Africa
    King's Manuscripts
    Papers relating to the state of British settlements in Africa, 1765.
County Record Office, Stafford, England
  Dartmouth Manuscripts
  H. M. Drakeford Manuscripts
Liverpool Record Office, Liverpool, England
  Clayton Tarleton Papers
  Holt and Gregson Papers
  Norris Papers
  Robert Bostock Papers
  Thomas H. Bickerton Papers
  Thomas Leyland Papers
  Tuohy Papers
  William Roscoe Papers
National Register of Archives, Edinburgh, Scotland
  Grant of Ballindalloch Manuscripts

Lennox of Woodhead Manuscripts
Public Record Office, London
  Chancery Papers
  Colonial Office Papers
  Treasury Papers
National Maritime Museum, Greenwich, England
  African Journal Manuscripts
  Duke of Argyle Journal Manuscript
  Sandown Manuscript
Scottish Record Office, Edinburgh, Scotland
  Ailsa Manuscripts
  Murray of Murraythwaite Manuscripts
  Alexander Nisbet Manuscripts
Sheffield Central Library, Sheffield, England
  Spencer-Stanhope Muniments
South Carolina Historical Society, Charleston
  Henry Laurens Papers
University Library, Keele, England
  Raymond Richards Collection

OTHER SOURCES

Mullin, Gerald. "Religion and Slave Resistance." Paper prepared for the
  American Historical Association Meeting, New Orleans, 1972.
Rudnyanszky, Leslie Imre. "The Caribbean Slave Trade: Jamaica and
  Barbados, 1780–1870." Ph.D. dissertation, University of Notre Dame,
  1973.

Index